the organic gardener

Christine and Michael Lavelle

the organic gardener

How to create flower, vegetable, herb and fruit gardens using completely natural techniques

Photography by Peter Anderson

LORENZ BOOKS

CONTENTS

Dedication
This book is dedicated to Mike Lavelle who would have loved to have seen this book.

This edition is published by Lorenz Books, an imprint of Anness Publishing Ltd, Blaby Road, Wigston, Leicestershire LE18 4SE

Email: info@anness.com
Web: www.lorenzbooks.com; www.annesspublishing.com

If you like the images in this book and would like to investigate using them for publishing, promotions or advertising, please visit our website www.practicalpictures.com for more information.

Publisher: **Joanna Lorenz**
Editorial Director: **Judith Simons**
Project Editor: **Felicity Forster**
Designer: **Lisa Tai**
Jacket design: **Balley Design Associates**
Additional text: **Richard Bird and Jonathan Edwards**
Additional photography: **Jonathan Buckley and Michelle Garrett**
Illustrator: **Liz Pepperell**
Production Controller: **Pirong Wang**

ETHICAL TRADING POLICY
At Anness Publishing we believe that business should be conducted in an ethical and ecologically sustainable way, with respect for the environment and a proper regard to the replacement of the natural resources we employ. As a publisher, we use a lot of wood pulp in high-quality paper for printing, and that wood commonly comes from spruce trees. We are therefore currently growing more than 750,000 trees in three Scottish forest plantations: Berrymoss (130 hectares/320 acres), West Touxhill (125 hectares/305 acres) and Deveron Forest (75 hectares/185 acres). The forests we manage contain more than 3.5 times the number of trees employed each year in making paper for the books we manufacture. Because of this ongoing ecological investment programme, you, as our customer, can have the pleasure and reassurance of knowing that a tree is being cultivated on your behalf to naturally replace the materials used to make the book you are holding. Our forestry programme is run in accordance with the UK Woodland Assurance Scheme (UKWAS) and will be certified by the internationally recognized Forest Stewardship Council (FSC). The FSC is a non-government organization dedicated to promoting responsible management of the world's forests. Certification ensures forests are managed in an environmentally sustainable and socially responsible way. For further information about this scheme, go to www.annesspublishing.com/trees

INTRODUCTION

The aim of this book is to show that organic gardening is gardening at its best. The most successful organic gardeners learn that the use of artifical chemicals for short-term gains leads to long-term losses and also that nature makes the best model. Whether you want to grow organic produce for your table, have a dazzling display of summer colour or create a wildlife paradise, the organic garden is for you. Many techniques may already be familiar to you and the change will be less difficult than you think. Going organic may not change the world immediately, but being an organic gardener means that you can make a difference to the wellbeing of the world.

Left: *A well-maintained ornamental garden will reward the keen organic gardener with a wealth of dazzling colour.*

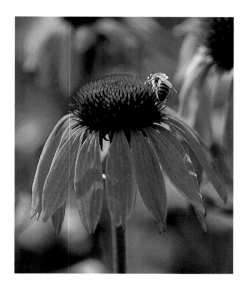

Above: *Organic gardens are highly beneficial to wildlife because they mimic natural environments.*

Above: *The organic garden is the ideal place in which to grow a selection of fresh healthy vegetables.*

Above: *Ornamental plants and flowers are perfectly at home and thrive in a garden that uses organic principles.*

WHAT IS ORGANIC GARDENING?

The term organic means of living origin. When applied to gardening, organic has come to mean the systematic use of techniques that mirror naturally occurring systems. Put simply, it is about finding environmentally friendly ways to cultivate the land, working with rather than against nature. Organic gardening refers not just to a system of techniques, however, but also to a whole philosophy of life.

Above: *The organic garden uses a range of natural materials, including by-products such as chicken manure.*

THE ORIGINS OF ORGANIC GARDENING

From the point of view of gardening, the "modern" organic movement began in the late1940s as a reaction to the increased use of pesticides and synthetic fertilizers in the years after the Second World War. In many respects, however, the principles of organic gardening have been practised for centuries. Ancient writers, among them Pliny and Virgil, commented on the importance of "good husbandry to the health of the land". Thomas Tusser, in his classic work of 1580 entitled *Five Hundred Points of Good Husbandry*, recommends crop rotation to maintain good health. The 17th-century English garden writer John Evelyn begins his *Kalendarium Hortense* with a section describing how to enrich the ground in mid-winter with "horse and sheeps dung especially, that you may have some of two years preparation".

Above: *Many of the plants that benefit wildlife also make showy and decorative additions to beds and borders.*

ORGANIC GARDENING IN THE 21ST CENTURY

Much of the current interest in organic gardening began in the 1960s, when there was increasing concern about the growing levels of environmental damage caused by pesticides and other agrochemicals. If they were causing so much damage to the natural world, then surely they must ultimately affect human beings?

The organic approach aims to reduce the effects that our gardens, farms and cities have upon the wider natural environment. Activities such as recycling, using sustainably produced materials and avoiding pesticides and other harmful agrochemicals all help in this. Organic gardening is often described as being a more natural way to garden. This can make it appear to be somehow revolutionary. In many ways, however, organic gardening could be said to be counter-revolutionary. It aims to avoid artificial inputs and gains. Instead it draws from a vast resource of wisdom and experience amassed over 10,000 years. Much of the so-called conventional wisdom is, in fact, very recent. We only have to look back as far as our grandparents to see that they were naturally organic gardeners. Organic gardening then is the marriage of good horticultural practice to an awareness of our impact upon our surroundings.

IS IT POSSIBLE TO BE WHOLLY ORGANIC?

The short answer to this would probably have to be … with great difficulty. But the purpose of this book is not to promote difficulty or set unattainable goals. The aim should always be to aspire to the ideal solution. Almost all of us face compromise on a daily basis and understand that practicalities outweigh personal ideals. With perseverance and practice, however, it is possible to become less compromised in the confines of your own garden. Simple planning and the observance of good

Left: *Organic gardens can be beautifully designed and can include a mixture of ornamental and edible plants.*

Above: *A well-designed and properly maintained organic garden can be both attractive and productive.*

gardening practice can steadily improve your organic credentials and, with time, a natural balance will be established in your garden. Ultimately, the aim of all organic gardeners, be they landscaping a city garden, tending a country estate or growing home-produced vegetables, is to make choices appropriate to their situation. It is better to move a few steps towards the organic way than to ignore it completely.

Above: *Vegetables need not be planted in rows. Here, the beds are arranged in an attractive geometric pattern.*

ORGANIC STANDARDS

Organic standards are set out to explain the requirements that farmers, growers, processors and others must meet in order for their products or services to be marketed as organic. The standards can be extensive and cover a wide range of farming, growing and food manufacturing practices.

Are organic standards the same worldwide? No. Different countries may stipulate their own standards. IFOAM is the International Federation of Organic Agricultural Movements that represents the worldwide body of organic agriculture and provides a platform for the global exchange of information and co-operation.

Are any chemicals allowed in organic production? Yes. In line with the legal framework of the country, a very limited number of chemicals are allowed on a restricted basis. Organic standards do not allow the use of artificial herbicides or fungicides. By comparison, in non-organic farming as many as 450 chemicals can be routinely used.

If organic gardening severely restricts the use of artificial chemical fertilizers and pesticides, then how do I keep my garden healthy? Organic gardeners rely on developing a healthy fertile soil and growing a mixture of crops. By following these basic practices, organic gardeners work in harmony with nature and aim to achieve a healthy natural balance within their gardens.

Do I have to achieve any standards to become organic? No. Commercial standards are very strict and not necessarily easy to achieve for the amateur. Everyone must make choices appropriate to their own situation.

Is the organic movement just concerned with growing food? No. Going organic is not just about organic food – it should become a way of life. Today, organic wood, clothing, gardening products and even restaurants can all be found. This means that other areas of your life can be organic as well as your garden. It does not always mean completely changing your life, but it can change lives.

WHY GO ORGANIC?

This commonly asked question is easy to answer. The primary reason to embrace the organic approach is health. This means the well-being of the individual as well as the health of the environment. Many pesticides can accumulate over time, both in our own bodies and in the wider environment, a poisonous legacy that can persist for decades. Organic gardening seeks to redress this damage by working with and encouraging nature. It is a long-term investment in the health and wellbeing of us all.

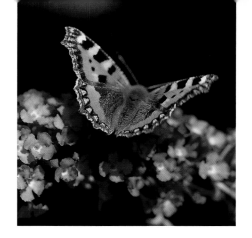

Above: *Butterflies are just one of the many different types of wildlife that can benefit from a pesticide-free garden.*

GREEN CUISINE

Hardly a day seems to go by without some new revelation about the benefits or detrimental effects of some food or other. Recent concerns about the "goodness" of the things that we eat have been a major incentive to supermarkets to supply a growing demand for organic produce. There can be little that equals the satisfaction to be derived from eating home-produced food, gathered fresh from the garden. What better than garden-fresh vegetables that are produced naturally and cleanly?

A GREENER, SAFER GARDEN

Although we think of our gardens as places of safe retreat we have used a cocktail of pesticides and agrochemicals on them that has stripped them of their natural diversity. Many of these poisons no longer control the beasts that they were intended to. All that suffers in this noxious onslaught is the garden, its wild occupants and ultimately

the plants. This cycle of pesticide use eventually turns your personal paradise into a potential health hazard.

HELPING THE ENVIRONMENT

For many of us it can seem that there is little that we can do to change the degradation of our environment. But the truth is that the actions of all of us have both positive and negative impacts upon the land. If every individual reduces his or her own negative impact upon the environment, then collectively we can make a difference. By changing the way you garden to a more organic way, you can begin the healing process, literally in your own backyard.

PROTECTING AND ENCOURAGING WILDLIFE

Be it a bird on a feeder or brightly coloured butterflies on a flower, most of us enjoy seeing visitors from the wild in our gardens. But many of the unsung heroes of our gardens – the insects, worms, amphibians

and mammals that crawl, slither and scurry out of sight – are equally important and may even be the reason why some of the larger visitors come. Organic gardening helps many of these and promotes a balance of wildlife that is both interesting and beautiful to look at.

SO WHAT IF I DO NOT GO ORGANIC?

While the intention of this book is not to dwell upon negative points, the cost of not adopting an organic approach may be seen all around us. This is most frequently noticed as fields and open spaces bereft of butterflies, bees, birds and other wildlife with very little diversity of plant species. It is unthinkable that we could hand this planet to successive generations in a denuded and impoverished state. Perhaps a garden free of "bugs" may sound attractive to some, but the long-term cost to the environment may be felt for generations and in the worst case may even be permanent.

Above: *Organic flower gardens, with their wide range of wildlife-friendly plants, can provide a balanced habitat for birds and insects that is diverse, interesting and beautiful to look at.*

Above: *Imaginative planting designs can result in beautiful contrasts of flowers and foliage, while also providing a wealth of flavourful, home-grown food for your table.*

IT'S A SOLUTION AND IT'S FUN!

Organic gardening is not the solution to all humankind's problems. However, it is a positive and valuable step that you as an individual can take. What's more, you can contribute positively to the wellbeing of your surroundings and to that of your wider environment by doing something that is also fun and rewarding.

WILL "GOING ORGANIC" MEAN THAT MY WHOLE LIFESTYLE HAS TO CHANGE?

Organic gardening is often presented as part of a more general "organic movement". This movement owes its origins to a range of social philosophies, some of which are more fundamentalist than others. The aim of organic gardening is to change the way that you garden and not your whole life. People frequently get confused about the meaning of words that are used as part of the wider organic movement. Four of these terms are explained below. Of these, three describe a whole philosophy that affects practitioners far beyond the confines of their own gardens. An understanding of the philosophies of others can help inspire your own lifestyle changes and all have their own points of interest. In the end, however, it is a matter of choice for you alone and it is best to decide just how organic you (and your family) wish to be.

Biodiversity literally means "the variety of life". It includes all the different plant, animal, fungus and microscopic species in the world. It also considers the genes they contain and the ecosystems of which they form a part. Biodiversity has been seen as the total complexity of all life, including not only the great variety of organisms but also their varying behaviour and interactions. An organic garden aims to maximize all these many different things which are vital to every part of the garden, but especially important when considering the soil. Soil biodiversity is the "lifeblood" of the organic garden and demands investment in order to yield a return.

Biodynamics is described by its practitioners as a science of life forces, recognizing the basic principles at work in nature and taking into account how our actions can bring balance and healing to the world. It is based upon the work of Rudolf Steiner and is said to offer an account of the spiritual history of the Earth as a living being. Its enthusiasts advocate a

Above: *The foliage and form of many types of vegetables can provide striking contrasts in the vegetable garden.*

broadening of personal perspective that includes an understanding of cosmic rhythms, natural healing, a respect for life forces and ultimately a shift away from centralized economic strategies.

Permaculture is a concept that was originally developed in the 1970s by Australians Bill Mollinson and David Holgreen. It was conceived as a response to increasing concerns over the deteriorating natural environment. They attempted to answer the question "how do we, as the human species, sustain ourselves and provide for the needs of the environment for an indefinite period of time?". The answer to this question is the basis for creating a permanent culture (Perma-Culture). This philosophy aims to unite practical, ecological design philosophies by incorporating natural systems and materials into human habitats. Permaculture rejects short-term gains in favour of long-term stability for the environment and those who live in it.

Self-sufficiency is an ideal rather than a reality for most that attempt it, as modern living usually dictates some degree of trade, even if it is limited. Advocates of self-sufficiency aim to produce everything that they need in order to support themselves. The only imports are those that cannot be produced by an individual.

REASONS FOR GOING ORGANIC

Below are just a few of the positive benefits that organic gardening may bring to you and your environment.

Human impact on the earth Organic systems reduce dependence on non-renewable resources. The world has an increasing population, but many of our resources are in limited supply. Using renewable resources helps to secure our common future.

Traditional methods with modern techniques Organic systems rely on a modern, scientific understanding of ecology and soil science. They also depend on traditional methods of crop rotation to ensure soil fertility as well as weed and pest control.

Local solutions to global problems The organic movement encourages individuals to act on a local level, while thinking about how this affects the world.

Best for biodiversity Organic growing is friendlier to the environment, so there is a greater diversity of birds, butterflies and plants in organic gardens.

Minimize your waste We produce a huge amount of waste, including packaging and kitchen and garden waste. Recycling and waste reduction are key issues for organic living.

Mimicking natural systems Organic gardening uses nature as its model and, by working in harmony with nature, aims to achieve a natural balance. By maintaining this equilibrium, organic gardens become very stable entities.

A more interesting garden Organic production is more sustainable and friendlier to the environment. By becoming involved in the whole natural cycle, you will gain greater satisfaction from your own personal Eden.

We are what we eat ... Organic systems recognize that our health is connected to the quality of our food and, ultimately, to the health of the soil.

UNDERSTANDING YOUR GARDEN

Plants, like all living things, flourish when given the right conditions. Certain plants will only thrive in a hot, sunny and dry garden, for example, while others may need cool, moist and shady conditions to prosper. If you are to have healthy plants, you need to choose those that are best suited to your garden and this means understanding exactly what conditions prevail and taking into account a range of environmental factors.

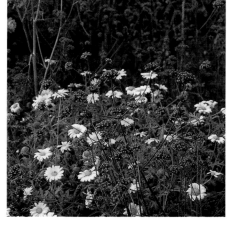

Above: *A hot, sunny spot is ideal for growing pretty summer flowers such as argyranthemums and verbenas.*

CLIMATE

The climate causes a variety of responses, depending upon the plant's location, its stage of maturity, the length of exposure and the intensity of the type of weather. Climate may have a dramatic effect on plant growth and development, especially when extreme weather conditions prevail.

TEMPERATURE

All plant species have their own maximum and minimum temperature tolerances, beyond which the life processes of the plant cease. As a general rule, the maximum temperature that most plants can tolerate is around 35°C (95°F), while the minimum is highly variable. The air and soil temperatures are also crucial in influencing dormancy within plants and this, in turn, largely dictates the length of the growing season.

Air temperature is affected by the degree of energy received from the sun. A sheltered site that benefits from the warming effects of the sun may be used for growing plants that are indigenous to warmer climates.

Soil temperature influences a plant's root development and the rate at which water and nutrients can be absorbed. Sandy soils warm up quicker and earlier in the season than clay soils, mainly because they are relatively free draining and do not hold as much water. Sites that receive a lot of sun, or with a slight incline towards it, will also warm up quicker than shady ones.

WATER

This is the major constituent of all plants. In most gardens, rainfall is the principal source of water for plants and it can be lost through evaporation or surface run-off, although much of it is soaked up by soil particles. This water may then be absorbed by the root hairs of the plant. A steady supply of water is essential for the plant to sustain itself and for optimum growth.

Water may also be held in the air and is referred to as humidity. The amount of water vapour in the atmosphere at any one time is referred to as the relative humidity and is measured as a percentage of the saturation point (100 per cent humidity). In areas that receive heavy rainfall, relative humidity is also higher. Many plants, such as ferns and mosses, thrive in such conditions. But high relative humidity can have undesirable effects on plants, often encouraging disease.

Waterlogging refers to the build-up of water that may occur in badly drained soil with poor structure. The roots of plants that are not adapted to these conditions will suffer and probably die through asphyxiation.

LIGHT LEVELS

Sunlight enables photosynthesis (the method by which plant food is made) to occur. As a result, it is vital to new growth as well as sustaining existing growth. Seasonal changes in light levels may also trigger different stages in the plants' development.

AIR CIRCULATION

Even moderate winds can increase a plant's transpiration rate. However, a light wind can also have beneficial effects, providing relief from extreme heat and cooling the foliage. It will also "change the air" around the plant, and thus help to alleviate a stagnant atmosphere that could promote disease.

ASSESSING THE CLIMATE

A range of climatic information is generally available for your local region. Weather forecasts are an obvious source, but long-term records are sometimes available. From these you should be able to get a picture of the average rainfall, snow, frosty days, wind direction and monthly temperatures.

Left: *A bog garden provides ideal conditions for a range of decorative moisture-loving plants.*

Right: *Blossom is both pretty and essential for good fruit-set. A sheltered site will also encourage pollinating insects.*

A TYPICAL GARDEN AND ITS MICROCLIMATES

Even a small garden can contain a wide variety of microclimates, ranging from cool, shady corners to hot, dry areas. A proper assessment of the growing conditions that prevail in your garden allows you to choose the right plants for the right place.

Shrubs | Dry stone wall | Cool, damp and dark area | House | Wisteria

Pond | Rockery

Brick wall

Grass

Dark and wet area

Wire fencing

Exposed, windy area

Patio

Panel fencing

A GARDEN'S MICROCLIMATE

The prevailing weather conditions in confined or discrete areas are termed the microclimate. For example, there will be a range of environments within a small domestic garden that may be very different from those weather conditions prevailing elsewhere in the locality. Observe what is going on in your own garden and keep a careful record of the position and influence of the following features.

Walls, hedges and fences may cause wind turbulence and dryness, depending upon their height and density. They may cause cold air to build up on sloping sites by preventing it from "draining away" downwards. This can create frost pockets that may have a crucial effect on the type and range of plants that may be grown.

Shadow projections from permanent features, such as buildings, walls, hedges and large trees, may create a range of dense shadow resulting in dark, dry and often cool conditions that will only suit certain plant species.

Hot spots may occur with aspects that are subject to high and prolonged levels of sunlight. Plants may struggle in the dryness created by such strong sunlight.

Damp areas may be anticipated where the ground is low-lying, especially on very heavy soils. During heavy rainfall you should also note the direction of water flow, including where necessary the route taken by excess surface water, which may in extreme cases be the cause of soil erosion.

Soil type and pH play an important role in the ability of a site to support particular plant species. The relative acidity or alkalinity can affect the availability of certain essential nutrients, leading to either shortage or toxicity in plants not ideally suited to the pH of a soil. It is always better to choose plants that thrive in the particular pH of a soil. Attempts to alter the pH by acidifying or adding lime are rarely satisfactory and neither are long-term solutions.

Existing habitat types on and around the garden indicate what plants are likely to thrive. Notes should be made on the range of species and the likely wildlife value.

The garden topography (the shape and aspect of the land) may also affect what you are able to do. If a garden slopes toward the

direction of the midday sun, for instance, it will be warmer than a flat site. Sloping or uneven gardens have their own problems, particularly if you wish to site a greenhouse.

RIGHT PLANT, RIGHT PLACE

Once you have assessed your garden environment, you will be able to choose the right plants for your site. Every garden has its own unique set of advantages and limitations, and these take time to evaluate, so trial and error is ultimately the most reliable method.

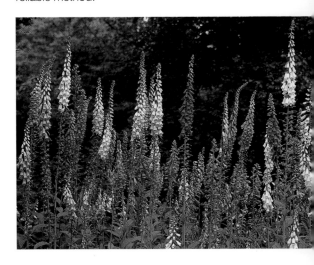

Right: *A shady corner of the garden provides the perfect place for shade lovers such as these foxgloves (Digitalis).*

THE ORGANIC CYCLE

Plants produce their own food using carbon dioxide from the air, water from the soil and energy from the sun in a process known as photosynthesis. The energy in this sugar powers all the growth, development and life-giving processes within the plant. Plants must also produce a range of other substances, including proteins, fats, oils and cellulose, for which they need nutrients such as nitrogen, phosphorus, and potassium. These are almost always taken up through the roots.

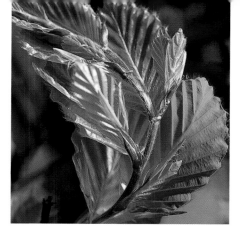

Above: *Plant leaves are remarkable structures because they are the factories in which a plant makes its food.*

WHAT PLANTS NEED

In natural systems, nitrogen, phosphorus and potassium are repeatedly taken up by the plant, used and returned to the soil when the plant dies, drops its leaves or is eaten by an animal. This process is known as nutrient cycling. Plant nutrients are covered in more depth later. For now we need only look at three of the most important cycles: water, carbon and nitrogen.

THE WATER CYCLE

The movement and endless recycling of water between the atmosphere, the surface of the land and under the soil is called the water cycle and is driven by the energy of the sun and the force of gravity.

Water vapour in the atmosphere condenses into clouds, which fall as snow, rain, sleet or hail. This water may be taken up by plants, stored in lakes, enter the soil or flow over the surface in streams. The sun causes water to evaporate back into the atmosphere, or gravity may pull it down through the pores of the soil to be stored as slow-moving ground water. Water can also return to the atmosphere indirectly through plants' leaves – a process known as

transpiration – this being highest during periods of high temperatures, wind, dry air and sunshine.

THE CARBON CYCLE

The movement of carbon, in its many forms, between the total living content of the earth, the atmosphere, oceans, and the rocks and

Above: *Plants rely on water, taken up through the roots, to support their life processes and facilitate growth.*

soils covering the surface, is termed the carbon cycle. It is complex and far reaching. The same carbon atoms in your body today have been used in countless other molecules since time began. Plants absorb carbon dioxide from the atmosphere during photosynthesis (food production) and release it back into the atmosphere during respiration (food use). This process is the great natural recycler of carbon atoms.

THE NITROGEN CYCLE

Nitrogen is used by living organisms to produce a number of complex organic molecules such as amino acids, proteins and nucleic acids, the "building blocks" of life. The largest store of nitrogen is in the atmosphere, where it exists as a gas. This store is about one million times larger than the total nitrogen contained in living organisms.

Right: *Left to develop naturally, grassland will become a rich and diverse habitat for a wealth of both plants and wildlife.*

NUTRIENT CYCLES IN A TYPICAL GARDEN

Even small gardens contain natural cycles. Elements and nutrients are cycled repeatedly both within the environment and as a result of the complex food chains and webs. This cycle of nature is essential in creating a balanced and healthy habitat.

Hawks

Garden birds

Fence with climbers

Pest insects

GARDEN FOOD CHAIN

Fox

NITROGEN CYCLE

Mole

Frog

CARBON CYCLE

Nitrogen in atmosphere

Blackbird

Fruit

Hedge

Carbon dioxide

Worm

Snail

Some carbon returned to atmosphere through respiration

Plant nectars

Flying insect

Recycled through composting

Carbon taken in by plants

Carbon and nitrogen contained in dead or recycled plant matter

Excess nitrates liberated as nitrogen by bacteria

Decomposers recycle all dead plant and animal material

Thrush

Nitrates taken up by plants

Bacteria fix nitrogen as nitrates, a form that can be used by plants

Hedgehog

Despite its abundance in the atmosphere, plants can only take up nitrogen in two solid forms: ammonium and nitrate. Most plants fulfil their needs using nitrate from the soil. Ammonium is used less frequently because it is toxic in large concentrations. Most ecosystems have nitrogen stored in living and dead organic matter, which re-enters the cycle via decomposition. Decomposers in the soil, such as bacteria and fungi, chemically modify the nitrogen found in this organic matter.

Almost all of the nitrogen found in any terrestrial ecosystem originally came from the atmosphere and is biochemically converted ("fixed") into a useful form within the soil by specialized bacteria. Members of the bean family (legumes) and some other kinds of plants form relationships with nitrogen-fixing bacteria. In exchange for nitrogen, the bacteria receive food from the plants and special root structures (nodules) that provide protection.

WHAT ARE ECOSYSTEMS?

Short for ecological systems, ecosystems are communities of plants and animals that consist of a given habitat (the place where an organism lives) and its community (all the plants and animals that live in it). Any group of living and non-living things interacting with each other (including those found in gardens) can be considered an ecosystem.

The chemical materials that are extracted from the environment and changed into living tissue by plants and animals are continually recycled within the ecosystem. These nutrient cycles are at their most efficient when an ecosystem has a good diversity of species. Such diversity tends to make a community stable and self-perpetuating.

FOOD CHAINS AND WEBS

The energy necessary for life reaches the earth as sunlight. This is made into food and stored in plants. Animals acquire some of the stored energy by eating the plants or by eating other plant-eating animals. Such sequences, called food chains, overlap at many points, forming food webs which show "who eats whom" in an ecosystem. If one animal or plant is affected, then the entire food web can be changed.

SOIL AND SOIL MANAGEMENT

Soil is the most precious resource in your garden. Some inherit a well-tended soil, while others, particularly those moving into new homes, inherit a rubble-filled mass. However, any soil can be improved through time and effort. If you regard your soil as a living entity, you will see that essential plant nutrients are cycled by a microscopic army of inhabitants and larger worms, insects and grubs. All these creatures need air, moisture and food. Using manure, garden compost and other sources of organic matter is the key to sustaining this soil life and keeping the soil healthy.

Left: *The key to developing a successful organic garden lies in the careful management of the soil.*

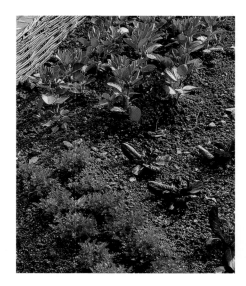

Above: *Newly planted crops must be kept weed free so that water and nutrients are freely available.*

Above: *Companion plants can help to protect crops naturally from pests, thus avoiding damage to the soil ecology.*

Above: *Crops that are grown in rows must be rotated on a regular basis in order to avoid soil-borne pests and diseases.*

TYPES OF SOIL

Soil is probably the most important constituent of any organic garden because it is vital for successful plant growth. Understanding your soil and knowing how this can help you to create a healthy, fertile growing environment for your plants should be a priority. The starting point in this process is an understanding of the different soil types and how they affect the plants you can grow. Once you understand the soil in your own garden, then you will be able to create a successful organic garden.

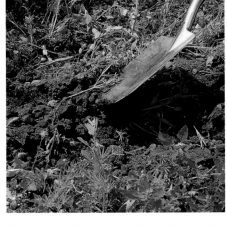

Above: *All soil types benefit greatly from the addition of organic matter such as this green manure.*

WHAT ARE SOILS MADE OF?

Both natural soils and some potting mixes for container-grown plants usually have five main components. These are mineral particles (the inorganic fraction), organic matter (the remains of living organisms), water (the "soil solution"), air (which fills the spaces between solid particles that are not filled with water) and living organisms. The proportions of these components vary widely according to the soil type, or the growing medium.

The proportions of water, air and organic matter can be readily changed by soil cultivation and other horticultural practices. A good topsoil will continuously supply plant roots with water, air and nutrients. Subsoil (the largely inert soil layer that lies beneath the thin layer of "living" topsoil) has less organic matter than topsoil. Plant growth will suffer when the proportions of water and air in the medium are out of balance. Too much air will have the same effect upon plant roots as a drought, whereas too much water causes waterlogging. Growth will also suffer if nutrient levels are too low, too high or if there is an imbalance in supply between different nutrients. In addition, soil that is too compacted for roots to grow will also adversely affect growth.

SAND AND SILT

Sandy and silty soils originate from river deposits, windblown sediments or from the erosion of sandstone outcrops. Their general properties are that they do not provide or retain plant nutrients; they are not cohesive and therefore possess a weak structure; and in most cases they are free draining.

Silts, unless well structured, will be waterlogged. Sand, on the other hand, is naturally free draining. The structure and texture of sandy soils means that they are only able to hold a very small reserve of water. Organic matter can improve the available water content but the real trick in avoiding drought-stress lies in ensuring that plants root deeply into the soil. Nutrient shortage can also be a problem on sandy soils which have a tendency to become acidic over time. Liming and the regular addition of organic matter will help alleviate these problems.

Sandy soils do have the advantage of "warming up" quickly in spring due to their lower water content and are easier to work early in the year. This means that you can grow a wider range of plants in a sandy soil. Planting or transplanting is also easier in the autumn.

Organic material is broken down very quickly in sandy soils due to good aeration and a temperature that favours rapid bacterial action. Many light soils naturally have less than two per cent organic matter and it is vital that organic matter be added regularly to sustain healthy plant growth.

PLANTS SUITABLE FOR DIFFERENT SOIL TYPES

Many plants have a type of soil in which they grow best. The list below gives a few examples of the soil preferences of some common species.

Plants suitable for acid soils
Rhododendron (all species)
Camellia (all cultivars)

Plants suitable for alkaline soils
Butterfly bush (*Buddleja* spp.)
Sage (*Salvia*)

Plants suitable for hot dry soils in sun
Yucca (all species)
Broom (*Cytisus*)
Lavender (*Lavandula*)

Plants suitable for damp or wet soils
Willow (*Salix*)
Dogwood (*Cornus*)
Plantain lily (*Hosta*)

Plants suitable for heavy clay
Weigela (all cultivars)
Crocosmia (all cultivars)
Daffodil (*Narcissus*)

Plants suitable for dry shaded soils
Flowering currant (*Ribes sanguineum*)
Pachysandra terminalis
Elephant's ear (*Bergenia cordifolia*)

COMMON TYPES OF SOIL

sand

silt

clay

loam

Sand A free-draining soil that is quick to warm up, but hungry and thirsty.
Silt River deposits can be sticky, but not as sticky as clay. Rich and easy to work.

Clay A heavy soil that is often difficult to work. Slow to warm up, but fairly rich.
Loam A moisture-retentive soil that warms up quickly and works perfectly.

HAND-TEXTURING METHOD

sandy   silty or loamy sand   loam   clay loam   clay

Finding out what type of soil you have is easy and does not require any specialist equipment. This test is ultimately a matter of judgement and will only give you a relative picture of the sort of soil you have. However, it is surprisingly accurate. Simply take a small amount of soil – about a teaspoonful will do – in the palm of your hand. Moisten with a little water (not too much but enough to make it just workable). Once moistened, try to form the soil into one of the shapes shown above.

1 Begin by forming a ball. If it stays together, then proceed to the next shape. If it does not form a ball, then you have a sandy soil.
2 If you can flatten the ball without it breaking up, then you have a silty sand or a loamy sand.
3 If you can roll the flattened ball into a thick sausage shape, then you have a loam.
4 A soil that can be rolled into a thin "sausage" is a clay loam.
5 If you can bend the soil into a horseshoe or ring shape, then you have a clay soil.

Above: *Plants such as alliums and eryngiums like well-drained soil and so will thrive together in the same site.*

CLAY

The particles found in clay are extremely small and are able to interact with, and directly affect, the chemistry of the soil. The individual clay particles are so tiny that they are actually bonded together by electrical charges which produce the characteristic plasticity of this type of soil. Clay is both water retentive and rich in nutrients. It has few pore spaces and those that are there have a tendency to become waterlogged. Clay is prone to swelling when waterlogged and shrinkage when dry. As a result, clays heave (swell outward and upward) when wet and crack when dry. They can also be subject to frost action which causes an increase in tiny, almost microscopic, airspaces (micro pores). Pure clay soils are rare, although some soils may be very rich in clay. They have the potential to be extremely fertile soils if they are well managed.

LOAMS

Loams are a mixture of sand, silt and clay that results in a blend of the characteristics of each constituent part. They are usually characterized by their clay content. Heavy loams are about 24–30% clay, whereas light loams contain about 12–18% clay. Heavy loams behave and should be treated like clay soils. Light loams should be treated like sandy soils. Medium loams are potentially the ideal mixture, exhibiting the advantages of both heavy and light soils without many of the disadvantages of either.

HUMUS

This is a stable form of partially decomposed plant material that gives topsoil its characteristically dark colour. Humus has a high nutrient-reserve potential (2½ x better than clay), retains water, increases the friability (suitability for cultivation) of heavy soils and its darker colour encourages soils to warm up more rapidly.

SOIL PROFILE

A typical soil profile usually consists of three main elements: an upper layer of dark, fertile topsoil; a middle layer of lighter, infertile subsoil; and a lower layer of bedrock, which ranges from a few to hundreds of metres (yards) deep.

Topsoil is the dark layer of soil that contains organic material. Keep as deep as possible, although usually only one spit (spade) deep.

Subsoil is usually lighter in colour and contains little or no organic material or nutrients. It should be broken to one spit depth, but not mixed with the topsoil.

Bedrock is usually below the level of cultivation.

MANAGING YOUR SOIL

Any soil has the potential to be a fertile growing medium in which plants will thrive if it is managed correctly.

Management of light/sandy soils
• Maintain levels of organic matter.
• Lime when required. (N.B. It is often easier to select species tolerant of the site conditions in the long term.)
• Fertilize well as light soils are usually infertile. (N.B. Some exotic and native plant species actually thrive under relatively poor nutrient conditions.)
• Irrigate frequently in the first year after planting, less so once deeper roots are established.

Management of clay soils
• Drainage is essential.
• Maintain lime status.
• Maintain levels of organic matter and fertilize when needed.
• Wise cultivation is needed to conserve winter or summer tilth produced by natural weathering, i.e. cracking due to wetting/drying cycle and breakdown by frost action.

SOIL STRUCTURE

Soils are made up of mineral and rock particles that give them their natural properties. The character of the mineral fraction cannot be changed but the way that these building blocks are organized within the soil can. Creating and maintaining soil structure is a key aspect of maintaining the fertility of the soil and supporting healthy plant growth. Even the most difficult soils can be modified to create a fertile growing medium for plants.

Above: *Even "difficult" soils can be transformed into a good growing medium by careful cultivation.*

WHAT IS MEANT BY SOIL STRUCTURE?

Soil structure is quite simply the way soils are organized. To use a simple analogy: if we see the soil particles (sand, silt or clay – the mineral fraction) as the building materials – like the bricks and mortar of a house, for instance – then the structure is the architecture. The building materials themselves cannot be altered, but the architecture can vary considerably from home to home. This is the key. It is possible to improve a soil's structure even if the mineral fraction remains unchanged. It is perfectly feasible to have a well-structured clay soil for instance. It all depends upon how well you manage it.

WHY IS SOIL STRUCTURE IMPORTANT FOR PLANT GROWTH?

In order to survive, plant roots need water, nutrients and air. Plant roots breathe in the soil, taking in oxygen and expelling carbon dioxide. A poorly structured soil may have too little airspace. This can have two negative effects. Fresh air (containing oxygen) may not be able to penetrate the soil very easily and the soil will tend to become waterlogged following rain. Waterlogging will also reduce the air available in the soil.

Below: *A rotavator is a useful and labour-reducing method of breaking up the soil to prepare it for planting.*

Structure is therefore very important in terms of maintaining the health of plant roots. Plant shoot development is directly linked to root health. A healthy root system ensures healthy shoots and will ultimately result in better growth and crop yields.

HOW DOES SOIL STRUCTURE DEVELOP IN NATURAL SYSTEMS?

Soil structure naturally develops in soils through the effect of weather cycles. Wetting causes soils to swell while drying causes shrinkage. This naturally causes soils to crack. The action of freezing and thawing is also important on clay soils in areas where frosts occur. They form particles known commonly as crumbs. The "crumb structure" of any soil develops over time and is important in terms of allowing the free passage of water through the soil and air that must be able to move in and out of the soil. In this way soils do not become habitually waterlogged and natural nutrient cycles – oxygen, carbon and nitrogen, for example – are not impeded. Plant roots and soil organisms, such as worms, naturally help to maintain soil structure, as does the natural addition of decaying plant material each autumn.

HOW TO ALTER SOIL STRUCTURE

Humans have learned over time that even an infertile area can be worked – and the structure of the soil improved – by cultivation. This is covered in more detail later but it is essential to understand now that cultivation is a way of rapidly accelerating the natural cycles that promote good structure. Digging and breaking down "clods" helps to introduce air and creates new pores in the soil. Adding organic matter helps to maintain these pore spaces, retains moisture (in dry soils) and encourages the action of soil-dwelling creatures such as worms. No-dig

Above: *If you need to work on wet soil, work from a plank of wood to ensure the soil is not compacted and its structure destroyed.*

systems aim to harness this natural cycle more closely, but the goal is the same – a rich, fertile and well-structured soil.

IMPROVING DRAINAGE

Soils that tend to become waterlogged often do so as a result of poor structure and because there is nowhere for the water to go. The vast majority of soils do not actually need (or benefit from) the installation of land drains. Often it is enough to dig over a site because much of the drainage problem may be due to surface compaction. Surface compaction severely reduces the passage of water into the soil and can result in a sticky surface that is prone to "puddling". Installing land drains is usually only done where the water table is very near to the

SECTION THROUGH A LAND DRAIN

This cross-section of a typical land drain shows the various layers of materials from which it is constructed, including the topsoil, an inverted turf or perforated plastic membrane, gravel, peabeach or crushed stone, and the land-drain pipe.

- Topsoil
- Inverted turf
- Gravel
- Land-drain pipe
- Peabeach or crushed stone

surface or the consequences of flooding are severe (if they threaten housing or use of the area for instance). Land drainage using pipes or "tiles" is a complex undertaking and may be best left to a contractor.

If you have a sloping site you can dig a "soak away" drain at the base of the slope and improve the structure of the soil to encourage the rapid dispersal of water following rain. If you have a fairly flat site, then you should consider making a raised bed for growing crops. Raised beds are easy to manage and avoid the inconvenience of installing (and maintaining) a drainage system.

IMPROVING SOIL STRUCTURE

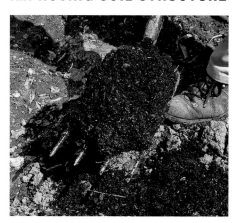

1 *One of the best ways to improve the structure of the soil is to add as much organic material as you can, preferably when the soil is dug. For heavy soils, this is best done in the autumn.*

2 *If the soil has already been dug, then well-rotted organic material can be worked into the surface of the soil with a fork. The worms will complete the task of working it into the soil.*

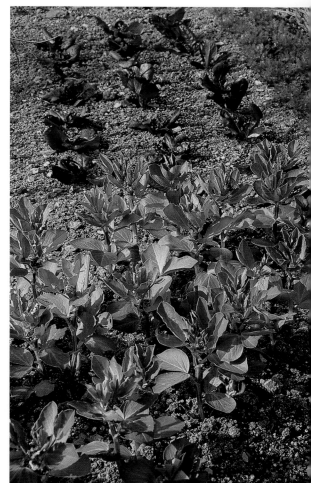

Above: *A well-prepared soil that is kept free of weeds and dug regularly will result in healthier, more vigorous crops throughout the growing season. A healthier crop will be more resistant to pest and disease attack.*

SOIL CHEMISTRY

While for many of us the word chemistry can be extremely off-putting, the truth of the matter is that everything in life is made up of chemicals. While the pure science of chemistry can be very complex, the chemistry of soil that organic gardeners must master is mercifully simple. A rudimentary knowledge of the chemicals that affect plant growth and how soil chemistry can be controlled and managed is all you need to grow healthy plants in an organic garden.

Above: *You can reduce the acidity of the soil by adding lime some weeks before planting. Test the soil first to see how much is needed.*

OXYGEN

The amount of oxygen in a healthy soil controls the type of life it will support. Nearly all organisms need oxygen to survive. Soils without oxygen are described as anaerobic. Most organisms can survive for short periods under anaerobic conditions, but this causes the accumulation of poisons that can become toxic at high concentrations.

A typical soil has about 50 per cent of its pore space filled by air and 50 per cent by water. Only certain bacteria can remain in anaerobic conditions for long periods of time, although some species of bacteria can readily switch from oxygen-rich to oxygen-poor conditions quickly to adapt to local conditions. Microbes use about 70 per cent of the oxygen in the soil and plant roots use the remaining 30 per cent. Under anaerobic conditions, the efficiency of microbes is poor and decomposition rates are much slower.

WATER

Soil water is vital for all soil life. Without it, microbes cannot grow or remain active and many will go into "hibernation" until water returns. Fungi, on the other hand, are more resistant to water stress than bacteria. With too much water, oxygen levels drop and the lack of air tends to slow down the nutrient cycles driven by microbes. Water is also the medium by which essential nutrients are able to enter the plant.

SOIL pH

The pH scale is an abbreviated form of "Potential of Hydrogen". It is a measure of the degree of acidity or the alkalinity of a solution as measured on a scale (pH scale) of 0 to 14. The midpoint of 7.0 on the pH scale represents neutrality. A "neutral" solution is, therefore, neither acid nor alkaline. Numbers below 7.0 indicate acidity; numbers greater than 7.0 indicate alkalinity.

The level of acidity or alkalinity (pH) of a soil can significantly affect the nutrient availability. Many nutrients become "unavailable" to plants when the soil is either too acid or too alkaline. Microbial activity in soil is also largely controlled by pH. Fungi tend to predominate in acid soils, bacteria in neutral or alkaline soils.

Soil pH is essentially a measure of the acidity of the soil water, although the soil itself is the deciding factor in respect of what this will be.

Most plants prefer or are tolerant of a specific pH range. Some plants, such as the hydrangea, exhibit a different flower colour depending upon the prevailing pH. Most garden plants, especially vegetables, thrive within a range of 6–7 which happens to be where the majority of nutrients are available. It is best to maintain this pH in order to optimize the availability of nutrients. Many garden plants, however, are not too fussy about the pH levels, so if you choose plants carefully, it will not usually be necessary to alter the soil acidity.

ACIDIFYING SOIL

Lowering the pH of a naturally limy soil is difficult because the soil often contains a reserve of calcium that is released immediately upon acidification. Lowering the pH involves the use of flowers of sulphur and is only usually successful over a short period of time.

TAKING A pH TEST

1 *Place the soil in a test tube until it reaches the mark on the side. For the most accurate results, dry the sample first, grind it into a powder and ensure it is free from stones.*

2 *Put a layer of barium sulphate powder into the tube level with the mark. This compound helps the solution to clear rapidly and makes the pH reading clearer.*

3 *Pour in a little of the indicator solution up to the mark shown on the tube. Be careful not to put in too much because this can make the solution dark and difficult to read.*

MAKING A NUTRIENT TEST

1 Place a small sample of the soil into the test tube up to the mark on the side.

2 Add a test solution (in this case one for nitrogen) up to the mark on the test tube.

3 Filter the solution to remove soil particles and leave just a liquid solution.

4 Decant the resulting filtered solution into another container for the final stage of the nutrient test.

5 Add a small amount of indicator powder. This will react with the solution and enable a colour reading to be taken.

6 Shake for about 10 seconds and compare with the chart. Here, the low reading indicates that a nitrogen-rich fertilizer will benefit this soil.

LIMING SOIL

It is generally easier to raise the soil pH than to lower it. Lime neutralizes soil acidity and is commonly applied as ground limestone, chalk or dolomitic limestone (dolodust). Lime requirement cannot be determined from soil pH because it is influenced by soil texture and organic matter content. Clay and humus act as a "buffer" because of their complex chemistry. If soil is known to be acidic, regular light application is preferable to heavier, more infrequent, doses.

HIGHLY ALKALINE SOILS

Soils that are too alkaline suffer trace element deficiencies of manganese, copper, iron, zinc and boron. Phosphates are also less available, their maximum availability being between pH 6–7. Disease organisms can be more of a problem in calcium-rich soils, as many disease-causing fungal agents prefer alkaline conditions. Some plants, such as rhododendrons, are intolerant of high pH and only grow on acid soils, while others, like helianthemums, thrive in highly alkaline soils.

GROWTH RESTRICTIONS IN EXTREMES OF PH

Many vital nutrients that are essential for healthy plant growth become unavailable in extremes of soil pH.

Nitrogen deficiency Most nitrates are released from organic matter and a low soil pH limits the rate of decomposition severely.

Phosphate deficiency Phosphate becomes unavailable outside the 6.5–7.5 pH range. Some plants form relationships with soil-borne fungi that release phosphates in acid conditions.

Trace-element toxicity and deficiency Trace elements, especially aluminium, iron and manganese, are generally more soluble in acidic conditions. Extreme acidity can lead to excessive quantities of trace elements and to plant death. Other trace elements, such as copper, boron and molybdenum, become less available at low soil pH. Molybdenum deficiency affects legumes, which will not grow in acid soils.

4 Add distilled water to the mark on the tube and shake the container vigorously for about a minute. Ensure the contents are mixed thoroughly and leave to settle.

5 Once sufficiently cleared, compare the colour against those on the chart, choosing the one that most closely matches that of the solution.

DIGGING AND CULTIVATION

Every organic gardener's goal should be a healthy soil to support plant growth and development. Digging is one of the commonest ways to create a rich, fertile and ultimately productive soil. It can be hard work at the outset, particularly on sites not cultivated for some time, but the results – in the form of healthier, more productive plants – are worth it. Quite simply, what you get out of your soil will depend upon what you put into it.

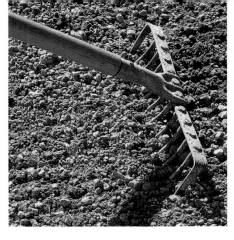

Above: *After a winter exposed to the weather, most soils can be easily broken into a fine tilth with a rake.*

THE BENEFITS OF DIGGING

Winter is the commonest time to dig, but soil can be dug at any time of the year if the conditions are right. Avoid working the soil when it is too dry and impenetrable, or too wet and sticking to your tools and boots. Clay soils may be best dug in mid- to late autumn to allow the action of frost to make the soil more suitable for final cultivation. Lighter soils are best dug in the spring or immediately prior to planting the site. Done properly, digging increases the amount of air space in the soil, which in turn benefits soil-dwelling organisms and plant roots due to the increase in oxygen available. It also lets you add organic matter that will feed these vital denizens of the soil and aid nutrient cycling. Calculate how much organic matter you will need before you start. You should aim to add about 30 per cent of the volume cultivated. A 20m² (220ft²) plot cultivated to one spade's depth will need 2.5 cubic metres (88 cubic feet) of manure or garden compost.

SINGLE DIGGING

This method involves digging down to the depth of one spade (this is called a spit). Single digging suffices on light free-draining soil as long as there is no layer of compacted stones in the topsoil. Much of the procedure is the same as for double digging, but the subsoil is left undisturbed. Mark out the position of the bed. Remove any turf or vegetation from the surface, put to one side and then bury it in the bottom of the bed as you proceed. Work across the bed, digging out a trench that is two spits wide and a single spit deep, and place the soil to one side. Remove stones and perennial weeds as you go. Fork well-rotted manure or compost into the trench. Begin digging a new trench behind the first. Throw the soil forward into the first trench, burying the organic matter. Repeat this process of trenching down the bed until the last trench has been dug. Add organic matter to the base and fill the trench with the soil dug from the first trench.

DOUBLE DIGGING

This is a method for deeply digging the soil, in which the soil is broken up to a depth of approximately 70cm (28in) or more. The method usually involves digging a quantity of soil and setting it aside while aerating and sometimes adding an amendment to the subsoil below, then returning the topsoil. There are several methods of double digging, all of which have their advocates. Two methods for double digging are described here.

First, define the area where the digging will take place, making an estimate of the area to be dug. Dig a trench, 30cm (12in) wide and a spit deep, across half the width of the bed. Place the excavated soil next to the other half, placing it on to a tarpaulin or similar covering if the surface needs protection.

When the trench is complete, fork the subsoil, rocking it back and forth, to loosen it down to a depth of about 30cm (12in). Then, spread a layer of garden compost over

---

SINGLE DIGGING

Single digging is the simplest method of cultivation. It is well suited to light soils or those soils that have been well worked for a number of years. It simply involves digging and inverting the soil to a single spade's depth, leaving the subsoil below undisturbed.

1 *Start by digging a single trench across the width of the plot. Put the soil from the first trench to one side because you will need to use it later in the final trench.*

2 *Put a layer of manure in the bottom of the trench. Dig out the next trench and cover over the manure in the first trench with the earth taken from the second trench.*

3 *Repeat this process of adding manure to each trench and filling in with earth from the next, breaking up the soil as you go and keeping the surface as even as possible.*

4 *Continue down the length of the plot until you reach the final trench. This should be filled in with the earth taken from the first trench, which was set to one side.*

DOUBLE DIGGING, METHOD ONE

Double digging is a good method for compacted, heavy or poor soils that are in need of rejuvenation. It involves a deep cultivation of both the topsoil and subsoil and is well worth the hard work, producing a wonderful soil in which plants will thrive.

1 *Dig a wide trench, placing the soil to one side to be used later when filling in the final trench.*

2 *Break up the soil at the bottom of the trench with a fork, adding manure to the soil as you proceed.*

3 *Dig the next trench in the bed, turning the soil over on top of the broken soil in the first trench.*

4 *Continue down the plot, ensuring that subsoil from the lower trench is not mixed with topsoil of the upper.*

DOUBLE DIGGING, METHOD TWO

1 *Keeping soil from each level separate, dig the first trench two spits deep and fork over. Dig the second trench one spit deep.*

2 *Add organic material to the first double trench and dig the lower spit of the second trench into it.*

3 *Dig an upper third trench one spit deep, and place the soil on top of that already placed in the first trench.*

4 *Continue, ensuring that the topsoil and subsoil do not mix. Fill in remaining trenches with soil taken from the first one.*

the exposed subsoil. Move over one spit's width in the bed, and begin to dig out another trench, moving and inverting the excavated soil into the adjacent trench that was just dug. When you get to the end of the bed replace the soil which was set aside.

When the digging is finished, level the site prior to planting. More garden compost (approximately 8cm/3in) can be spread over the surface and forked in at this stage.

You do not have to dig the entire garden all at once. Instead, work on small areas, say, one metre (yard) square, whenever you wish. Once you double-dig a bed, it is important not to walk on it. After all, the whole point of double digging is to loosen the topsoil and the subsoil to a sufficient depth so that the roots of the plants can grow unrestricted and water can readily percolate through the soil. Walking on the soil will simply pack it down again.

There is a second method of double digging that is less commonly used, which enriches the soil to a greater depth.

SECONDARY CULTIVATION

This normally involves the nourishing of the soil after it has been cultivated by digging and usually entails the addition of some form of organic matter during, or immediately after, its completion. Secondary cultivation also describes light digging used to control weeds or incorporate green manures. The tool generally used for this is a fork. Light forking is often the best method to use in areas with permanent plantings of perennial plants or shrubs.

USING A ROTAVATOR

A rotavator is a useful labour-saving device for breaking down dug clods and creating a fine, free-running "tilth" that can easily be levelled for planting or seed-bed preparation.

TIPS FOR DIGGING

Digging can be hard work, but simply following the tips given below will help you to avoid strains and injuries.

- Start with a small area, pace yourself and avoid straining your back.
- Use a spade that is right for you and the job. It should be a little higher than hip height when held vertically.
- Do not try to lift more than you can handle. You will dig for longer periods of time by taking smaller amounts.
- As you work, try to establish a rhythm that you can maintain at all times.
- When doing a lot of heavy digging, scrape the blade clean now and then, and, if necessary, use a file to sharpen the end of the spade, following the original bevel of the blade.

NO-DIG GARDENING

As the name suggests, no-dig gardening is a method of growing plants without cultivating the ground they occupy. While this may seem unnatural to some confirmed tillers of the soil, it is actually the most natural method available. No-dig gardening mimics the natural cycle. After all, plants have grown on the earth's surface for over 400 million years without people digging the soil for them. This approach also has the advantage of being less labour-intensive.

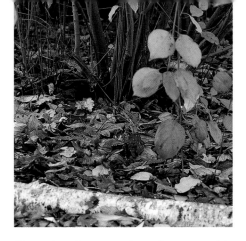

Above: *In nature, organic matter accumulates on the soil surface, breaks down and is worked into the soil by worms.*

ESTABLISHING A NATURAL CYCLE

Essentially no-dig gardening relies upon natural soil processes combined with the action of soil organisms to produce a good soil structure and natural nutrient cycles. There are numerous ways that this can be done, but all rely upon inputs from the top down. A thick top-dressing of organic matter is placed on the surface to be absorbed by the soil itself. Less laborious than digging, the no-dig method does need planning and careful input in order to be successful, although a properly prepared no-dig bed will be every bit as effective as a conventionally cultivated one.

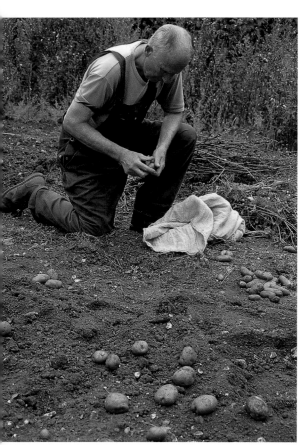

WHAT ARE THE BENEFITS?

Assuming weeds can be controlled, most vegetable crops can be grown with reduced tillage. The key features of a no-dig vegetable-growing system are to keep the soil covered with organic mulch as much of the time as possible and to keep off the soil. The beds are left permanently in place, and there is no cultivation.

Plants grown without tillage use water more efficiently, the water-holding capacity of the soil increases, and water loss from run-off and evaporation are reduced. For crops grown without irrigation in drought-prone soils, this more efficient use of water can translate into higher yields.

In addition, the organic matter in soil and populations of beneficial insects are maintained, as are earthworm populations and microbial activity. Soil and nutrients are less likely to be lost from the ground, less time is required to prepare the soil for planting, and, since there is less bare soil, there will be fewer opportunities for weeds to get established. The mulch of organic matter also helps to keep weeds down.

WHAT ARE THE DISADVANTAGES?

Potential problems associated with the no-dig method are compaction, flooding and poor drainage. However, if the water-holding capacity of a soil improves, no-till systems may produce higher yields. Soil temperatures under organic mulch can be several degrees lower than bare soil or soil under a plastic mulch. Although the lower temperature can be an advantage, especially in the summer when soil temperatures under plastic can be excessive, it can delay crop development.

Left: *Many organic gardeners grow crops such as potatoes quite successfully without ever resorting to digging.*

WHAT ARE THE BENEFITS OF NO-DIG SYSTEMS TO THE ORGANIC GARDENER?

Although no-dig beds may require a little longer to establish initially than cultivated plots, they do offer considerable labour-saving advantages to the organic gardener. They also suffer very few disadvantages when these are weighed against the considerable advantages.

Advantages
- Plants use water more efficiently.
- Better water-holding capacity of the soil.
- Reduced water loss from run-off and evaporation.
- Higher crop yields in areas prone to drought.
- Organic matter in the soil and soil organisms are maintained at higher levels.
- The lower temperature can be an advantage, especially in summer when soil temperatures under plastic can be excessive.
- Soil and nutrients are more easily maintained.
- Less time is required to prepare the soil for planting.
- Fewer weeds become established due to the mulch of organic matter and the lack of bare soil.

Disadvantages
- Soil can become compacted or poorly drained if it is not properly managed.
- Soil temperatures under an organic mulch can be several degrees lower than bare soil, which can delay the development of crops.

MAKING A NO-DIG BED

A bed system which includes permanent paths is essential if digging is to be eliminated from gardening tasks. Planning the area so that all parts of the bed can be reached from the paths means that you can grow your crops closer together (you do not need to leave extra space for access) and you will be able to harvest more from a smaller area.

Mark out the beds on the ground or build simple raised beds with wooden sides. Alternatively, those wishing to make a more permanent edge could consider a low brick wall. By raising the bed it is possible to create a deep bed of good-quality soil that will warm up more quickly than the surrounding soil. A raised bed also means you do not have to bend down so far to carry out routine tasks and the method is tailor-made for disabled gardeners. Raised edging is also useful for attaching supporting hoops, crop covers and cloches. Edges such as these are also ideal for providing barriers for pests. Devices such as water traps or copper paper are easily attached to them to prevent slugs and snails from entering the bed.

Beds should be no more than 1.2m (4ft) wide and paths at least 30cm (12in) wide with every other path double this width to allow for easy wheelbarrow access. Individual beds should be no longer than 3.5m (12ft) otherwise you will waste a lot of time walking around them. The beds can be of any design, from a simple series of parallel rectangles to a more complex design of interlocking shapes. Whatever design you choose, try to follow the same recommended bed and path widths, remembering that narrow angles and very small beds are more difficult to construct and use space less efficiently.

Right: *Green manures are usually dug into the soil, but they can still be used in a no-dig system. The manure can be cut down and left as a mulch.*

PLANTING POTATOES IN A NO-DIG BED

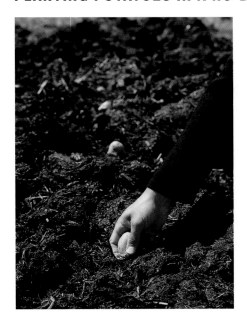

1 *Place a thick layer of well-rotted manure or garden compost on the bed to be planted. This should be quite deep – at least 15–20cm (6–8in) – as it will quickly decompose during the growing season. Early planting is possible by manuring in winter and covering with plastic sheeting to warm the soil. The potatoes are planted directly into this and may be more closely spaced than those planted in soil, perhaps as close as 30cm (12in) apart.*

2 *Apply a generous mulch of straw once the bed is planted to give cover to the tubers and to suppress weed growth on the manure or compost. Spread a second layer of composted organic material over the straw. Add another layer of straw and composted material. Water the bed well. Once the potato plants begin to emerge, more straw can be laid down on to the bed, as the material put down earlier in the season will begin to compost down.*

3 *As the potato stems grow, mulch heavily in order to ensure that no light reaches the developing tubers. The potato crop will mature at the same rate as potatoes grown in ordinary soil. The no-dig system is possibly the best method for heavy clay soils that are prone to waterlogging. Potatoes grown in this way are also easy to harvest as there is no digging and the potatoes are cleaner once they are ready for harvesting.*

SOIL CONDITIONERS

There is quite a range of conditioners available to the organic gardener for improving the soil. Some are free (if you do not count the time taken in working and carting them), others are relatively cheap, while those bought by the bag can be quite expensive. The best option for the organic gardener begins with using the materials that are closest to hand. Smaller gardens or those that are newly established may require soil conditioners to be brought in. This section looks at some of the options.

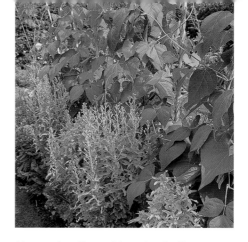

Above: *A well-conditioned soil will pay dividends in terms of enhanced plant growth and development.*

FARMYARD MANURE

This is usually freely available, although these days it comes increasingly from stables rather than farms. It contains a small amount of nutrients although it usually makes the soil more acidic as it decomposes and should always be well rotted before use. It can also contain lots of weed seeds, which often come from the bedding used for the animals. Occasionally there can be problems if the straw used has been sprayed with pesticides, so always be sure of your source. Farmyard manure is usually cheap or occasionally free for the taking.

BURYING GREEN WASTE

If you have space, you can simply open a trench in the soil and bury your green waste 20–30cm (8–12in) deep under the soil. It will take perhaps two to three months during the warm season to break down. Avoid planting crops in the soil above until the material has decomposed properly.

Left: *Spent mushroom compost is an ideal material for improving the structure of many types of soil.*

LEAF MOULD

Many gardeners believe leaf mould to be the finest addition to any soil. The product itself forms naturally under the closed canopy of forest trees. It is, as the name suggests, the rotted product of fallen leaves. It is not particularly rich in nutrients but it has an extremely good ability to condition a soil and encourages natural nutrient cycles in your soil. It is usually made by the gardeners that wish to use it and is rarely sold on. Anyone who has a ready supply of leaves will find this an easy material to make.

Start by gathering up leaves in the autumn and stack in a chicken-wire cage to prevent them being blown back over the garden. Do not add any greens or other materials to the pile. The heap will rot down slowly and be ready for use in one to two years. It can be sited in a dark corner where nothing else will grow, but you must ensure that you keep the pile moist all year round. The wire cage can be removed after two months or so and used again the following

Left: *Animal manures can provide both nutrients and valuable organic matter when added to your garden soil.*

autumn. Alternatively, two permanent pits, sited side by side, can be filled (or emptied) in alternate years. Smaller quantities of leaves can be pushed into black plastic sacks with the top closed and with holes pierced by a garden fork around the sides and bottom of the bag to allow some airflow.

SPENT MUSHROOM COMPOST

This is one of the few types of organic matter to have a slightly alkaline effect on the soil. It is a uniform and friable mixture of stable organic materials that is a waste product of the mushroom-growing industry. It is usually quite inexpensive. The composting and growing processes that produce this material bind nutrients to the organic matter, resulting in a substance that holds on to nutrients more readily than fresh or non-composted organic wastes. In addition, the compost has good moisture-holding abilities.

Spent mushroom compost is slightly alkaline with a pH ranging from 7–8 but generally around 7.3. There are few weed seeds, insects or pathogens because the compost is pasteurized before it is removed from the mushroom house. The addition of spent compost to garden soil can result in a

BUILDING A LEAF MOULD PIT

1 *Drive in four 1.5m (5ft) posts to form the four corners of a square on the ground. The posts should be spaced about 1m (3ft) apart and there should be just over 1m left above ground once the posts are driven in.*

2 *Attach chicken wire – a 1m (3ft) wide roll is needed for this – to the stakes using "U"-shaped fencing staples, hammered in firmly. Pull the wire tight across the length of the roll before attaching it to the next post.*

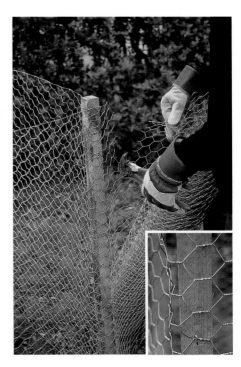

3 *Once the wire has been securely stapled to the posts all the way around, cut it with wire cutters, folding the sharp ends under the attached mesh so that they cannot cut you.*

4 *Place fallen leaves into the "pit" until it is full. Firm the leaves lightly in layers as you go, so that the pit is completely packed with leaves but still contains a little air.*

5 *After a year or two, the leaf mould is ready and should be applied to the soil in late winter or early spring in order to gain the most benefit.*

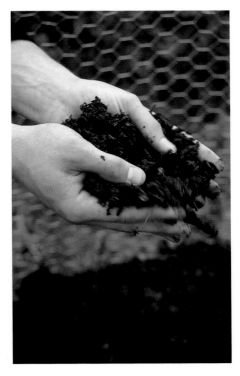

6 *It is a good idea to build two or more pits and rotate their use as a single pit will not be emptied in time to receive the new lot of leaves in the following autumn.*

Left: *Beans and other leguminous plants are an important part of a successful organic vegetable garden, "fixing" their own nitrogen and so helping to raise levels of soil fertility.*

or sickly cocoa, is often enough to put people off. They are sometimes marketed commercially although they may be available as a local by-product of industry. Whatever product you use, it should be well rotted before it is used as a soil conditioner.

WORM COMPOST
Worms can be used to compost your kitchen waste both indoors and outdoors, although both methods have their limitations and advantages.

The materials that are being composted are consumed by the worms and then excreted as worm casts. This process binds the nutrients consumed into a form that can be used by plants and reduces the volume of the original materials. These worm casts are covered with slow-dissolving, semi-permeable mucus that acts as a time-release mechanism for the nutritional content of the worm casts and also gives the finished compost good water-retentive qualities.

higher pH, increased nutrient-holding capacity and better soil structure. The main disadvantage occurs when the compost is first mixed with soil, as bacteria convert the proteins in the compost to ammonia, which can be toxic to young plants. Always ensure the source of your compost is an organic mushroom grower where possible.

VEGETABLE INDUSTRIAL WASTE
Some by-products of the food industry, such as spent hop waste and cocoa shells, can be beneficial as soil conditioners in the organic garden. They are useful in terms of their ability to improve soil structure. However, their smell, which may be described as rancid ale or beer with hops,

Above: *Brandling or tiger worms readily reduce vegetable matter into a useful compost material within a wormery.*

A WORMERY

Worms are an effective way to break down kitchen waste such as vegetable scraps. They will eventually eat their *bedding as well as the kitchen waste. The resulting worm casts are a nutrient-rich soil conditioner.*

Decomposing waste (strong manure, leaf mould, shredded newspaper, old garden compost)

Planks of wood to separate compost from gravel

Drainage holes

Damp newspaper

New kitchen waste

20cm (8in) bedding material

15cm (6in) gravel

Worm colonies can be built in a similar way to a cold pile compost heap, with materials added as they become available. Excessive heat and frequent pile turning are not needed. Too much heat will actually kill the worms. Alternatively, a purpose-built wormery can be used. Both methods require materials to be placed in a shaded, cool and moist location. The worm colony must not become heated by the microbial action that takes place in normal composting. If the colony does get hot, it may cause the loss of the worms if they do not have cooler areas to which they can escape.

For an indoor worm colony, the wormery (a sealed, ventilated box with a close-fitting lid) is filled with bedding materials (usually damp shredded newspaper or similar) and the worms are added. Vegetable waste from the kitchen is placed on top or a few inches under the bedding where the worms can find and devour it. Eventually, the worms eat their bedding as well as the vegetable scraps. The finished worm castings can be removed and used. New bedding and kitchen scraps are then placed

in the container and the worms returned to make a new batch of compost. Many purchased wormeries have the facility to collect the liquid by-product of the worms' activities, which makes an excellent liquid plant food.

It is advisable to check the pH level of the wormery every now and then. Thin, white, thread-like cotton worms are usually

Above: *Leafy crops benefit from the addition of organic matter because it encourages nitrogen-fixing bacteria to do their all-important work in the soil.*

an indication that the pH is too low. Adding some calcified seaweed can help to counter this acidity, as can a regular addition of eggshells.

Above: *Place a thick layer – about 8–10cm (4–5in) – of well-rotted organic matter into the base of a trench dug to a spit's depth (the depth of a spade blade). Use a fork to break up the material and to ensure that there is plenty of air space in the soil to aid the breakdown of the material and help soil organisms to cycle the nutrients.*

THE BENEFITS OF ADDING ORGANIC MATTER
Using organic matter as a mulch or soil conditioner will help to warm up the soil earlier in the spring. This in turn will allow for the earlier planting of some types of plant.

- Organic matter inoculates the soil with vast numbers of beneficial microbes and provides the food source that soil-dwelling microbes need to live. These microbes are able to extract nutrients from the mineral part of the soil and eventually pass the nutrients on to plants.
- Adding organic matter to your soil improves the way in which water interacts with the soil and improves the overall soil structure. All soils can benefit from the regular addition of organic matter.

To sandy soils
- Organic matter acts as a sponge to help retain water that would otherwise drain down below the reach of plant roots. This has the benefit of protecting plants against drought.

To clay soils
- Organic matter helps to increase the air space within the soil, making it drain more quickly. This ensures that the soil does not become waterlogged or dry out into a brick-like substance.

MAKING GARDEN COMPOST

Every organic garden should have at least one compost heap, where garden and kitchen waste can be broken down by microbes and other soil-dwelling creatures to produce a good medium-fertility soil improver. Making compost is not difficult and is an excellent way to recycle waste. Many gardeners take great pride in their home-produced compost and all gardens can benefit from this sustainable approach to soil improvement.

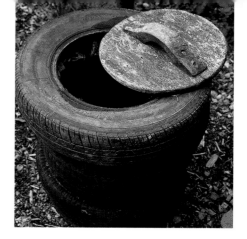

Above: *Even a stack of old tyres can be recycled and used to make an effective compost heap.*

THE SITE

A position in full sun will give the compost heap additional heat, allowing the contents to decompose more rapidly. If time is not a key factor, partial shade or even full shade will do. Compost is easily made in a freestanding pile in a sunny or partially

shaded area in the garden. Alternatively, a simple structure can be used to contain the pile. A variety of materials can be used to make these structures, including wood, bricks, pallets, a wire cage or even a stack of used tyres. Whichever method you use, you must provide good drainage. An average heap should be around a cubic metre (10 cu. ft). It can be much larger, but any smaller and it will not be as effective.

When adding waste materials to the heap, the items should be as small as you can make them. The more surface area that is exposed, the quicker it will decompose. A chipper or shredder is a big help. Many gardeners are keen advocates of adding a small amount of good topsoil in order to introduce microorganisms that will kick-start the process of decomposition. Compost heaps in containers can be built

Left: *Composting your garden and kitchen waste ensures that you return essential nutrients to the soil.*

up with successive layers of "green" and "brown" materials, separating these with thin layers of topsoil.

Sifting the pile is the final stage of the process, with any large pieces of residue being returned back to the new heap.

COMPOST INGREDIENTS

The potential ingredients for your compost heap will be either "brown" or "green". Browns are dry and dead plant materials, such as straw, hay, dry brown weeds, autumn leaves, nutshells, shredded paper, pine needles, tough plant stems and wood chips or sawdust. Because they tend to be dry, browns often need to be moistened before they are put into a compost system.

Greens are fresh (and often green) plant materials, such as green weeds from the garden, fruit and vegetable scraps, green leaves, grass clippings, tea bags, coffee grounds, seaweed, eggshells, fish scraps, green manures and fresh horse manure. Compared with browns, greens contain

---

MAKING A HOT PILE COMPOST HEAP

1 *Starting with an empty compost bin, place a layer of "browns" – straw, old leaves and chipped wood are ideal – in the base of the bin. If the bin is positioned over bare soil, include some fine twiggy material to help to circulate air to the base of the pile.*

2 *Add a layer of brown compost materials, such as autumn leaves, plant stems and wood chips, which should be approximately 15cm (6in) deep, and ensure that it is of an even thickness. The material should be lightly firmed in.*

3 *Add a new layer of "greens" to the compost bin. Most plant material can be used for this, although you should avoid too much fibrous or woody material such as plant stems. Never include weed seeds if possible.*

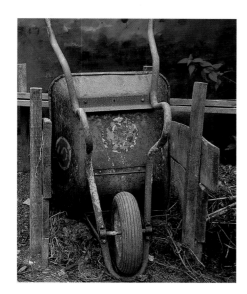

Above: *It is often advisable to have two or more compost heaps at any one time in order to ensure a steady supply.*

the heap with cardboard or old carpet and peel this back to stir in any greens. In this type of composting, there are never enough high-nitrogen greens to get the pile really hot. Turn the pile a minimum of once a month if you have not recently added any greens, thereby breaking up the decaying mass and making it friable. If you do use this method, be sure you always have at least as much browns as added greens, as too many greens will just create a slimy, smelly mess. Some compost heaps (those with lots of greens added) may reach very high temperatures, some even reaching 70°C (158°F), thereby killing weed seeds. Cold piles, on the other hand, do not and it is best not to add any weed wastes that will contain seeds. If you do, you could risk spreading weed seeds across your garden in their own growing mix when you come to use the compost.

THE "HOT PILE" METHOD
Wet the ground under the pile and add twigs or other un-shredded browns to provide some aeration at the base. Layer the rest of your materials, alternating green and brown layers of about 15cm (6in) thickness, and add water as you go. Topsoil can also be added as a 2cm (¾in) layer between each cycle of green and brown materials. Finish the pile with a layer of browns. Cover the pile with a lid or piece of carpet to keep out rain and conserve heat. Check to see that your pile becomes hot within a few days. Turn the pile to decrease composting time. This action allows all the material to be exposed to the

COMPOSTING MATERIALS
Many items can be composted into valuable soil conditioners. Whether because of toxins, plant or human diseases or weed problems, some things should never be used.

Good compost materials
Animal manure
Fallen leaves
Grass/lawn clippings
Hay and straw from organic farms
Kitchen waste
Prunings from the garden
Sawdust
Shredded browns
Soot and charcoal
Spent hops or cocoa shells
Spent mushroom compost
Weeds and other garden wastes

What not to compost
Chemically treated wood products
Diseased plants
Human and pet waste
Meat, bones and fatty food wastes
Pernicious weeds

more nitrogen. Nitrogen is a critical element in amino acids and proteins, and can be thought of as a protein source for the billions of multiplying microbes.

A good mix of browns and greens is the best nutritional balance for microbes. This mix also improves the aeration and level of water in the pile.

THE "COLD PILE" METHOD
Make a pile of "browns", such as autumn leaves, moisten them well and then slowly incorporate "greens" such as kitchen waste or lawn clippings over the next year (this method can take a full year to finish the compost). If it gets very cold in winter, cover

hot centre, thereby increasing aeration. Do this once a week in the warmer season, and once a month in cooler periods. The pile's heat should peak every time you turn it, although the peak temperature will be lower with each turn. Always make sure that the pile remains moist, but avoid over-wetting.

4 *Continue adding greens until you have a layer about 15cm (6in) thick, the same depth as the browns below. Lawn clippings should be placed in layers of about 10cm (4in) or mixed with other green waste to avoid the layer becoming slimy and airless.*

5 *Kitchen refuse, such as vegetable waste, can also be added and is usually classed as a "green". You can include a thin layer of soil to add microorganisms before the next layer of "browns". Continue layering until the bin is full, then water and cover.*

6 *After two to three months, you should have well-rotted garden compost, which, due to the heat of the pile, will be largely free from weed seeds, pests and diseases. Once the bin has been emptied, it can be refilled in the same way.*

GREEN MANURES

Sometimes referred to as "cover crops", green manures are plants that are grown to benefit the soil rather than for consumption or display. Green manures replace and hold nutrients, improve the structure of the soil and increase its organic material content. They also smother the soil and so prevent weed growth. Green manures also "fix" atmospheric nitrogen. They are easy to grow and can be used to improve the soil when manures are not readily available.

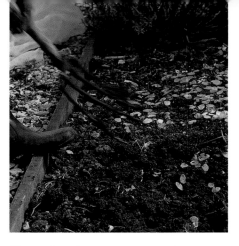

Above: *Growing a green manure is an easy and effective way in which to add some organic matter to the soil.*

BENEFITS OF GREEN MANURES

At any time of year, but especially in winter, the soil loses nutrients if it is bare for six weeks or more. Green manures help to counteract this and maintain a more even soil temperature and moisture content. Many green manures grow deep roots to tap resources unavailable to some crops. Others produce a fibrous root system to help build structure in the soil, while many have flowers that attract pollinating insects.

TYPES OF GREEN MANURE

Some green manures are nitrogen-fixers, using bacteria that colonize the nodules on their roots. These microbes take nitrogen out of the air and convert it into a form that plants can use. Green manures are usually divided into two groups: legumes and non-legumes. Leguminous manures include clover, peas, fava beans and alfalfa. Despite their nitrogen-fixing abilities, legumes have slow autumn growth and add less organic content. They can also be less winter hardy.

Winter rye is the most commonly grown non-leguminous cover crop, but oats, wheat, oilseed rape and buckwheat are also used. Although they do not add nitrogen to the soil, they help maintain levels and have the additional advantage over legumes of growing faster through the autumn, thereby giving better weed suppression. They also tend to break down more slowly than legumes and add more organic matter to the soil. You may wish to use a combination of green manures in order to balance the benefits of the different types.

DEEP-ROOTED GREEN MANURES

The roots of certain green manure "crops" work through the soil, holding it together as they grow. Once dug in, however, they help to make it crumbly and friable as they rot. Some green manures have very deep roots that reach down into the subsoil and can harvest nutrients that are unavailable to other garden plants. In this respect they are a form of biological double digging.

PLANTING GREEN MANURES

Winter green manures should be planted early enough to give about four weeks of growth before cold weather stops their growth. Spring or summer crops must be given sufficient time to develop before they are dug in. After preparing the soil, plant large-seeded cover crops in shallow, closely spaced furrows. Smaller seeds can be broadcast over the surface and covered with a light raking, watering if needed until they germinate. Dig the crop in once it is ready, allowing at least three weeks before you intend to plant to give time for the material to rot down. It is best not to allow green manures to go to seed as they all have the potential to become weeds.

Gardens are traditionally dug over and manured in autumn, then left bare over winter. Many nutrients can be lost during this time due to the leaching action of rain. A hardy green manure sown in the autumn can be dug in the following spring, yielding nutrients to a newly sown or planted crop.

USING GREEN MANURES

1 *Sow the seed evenly across the area where you plan to grow the green manure. Either broadcast the seed or sow larger seed thinly in shallow drills and close rows.*

2 *Lightly rake in the seed so that it is covered and will germinate quickly. Water the area thoroughly if there is no rain due or if it does not rain for the following 48 hours.*

3 *Once the seed germinates, allow it to grow a little before digging it into the soil. Never let green manure crops set seed or they will become a weed in later crops on the site.*

TYPES OF GREEN MANURE

Green manure for growing over winter

These species can withstand moderate to hard frost for a long period and can be cut down in the spring, prior to cultivation. The shorter types can also be used as catch (cover) crops around winter vegetables or biennial crops for harvest in the early spring. This protects bare soil, prevents nutrient leaching and creates a more stable soil environment.

GREEN MANURE	SOWING TIME AND METHOD	HEIGHT	WINTER HARDY?	NITROGEN-FIXING ABILITY	TERMS OF GROWTH	DIGGING IN	OTHER NOTES
Alfalfa *Medicago sativa*	Early spring to mid-summer; broadcast at 3g (¹⁄₁₀oz) per square metre (yard).	100–150cm (3–5ft)	Yes	Yes but poor	Perennial. Grow for several months or more than one season.	Any time. Medium effort if young. Hard if left for more than one season.	Very deep rooting. Will grow on most soils. Dislikes acid or waterlogged soils, but drought resistant.
Asilke clover *Trifolium hybridum*	Mid-spring to late summer; broadcast at 3g (¹⁄₁₀oz) per square metre (yard).	30cm (12in)	Yes	Yes	Several months	Any time. Medium effort.	Will withstand wetter soils than other clovers but more prone to drought. Shallow rooted.
Essex or red merviot clover *Trifolium pratense*	Mid-spring to late summer; broadcast at 3g (¹⁄₁₀oz) per square metre (yard).	40cm (16in)	Yes	Yes	Several months	Any time. Easy, little effort.	Prefers good loamy soil. Can be mown or cut several times per season and used for compost.
Grazing rye *Secale cereale*	Late summer to late autumn; broadcast at 30g (1oz) per square metre (yard) or thinly in rows 20cm (8in) apart.	30–60cm (12–24in)	Yes	No	Autumn to spring	Before flowering. Hard work.	Grows in most soils. Keep watered during germination, else yield is poor. Sow thickly to smother weeds.
Phacelia *Phacelia tanacetifolium*	Early spring to early autumn; broadcast at 3g (¹⁄₁₀oz) per square metre (yard) or thinly in rows 20cm (8in) apart.	60–90cm (12–36in)	Yes	No	2 months in summer; 5–6 months over winter	Before flowering. Easy, little effort.	Grows in most soils. Quick to grow in summer. If left, will produce mauve flowers that bees love.
Trefoil *Medicago lupulina*	Early spring to late summer; broadcast at 3g (¹⁄₁₀oz) per square metre (yard).	30–60cm (12–24in)	Yes	Yes	Several months to a year	Any time. Medium effort.	Will grow in most soils but dislikes acid. Can be used for undersowing. Dense foliage.

Green manure for warm-season growing

Plants for use in the spring and summer have to be quick growing in order to cover the ground and yield benefit within a short period of time. They are generally slightly tender, although lower-growing species can actually be used as a catch crop around other seasonal crops.

GREEN MANURE	SOWING TIME AND METHOD	HEIGHT	WINTER HARDY?	NITROGEN-FIXING ABILITY	TERMS OF GROWTH	DIGGING IN	OTHER NOTES
Bitter lupin *Lupinus angustifolius*	Early spring to early summer 4cm (1½in) deep; 3cm (1¼in) apart; in rows 15cm (6in) apart.	50cm (20in)	Mild winters	Yes	2–3 months	Before flowering. Easy, little effort.	Prefers light slightly acidic soil. Foliage not very dense. Deep rooted.
Buckwheat *Fagopyrum esculentum*	Early spring to late summer; broadcast at 10g (¹⁄₃oz) per square metre (yard) or thinly in shallow rows 20cm (8in) apart.	80cm (32in)	No	No	2–3 months	Before or during flowering. Easy, no effort.	Grows on poor soils. If allowed to flower, attracts hoverflies to aid pollination of crops.
Crimson clover *Trifolium incarnatum*	Early spring to late summer; broadcast at 3g (¹⁄₁₀oz) per square metre (yard).	30–60cm (12–24in)	Mild winters only	Yes	2–3 months or over winter	Before flowering. Medium effort.	Prefers sandy loam soil but will tolerate heavy clay. Large red flowers attract bees.
Fenugreek *Trigonella foenum-graecum*	Early spring to late summer; broadcast at 5g (¹⁄₅oz) per square metre (yard) or thinly in 15cm (6in) shallow rows.	30–60cm (12–24in)	Mild winters	No	2–3 months	Any time before flowering. Easy, little effort.	Prefers good drainage but will tolerate heavy or light soil.

BASIC TECHNIQUES

Most gardening techniques, from weeding and feeding to pruning and propagation, are straightforward and and easy to achieve if you plan and organize the task in hand. The procedures described here will help you to master the basics of organic gardening. You may well develop your own methods in time, based upon the techniques shown here as well as those you that learn from other gardeners. Always make sure that you are clear what you want to do and always approach a task positively. Gardening should bring enjoyment as well as a sense of satisfaction that comes from creating a thriving organic paradise in your own backyard.

Left: *A flourishing garden plot is the end result of careful planning and preparation as well as regular maintenance.*

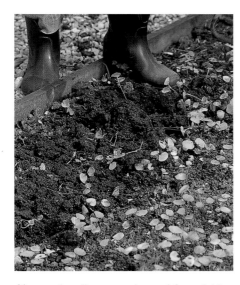

Above: *A well-prepared, weed-free plot is the ideal starting point for successful plant growth and development.*

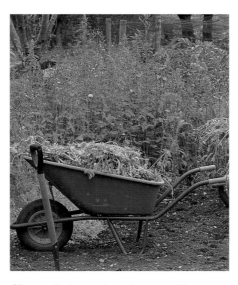

Above: *Both weeds and crop residues can be recycled in the organic garden by composting and then returned to the soil.*

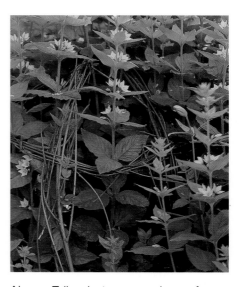

Above: *Taller plants may need some form of support. In this case, willow branches have been used to support* Lysimachia.

WEEDING AND WEED CONTROL

Many people are put off organic gardening because they do not like the idea of weeding. Not having the "quick fix" of weed-killing chemicals can make this task seem daunting. It is, however, worth considering that a well-maintained garden has less weeding to do than you might think. In addition, it can be a relaxing, even therapeutic, task and there is very little that is more satisfying in the garden than a freshly weeded plot.

Above: *Hoeing is an effective way of keeping a garden plot free of weeds. Pull a draw or swan-neck hoe towards you in a series of chopping movements.*

WHAT PROBLEMS DO WEEDS PRESENT?

Weeds compete with garden plants of all types for essential nutrients, light and water. Uncontrolled weed growth may kill plants that are less vigorous or seriously inhibit their development. Weeds also act as "host" plants for animal pests or diseases that may, in turn, affect the desired plants. Finally, weeds are controlled because they often look unsightly.

CAN WEEDS BE TOLERATED?

There is no easy answer to this question. It depends upon what exactly you want out of your garden. Aesthetic considerations aside, most gardens can survive quite healthily with some weeds. The majority only become a real nuisance when they start to take over or if they set seed. The simple rule is the fewer weeds in the garden the better.

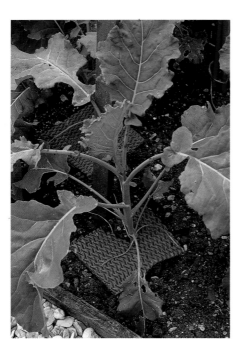

GOOD CULTIVATION

The secret of organic weed control is good cultivation. This begins with thorough ground preparation to reduce the build-up of weeds and weed seeds before planting. Fallowing is commonly used to do this. After the ground has been prepared, it is left bare for a period of a few weeks to a few months. The weed seeds are allowed to germinate and are then removed as they appear. This method will never remove all the seeds because they can survive for several years in a dormant state. But the majority of them will have germinated and the task of weed control made easier for the future.

Vigilance is important throughout the growing season, but never more so than in spring and early summer. Tackle weed seedlings as they appear. Some methods of control, such as hoeing, may damage garden plants, so use a hand fork for close work or in areas where hoeing is difficult. A hoe, for example, can sever the roots of surface-rooting shrubs such as rhododendrons. These weeding methods are relatively slow and labour-intensive. The trick is to do it little and often.

Flails, brush cutters, mowers, rollers, burning and other mechanical means are occasionally used. Although strimmers can be used in shrub borders, those that cut using nylon cords can damage woody stems.

MINIMAL CULTIVATION

Many weeds are plants of cultivation, thriving in disturbed ground. Minimal cultivation reduces disturbance and relies on creating a ground-covering layer of vegetation. The plants literally out-compete the weeds, which can be removed as they appear.

Left: *Weed-free plots can be attractive to crop pests. Here, plant collars have been used to prevent root flies attacking the crop.*

COMMON WEEDS

Weeds can be divided into three groups. Annual weeds germinate, grow, flower and set seed in one growing season. Certain annuals, which are known as ephemerals, complete their lifecycle well within this period and can produce several successive generations within the space of one season. The third type of weeds are perennial species. Perennial weeds initially establish from seed, but tend to persist for several seasons, sometimes dying down during adverse seasons only to re-emerge as conditions improve. They are much more difficult to eradicate once established than annual weeds and many are a serious problem in gardens.

Ephemeral and annual weeds
- Annual meadow grass
- Bittercress
- Chickweed

Perennial weeds
- Blackberry (in Australia)
- Couch grass
- Creeping buttercup
- Dock
- Ground elder
- Groundsel
- Nettle

Meadow grass

Chickweed

Creeping buttercup

Dandelion

DIFFERENT TYPES OF MULCH

Mulches provide a physical barrier to weed seeds that would otherwise land on the soil surface. The materials that can be used for mulching are varied in their composition and the effects they have. They are generally classified into synthetic and natural types.

Bark chippings

Newspaper

Dried bracken

Gravel

Old carpet

Sawdust

Woven plastic

Cocoa shells

MULCH

This is a layer of material that is laid over the surface of a soil or other growing medium. While often cited as a means of weed control, applying mulch has other functions that are beneficial to growth. Mulches help to keep the plants' roots warm in winter and cool in summer, greatly assisting new growth in the spring. They also reduce water loss from the soil in two main ways: by shading the soil surface and by slowing down evaporation of water from the soil.

In general, most mulches reduce the number of weeds growing in a planted area. They act by inhibiting the germinating weed seedling from reaching the sunlight or by "drawing up" the weed so that it is spindly and can be easily removed or "pulled". Mulches should be laid on a bare surface, as they will not inhibit established weeds, especially vigorous perennial ones.

If a mulch is laid to an even depth of around 5cm (2in), it will develop a dry dusty surface that will deter the germination of weed seeds that land on it. This is only a temporary measure, but can help reduce weeding at the busiest times of the year.

TIMING AND APPLICATION

Mulches should be laid on warm, moist soil. Autumn is the ideal time, but they can be applied in the spring after the soil has warmed up. Applied too thickly (over 10cm/4in), they may affect water infiltration into the soil. Materials containing an excessive amount of fine humus or soil-like material ("fines") may encourage weed seedlings to establish. In poor-draining soil, mulch may keep the soil waterlogged and this will be detrimental to plant growth. Synthetic materials, especially if they are impermeable such as black plastic, will inhibit oxygen and water infiltration into the soil. Some materials, such as grass clippings, can "pack down" on the surface and form a water-shedding layer.

As mulches encourage surface-rooting, application must be continued once started, otherwise the plants will suffer later. Many ornamental plants, such as rhododendrons, are naturally very shallow-rooting and thus need the protection of mulch for good growth. They benefit from an organic mulch that conserves soil moisture. Some mulches, such as manure and compost, also aid plant development by supplying nutrients.

MULCHING TO CONTROL WEEDS

1 Grass clippings are a cheap, effective mulch. Apply them at a maximum depth of 5cm (2in) or the heat they create as they decompose may harm the stems. Do not use mowings from grass that has gone to seed.

2 Chipped bark should be composted or stored for several months to let it release any resin and start to decompose. Some gardeners worry that it introduces fungal diseases, but the spores are already in the air.

WATERING

In order to cultivate a successful organic garden, it is crucial to recognize the water requirements of different plants. It is of vital importance that you know when and how to provide the right amount of water as well as how to avoid either drought or waterlogging. Conserving the water in the soil as well as storing and recycling this valuable commodity are of key importance in the organic garden, especially in areas where rainfall is seasonal and droughts are common.

Above: *Water that runs off the roof can be collected in a custom-made rainwater butt, and stored for later use.*

PRINCIPLES OF WATER MANAGEMENT

After rainfall or irrigation, all the soil pore spaces are filled with water. The air is displaced and the soil saturated. If the rain or irrigation were to continue, then surface pooling or runoff would occur. The rate at which a soil can absorb water is influenced by its texture and structure.

Water drains from the soil through the pore system and is replaced to some extent by air. After draining has removed the excess water, the remaining water may be lost either through evaporation or taken up by the plant and lost through its leaves.

All sands and loamy sands tend to have a low available water capacity. Loams and clay have a medium capacity while very fine sandy loam, silt loams, peats and any soil with a high water table have high available water capacity. Clay soils often have a large amount of water within them, but it is held so tightly that plants are not able to obtain it.

WATER AND THE PLANT

All plants are largely made of water and it is critical that water levels are maintained if the plant is to grow and develop. Soft fleshy subjects, such as many bedding plants and some vegetables, use large quantities of water, particularly during establishment. Plants with large leaves or with extensive branch systems, such as large trees, will remove gallons of water from the soil in the course of a hot sunny day.

WATERWISE GARDENING

Since water supplies are limited, we need to do all we can to conserve soil moisture. As the top layer of soil dries out, the dry soil acts as an insulation to further rapid moisture loss. Take advantage of this by avoiding over-cultivation, particularly during the summer, as this may bring moist soil to the surface to dry out. Always try to maintain a well-structured soil and avoid capping (a hard, partially compacted surface layer) as this can prevent the absorption of rainfall by the soil, leaving puddles that quickly evaporate. Mulches help to conserve moisture either by holding water or acting as insulation provided that they are deep enough. Keep the soil surface weed-free and provide shelter from drying winds. Maintain drainage, as poor drainage leads to limited root growth of the plant and poor soil structure.

STORING AND RECYCLING WATER

Water is a precious resource that is sometimes in short supply. Plants in open ground may acclimatize to the soil conditions, but those growing in pots are more susceptible to drought. Mains water can provide an answer but there is a cost involved and supplies can be restricted. Saving water from rainfall or recycling waste water (which is sometimes called "grey water") can overcome the worst ravages of summer drought.

METHODS OF WATERING

1 *When watering by hand, be patient and give the ground around the plant a good soaking. If in doubt, dig a small hole in the soil and check that the water has soaked through to the roots.*

2 *Turning on a sprinkler allows you to leave it and get on with something else. Place a jar under the spray to gauge how much has fallen. There should be at least 2.5cm (1in) of water for the sprinkler to have done any good.*

3 *A spray attached to a garden hose delivers at a greater rate than a sprinkler but it must be held in place until the ground is soaked. It is easy to under-water using this method. Spray the leaves to wash away dirt or dust.*

4 *A seep hose with holes in it is snaked around plants that need to be watered and left in position. When connected, it provides a gradual but steady flow of water that penetrates deeply into the soil.*

AUTOMATIC WATERING SYSTEMS

1 *You can bury a pipeline beneath the surface and plug in various watering devices. A sprinkler can be pushed on to this fitting, which lies flush with the turf.*

2 *Control systems can be fitted to the hose system so that you can alter the pressure of the water. These can also act as a filter.*

3 *Drip-feed systems can be used for beds, borders and containers. "T"-joints allow tubes to be attached for individual drip heads.*

4 *The delivery tube of the garden hose can be held firmly in position with a pipe peg that is inserted into the ground, if this is necessary.*

Storing and recycling household water is a relatively complicated undertaking that is usually best left to specialist contractors. The potential health risks mean that it is not usually wise to store this type of water for any length of time, but it can be used fresh to water non-food plants. Try keeping your bath water and using it to water ornamental plants. It can be used to fill watering cans and is ideal for watering outdoor pot specimens or plants in open ground.

Rainwater may be a viable alternative and some contractors will be able to install large underground tanks to contain seasonal rainfall. The quicker and easier alternative is to install water butts to collect water from downspouts from roof drains. This method will rarely provide enough water for your whole garden, but is often plenty to water (or supplement the watering of) plants in containers, particularly edible plants such as herbs. Rainwater is naturally acidic and is, therefore, not likely to contain many harmful bacteria. Its acidity also makes it the ideal choice for misting plants under glass on hot days (as it will not mark the leaves with lime) and suits many species sensitive to domestic water additives. Rainwater is also a must for people wishing to grow "acid-loving" specimens in pots.

WATERING PLANTS

In areas where seasonal water shortage is a regular problem, choose drought-tolerant species where possible. Seasonal crops (such as vegetables) and displays (summer or spring bedding) tend to suffer the most from drought due to the limited time that they have to develop extensive root systems. If you wish to grow these seasonal plants in drier areas, they will need to be watered regularly to survive prolonged dry periods. Perennials, on the other hand, may actually become more drought-tolerant if they are watered less. This is because they will have to root deeper to find water. Perennials will need to be watered in their first season following planting to ensure their long-term survival. Remember that applying a good drench on a more occasional basis allows the water to penetrate more deeply and have a better long-term effect because it encourages deeper rooting. Watering little and often can prove detrimental in drier climates by encouraging surface roots that may become very drought-prone. After the first growing season following planting, they are better able to cope if not watered at all.

WATERING METHODS

Plants can be watered in many ways, but all generally fall into two categories: hand watering or automatic systems.

Hand watering The commonest "tool" here is the watering can. Numerous designs exist but they all rely upon a gradual delivery through a spout. A rose ensures that a fine spray is delivered that will not wash away soil or damage plants. Hoses can also be used for hand-watering and many nozzles have been designed to deliver a shower of water rather than a jet.

Automated systems There is an array of devices to choose from, some of which can deliver doses of water at set times of the day or week. Even the most complex of these use relatively simple water-delivery methods such as seep or drip hoses and sprinklers. Seep and drip hoses are essentially "leaky pipes" that gradually release water into the soil. Sprinklers shower an area of garden repeatedly until the ground is well soaked. There are many designs for both and the amount of time they need to be left on depends upon the manufacturer's recommendations and the available water pressure. Both hoses and sprinklers offer the benefit of gradual delivery over a large area and both can be operated manually from a mains water supply. A good watering every few days can be extremely beneficial to most plants, especially if recently planted.

WATERING PROBLEMS

These are usually the result of either too much or too little water being applied to the plant. Both over- and under-watering have similar symptoms because both are related to root death. An over-watered plant's root system begins to die off due to a lack of oxygen. The plant becomes short of water and wilts. Other problems can result from the wetting of foliage and flowers. Watering in full sunlight can give plants a scorched appearance, so it is best not to water in hot sunny conditions.

RECYCLING WATER

The suitability of the water left over from washing, bathing and other household activities depends on how much waste matter it contains. Ordinary bath water, for instance, is useful for watering a variety of plants, but the main problem lies in its storage. Waste water always carries the risk of bacterial infestation. Specialist storage methods and filtration can be used, but it is easier to use it immediately (once cooled), and to avoid using it on houseplants or edible crops.

FEEDING

In order for plants to grow and sustain their life processes, they require water and air as well as a range of naturally occurring elements. At least sixteen different elements are needed by all plants for successful growth and development. Three of these elements – carbon, hydrogen and oxygen – are obtained from the carbon dioxide in the air and from the water and oxygen in the soil. In addition to these, plants also need a selection of other important nutrients, which are described here.

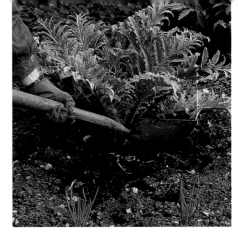

Above: *Top-dressing with organic matter provides the soil with nutrients and encourages nutrient cycles.*

IMPORTANT PLANT NUTRIENTS

In addition to carbon, hydrogen and oxygen, plants need other important nutrients, which they obtain directly from the soil or compost. These nutrients are commonly divided into two groups, depending upon whether they are found in plants in high or low concentrations. When they are found in high concentrations and are needed in large amounts, they are known as macro or major nutrients. There are three of these: nitrogen (N), phosphorus (P) and potassium (K). Every organic gardener must be fully aware of the functions of the "essential three". Nitrogen is essentially the shoot and leaf maker and is especially important early in the growing season; phosphorus is important in the formation of roots; and potassium plays a vital role in flower and fruit formation and is also important in promoting hardiness in overwintering plants. Elements that are needed in relatively small amounts are the micro or trace elements, of which there are ten. Among the most important of these are calcium, magnesium and sulphur, although all play a vital role in the growth and development of the plant.

SYMPTOMS OF DEFICIENCY

Plants exhibit varying symptoms to a nutrient deficiency. General ones are stunted growth, discoloured leaves, including mottling and inter-veinal coloration, and the premature death of leaves or other parts of the plant. Plants may also display twisted or distorted growth as well as poor root growth and development. In many cases, the symptoms are often seen first in the plant's extremities, such as the tips of the shoots, as these are furthest away from the nutrient source. If a plant cannot obtain enough of any nutrient from a soil it will be because there is either little or no nutrient present in the soil, or the nutrient is not "available" to the plant.

Any element can also be toxic to the plant if it is present in sufficiently high amounts or out of balance with other elements in the growing medium.

FEEDING PLANTS ORGANICALLY

Numerous organic nutrient supplements are available. All have their relative advantages, but they should be used only as part of a combined strategy that aims to harness natural nutrient cycles. This usually involves top-dressing the soil with well-rotted organic matter. This is the catalyst to nutrient cycling in the soil as it feeds the

ORGANIC FERTILIZERS

A wide variety of organic substances can boost nutrient levels. They should be used in addition to composts and manures.

Animal manure Bird manure is a good source of nitrogen. Use in pellet form, as the fresh substance will burn plant roots.

Bonemeal Promotes strong root growth due to its high phosphate content. Use it as a base dressing prior to planting perennials.

Calcified seaweed This raises the pH of the soil and adds calcium, like limestone, but also contains magnesium.

Fish, blood and bone A general fertilizer that is normally applied in the spring to promote root and shoot growth.

Ground limestone This raises the pH and supplies calcium where there is a deficiency. It is applied as a powder when it is needed.

Gypsum This supplies calcium to soils where there is a deficiency, but does not alter the pH. It is added in a 4:1 ratio to "lighten" clay soils.

Hoof and horn This material gives a slow release of nitrogen where strong growth is needed and is applied in the spring or early summer.

Rock phosphate Used mostly to counter phosphate deficiency and as an alternative to bonemeal.

Seaweed meal Helps to build up humus levels in the soil and is used on a wide range of plants.

Wood ash An excellent source of potassium that can be added directly to the soil or to a compost heap.

Bonemeal

Fish, blood and bone

Hoof and horn

Calcified seaweed

MAKING COMFREY TEA

1 *Cut a large bundle of comfrey leaves from the patch in your garden. Choose good, green, leafy growth. Remove the leaf and stem, but avoid using the crown.*

2 *Place in a plastic container with holes in the base. Weigh down the leaves. Line a second larger container with a plastic bag and place the first container inside. Tie the bag at the top.*

3 *The thick dark liquid from the decomposing comfrey leaves collects in the bag below. The lower bucket allows this to drip down and stores it until the process is complete.*

4 *Decant the finished liquid into a jam jar for later use. The liquid feed must be diluted before it is applied to plants at a ratio of about 10 parts water to 1 part concentrate.*

vast array of soil organisms that naturally make use of essential plant nutrients. The majority of garden composts do not contain especially large amounts of the major plant nutrients; it is their long-term ability to feed soil life that makes them so valuable.

Despite the best intentions, plants can become short of a certain type of nutrient. This is usually avoided by giving the plant a supplement of a "plant food" that is rich in that particular nutrient. This can be applied to the soil as a top-dressing, lightly worked in with a fork, or applied as a foliar feed. Foliar feeding involves spraying a fine mist of a low-strength solution of the feed. The exact concentrations vary according to the feed being used, but a rough guide would be to use a quarter strength of that which you would apply as a liquid feed to the soil. The nutrient will be taken up quickly and the residue is best washed off after a couple of days because any soil-applied fertilizer will have been taken up by then. Applying a weak solution of Epsom salts as a foliar or liquid feed is an example of applying such a tonic.

LIQUID FEEDS AND TEAS

Compost tea is easy to make. Comfrey is ideal for this, but stinging nettles are also very good. You could also use sheep or goat manure, or finely sifted compost from the heap. Simply fill an old pillowcase or burlap bag with your chosen material (comfrey, nettles, compost or manure) and sink it into a large bucket or barrel of water. Cover the container and let it steep for a few days. Remember, the longer you steep, the stronger the tea will be. You may use the final "brew" as a light liquid feed. It can also be used as a foliar feeding medium, provided that it is well diluted. Use the residue in the bag as mulch. An alternative method is shown above.

Worm colonies in containers also produce a liquid feed that is a tonic for your plants. It should be diluted to a ratio of about 10 parts water to 1 part liquid feed. It is generally high in potassium and phosphorus.

OTHER FEEDING METHODS

1 *An alternative method of feeding is to use a liquid feed. This is most useful for plants that are growing in containers. Add the organic fertilizer of your choice to one of the waterings, according to the manufacturer's instructions.*

2 *Organic granular fertilizer can be applied by hand, spreading it over the area covered by the roots below. Follow the manufacturer's instructions. You may wish to protect your hands when applying the fertilizer by wearing a pair of gloves.*

3 *Apply a layer of well-rotted organic material, such as farmyard manure or garden compost, to the surface of the soil around the plant. If the plant is not shallow-rooted, lightly fork the material into the top layer of the soil.*

PLANT NUTRIENTS

The following table highlights the characteristics of the soil nutrients. Symptoms of deficiency may be seen on different parts of the plant at different stages of growth, although it may not always be immediately obvious that a plant is suffering from a nutrient deficiency. Some of the more important symptoms that can be seen on plants are listed below.

PLANT NUTRIENT	NATURAL ORGANIC SOURCE	PLANTS MOST IN NEED	SOILS MOST IN NEED	SIGNS OF SHORTAGE	HOW TO AVOID SHORTAGE	TOXICITY CAUSE
Major plant nutrients						
Nitrogen (N) The "leaf maker"	Bird manure, blood and bone, grass clippings	Grass, vegetables grown for their leaves, and root-bound plants	Sandy soils in rainy areas	Stunted growth; small pale green leaves; weak stems	Apply a base dressing before sowing or planting. Top-dress in spring and summer with organic matter.	Excessive use of nitrogen-rich fertilizer
Phosphates (P₂O₅) The "root maker"	Comfrey, seagrass, horse manure, blood and bone	Young plants, root vegetables, and fruit and seed crops	Sandy soils	Stunted roots and stems; small leaves with a purplish tinge; low fruit yield	Apply a base dressing of bonemeal. Use fish, blood and bone when top-dressing plants.	Excessive use of fertilizer
Potash (K₂O) The "flower and fruit maker"	Comfrey, horse manure, seagrass	Fruit, flowers and potatoes	Sandy soils	Leaf edges turn yellow, then brown; low fruit yield; fruit and flowers poorly coloured	Apply a compound organic fertilizer or wood ash as a base dressing or top-dressing.	Excessive use of fertilizer; lack of magnesium
Minor plant nutrients						
Boron (B)	Beetroot leaves, horse manure, compost, seagrass, untreated sawdust	Root vegetables, top fruit (apples, pears etc.)	Sandy soils	Brown heart (roots); narrow leaves; corky patches on fruit	Top-dress with compost or apply borax in severe cases.	Irrigation water
Calcium (Ca)	Dandelion, lucerne hay, comfrey, horse manure, compost, blood and bone	Fruit, flowers, vegetables	Acid and potash-rich soils	Similar to nitrogen shortage – stunted growth and pale green leaves	Apply lime or use gypsum or calcified seaweed.	High pH causes toxicity for some acid-loving plants
Copper (Cu)	Nettles, yarrow, horse manure, dandelion, chickweed, compost, untreated sawdust	Fruit, vegetables	Sandy soils	Dieback; brown spots on leaves	Top-dress with compost.	Copper-based fungicides
Iron (Fe)	Stinging nettle, compost, dandelion, horse manure, spinach and seaweed	Rhododendrons, azaleas, camellias	Chalky soils	Yellowing of younger leaves	Trouble can occur on chalky, peaty, very light and acid soils. Iron shortage in chalky soils is due to lock-up by calcium and difficult to avoid.	Rare
Magnesium (Mg)	Grass clippings, seagrass	Roses, tomatoes	Sandy, peaty and potash-rich soils	Yellow or brown patches between veins of older leaves	Apply a mulch of compost or Epsom salts if deficiency is severe.	None
Manganese (Mn)	Chickweed, compost, untreated sawdust	Rhododendrons, azaleas, camellias	Chalky soils	Yellowing between the veins of older leaves	Shortage in chalky soils is due to lock-up by calcium (see iron). Acidification for some plants.	None
Molybdenum (Mo)	Cornstalks, compost, grass clippings	Brassicas	Acid soils	Narrow leaves	Apply lime and top-dress with compost.	None
Sodium (Na)	Seaweed	Root vegetables, fruit	Sandy soils	Very rare except in a few seaside-loving plants	Not usually warranted.	Land reclaimed from sea
Sulphur (S)	Cabbage leaves	All plants	Soils in rural areas	Stunted growth and pale green leaves	A light dusting of flowers of sulphur during the year.	Industrial sites and acid rain
Zinc (Zn)	Horse manure, corn stalks, garden compost, untreated sawdust	Fruit, vegetables	Sandy soils	Dieback	Top-dress with compost.	Leaching from containers

BASIC PRUNING

The task of pruning can seem a daunting prospect to some gardeners, but there is, in fact, no great mystery surrounding pruning and a few basic rules are all you need to get started in most cases. At its simplest level, pruning should be regarded as a way of introducing some order to your garden, giving your plants space to grow and look their best, while also controlling them within a set space. The following section provides some basic advice to enable you to prune with confidence.

Above: *Regular dead-heading keeps shrubs tidy and promotes further flowering. Cut flowering stems back to a bud or stem division.*

WHY IS PRUNING NECESSARY?

Pruning is usually carried out to control the growth of stronger subjects that may otherwise damage those of a weaker habit growing alongside; it also ensures plants do not outgrow their allocated space and cause an obstruction. Pruning is also used to train a plant to a specific shape or form; to maintain or improve flowering; and to improve the shape or "balance" of an individual shrub or tree. Finally, it is used to remove dead, damaged, diseased or pest-infected growth. This last type of pruning is referred to as hygienic pruning and helps maintain plant health and vigour.

Constant pruning, however, is not always necessary for the good cultivation of plants. Once a plant has become established and the initial framework has been formed, pruning is often reduced to a minimum. The major exceptions to this include plants that are pruned annually in order to improve flowering, fruiting or quality of foliage. Apples, peaches and other fruit trees and bushes are regularly pruned to increase the yield of fruit. Roses are a good example of an ornamental shrub that benefits from regular pruning, having more vigorous and prolific flowering as a result of cutting back on a yearly basis.

SUCCESSFUL PRUNING

There are arguably two hallmarks of good pruning: a well-planned, careful and methodical approach to the work undertaken and a good working knowledge of the requirements of the plants that are to be pruned. The real results may not always be apparent for months and, in the case of trees, for years.

With secateurs (hand pruners), always try to place the thin blade on the trunk/branch side of the cut. This will result in a short stub and will also prevent a layer of damaged cambium tissue being left immediately under the line of the cut.

GOOD AND BAD PRUNING

1 *A good pruning cut is made just above a strong bud, about 3mm (⅛in) above the bud. It should be a slanting cut, with the higher end above the bud. The bud should generally be outward bound from the plant rather than inward.*

2 *If the stem has buds or leaves opposite each other, make the cut horizontal, about 3mm (⅛in) above the buds.*

3 *Always use a sharp pair of secateurs (hand pruners). Blunt ones will produce a ragged or bruised cut, which is likely to introduce disease into the plant.*

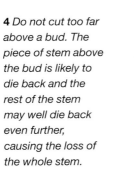

4 *Do not cut too far above a bud. The piece of stem above the bud is likely to die back and the rest of the stem may well die back even further, causing the loss of the whole stem.*

5 *Do not cut too close to the bud otherwise the bud might be damaged by the secateurs or disease might enter. Too close a cut is likely to cause the stem to die back to the next bud.*

6 *It is bad practice to slope the cut towards the bud as this makes the stem above the bud too long, which is likely to cause dieback. It also sheds rain on to the bud, which may cause problems.*

HARD PRUNING SHRUBS

1 *There are a few shrubs – buddleias are the main and most obvious example – which benefit from being cut hard back each spring. This treatment improves the development of the foliage. Elders (Sambucus) and the purple smoke bush (Cotinus) should also be treated in this way. Rosa glauca also responds very well to this type of hard pruning.*

2 *Cut the shoots right back almost to the ground. It is important to ensure that you make the cuts just above an outward-facing bud. Cutting back will leave little more than a stump. It may seem a little drastic, but the shrubs will quickly grow again in the spring. If they are not cut back, they become very leggy and do not make such attractive bushes.*

3 *Several plants that have attractive coloured bark in the winter are best cut to the ground in the spring. So, by the following winter, attractive new shoots will be displayed. The various coloured-stemmed Rubus, such as R. cockburnianus, as well as some of the dogwoods (Cornus) and willow (Salix), are good candidates for this treatment.*

Cuts should always be made immediately above a bud and should be done as cleanly as possible. Use well-maintained secateurs that are regularly sharpened. Make sure that you do not position your blade too close to the bud or the tissue that connects the bud to the main plant body could be damaged. As a guide, you should cut 3mm (⅛in) above a bud and always ensure the bud is not damaged when cutting.

Be careful when using a saw close to a trunk or stem to remove heavier thicker branches. The weight of the branch can sometimes cause splitting and tearing to the main stem wood or bark. These injuries can allow the entry of disease-causing organisms and damage the plant.

The typical order of cuts to follow when pruning any tree is to remember the D's. These are: dead, dying, diseased,

displaced or deformed branches. All of these must be removed as the first stage of any pruning work. Then add to this list the C's: criss-crossing branches and crowded growth.

The next stage is to remove any unwanted growth. Care must be applied at this critical stage to ensure that you do not remove too much growth. Finally, once you have cleared this material, it is possible to

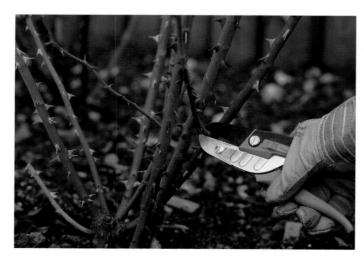

Above: *When cutting out crossing stems, cut out the stems while they are still young and free from damage and disease. Using secateurs (hand pruners), cut the stem at its base where it joins the main branch.*

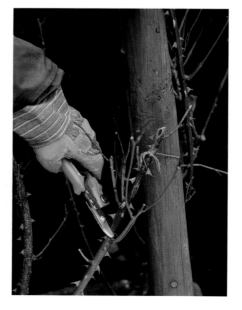

Left: *Tips of stems often die back, especially those that have carried bunches of flowers. Another cause is the young growth at the tip of shoots being killed by frost. If this dieback is not cut out, it can kill off the whole shoot. Even if dieback proceeds no further, the bush looks tidier without these dead shoots. Cut the shoot back into good wood, just above a strong bud.*

PRUNING OUT DEAD WOOD ON A CLIMBER

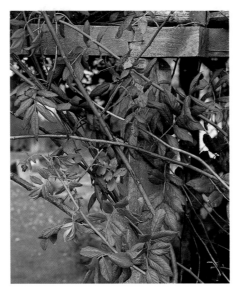

1 *Most climbers produce a mass of dead wood that has to be removed so that the plant does not become congested. Dead wood is normally quite clearly differentiated from live wood by its colour and lack of flexibility.*

2 *Thin out all of the dead wood that the climber has produced, removing it very carefully in sections, if this is necessary, so that the remaining stems are not damaged when the dead stems are eventually pulled out.*

see what further work needs to be done. Many species have specific pruning requirements, which need to be carried out if the plant is to reach its full potential. Creating balance, form and a pleasing shape in the pruned specimen requires a keen eye, as well as an understanding of the plant's growth habits and tolerances. It is worth taking a little time over this and planning what you are going to do before

starting. Acting too hastily now can easily spoil the job. Pruning is one of a few tasks in the garden that are best viewed intermittently from a distance. Remember, you can only cut a branch once. If you cut the wrong branch, you cannot rejoin it effectively to the plant from whence it came. Always check that you know the full extent of a branch and what effect its removal will have prior to making the cut.

Above: *Up to a third of the old wood should be removed to encourage the climber to produce new growth. If possible, cut some of this out to the base; also remove some of the upper stems, cutting them back to a strong growing point.*

Above: *Remove any wood that has become diseased, cutting it back to a point on the stem where the wood of the climber is healthy. If the cut end shows that the wood is still diseased on the inside of the stem, cut back further still.*

PLANT PROPAGATION

Despite the large variety of methods employed, there are really only two basic types of plant propagation: vegetative – taking cuttings, for example – and sowing seed. All of the techniques used fall into one or other of these categories. Raising your own plants is one of the most rewarding activities that any gardener can do. It can also be particularly beneficial for the organic gardener because, unlike with bought-in plants, you can be assured that self-raised stock will be pesticide-free.

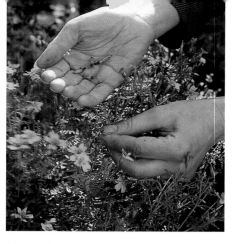

Above: *Collecting your own seed can be very rewarding and ensures that your new plants are free of any pesticide residues.*

POTTING MIX FOR PROPAGATION

Seed and cutting potting mix should be almost free of nutrients – the plants do not need soil-derived nutrients until they have rooted. Numerous proprietary brands are available for organic propagation. Alternatively, you can make your own potting mix using finely sifted compost or leaf mould mixed with equal parts of sharp sand or grit. Mixing this is comparatively easy but problems can arise if the organic matter is not thoroughly sterilized. Unless you are able to do this, there is always the possibility of fungal diseases affecting the plants. Worm compost can be good for making potting mix but the easiest way to get sterilized potting mix is to use compost that was made in a hot pile. Use material from near the middle of the pile to get the most sterilized matter.

PROPAGATION FROM SEED

Seeds are nature's way of introducing variety into plant material. Fertilizing the female part of a flower with pollen from the male part produces a seed. Seeds are a resting and survival stage in the plant's life that help it survive adverse conditions in nature. Seeds can survive conditions that kill plants. A seed consists of three things: an embryo (a young plant at its most immature stage); a food supply (to maintain the embryo and provide energy after germination); and a protective seed coat. The embryo consists of a young root system (radicle); the young shoot system (plumule), which carries the seed leaves (cotyledons); and the hypocotyl, which is the junction between the root and shoot systems.

Some seeds need special treatment to germinate. One such treatment is stratification. To stratify seeds, cover them in some damp material, such as damp compost, and keep them in a refrigerator at about 4.5°C (40°F) for up to three months. After this treatment, the seeds are ready to germinate. Seeds that germinate better after stratification are oaks and hellebores.

Seeds require moisture, warmth and oxygen to germinate. Because a seed needs oxygen as well as moisture, it is important not to keep the seeds too wet.

On the other hand, the seeds must not dry out. Most seeds germinate best between 18.5–24°C (65–75°F). Most seeds will germinate well in light; however, some seeds, such as those of periwinkle, pansy and verbena, germinate best in the dark.

Many seeds have specific germination requirements that require knowledge of the particular species. Certain generalizations are possible and although it is always advisable to follow the instructions on packets you buy, self-collected seed may require a bit of guesswork. If it is a small dust-like seed (thyme and basil, for example), it probably needs light to germinate. Make sure the seed is well pressed into the moist mixture, but do not cover. Larger seed should be covered to twice its thickness in the soilless mixture. If the seed packet says to scarify, make a scar in the seed by nicking the seed coat in some way. Lightly rubbing the seeds with sandpaper usually accomplishes this. The reason for scarification is to speed up the lengthy process of letting the water past the waterproof seed coat.

MAKING ORGANIC PROPAGATION POTTING MIX

1 *Take equal quantities of an organic material, such as coir or finely sieved leaf mould, and a free-draining material such as vermiculite or perlite.*

2 *Mix the organic material and vermiculite or perlite together thoroughly, ensuring that there are no lumps and that the mixture is open and "free running".*

3 *This organic potting mix for propagation is now ready for use and does not need any additional fertilizer. It can be used to propagate seeds and cuttings.*

SOWING SEEDS IN CONTAINERS

1 *First gather together the basic equipment. You will need pots, potting mix, labels, a pencil, a firming board and a plastic bag.*

2 *Fill the container with the potting mix, gently tapping the pot to ensure that there are no air spaces in the mix.*

3 *Gently firm and flatten the potting mix with the firming board. Take care not to over-firm the potting mix.*

4 *Sow the seed evenly over the potting mix surface. Large seed can be placed, but smaller seed must be scattered.*

5 *With larger seed, lightly cover the seed with finely sieved potting mix. Sieved vermiculite or perlite can also be used.*

6 *Water the pot using a fine rose on a watering can. If the seed is small, water the potting mix prior to sowing.*

VEGETATIVE PROPAGATION

The vegetative parts of the plant (stem, root or leaf) can also be used to produce a new plant. Most fruit trees are propagated asexually, using a bud or a twig from a tree that produces exceptionally good fruit. When this bud or twig becomes an adult tree, it has the same qualities as the "mother" tree. By propagating asexually (cloning), we reproduce the "mother" plant.

PROPAGATING PLANTS FROM SPECIALIZED ORGANS

Plants may be propagated from many different plant parts. Specialized roots, stems and leaves that occur naturally make asexual propagation easy.

Bulb This consists of swollen leaves on a short stem. Bulbs can be propagated by removing small bulblets or offsets that form at the base of the parent bulb. These small bulbs take two or three years to mature into plants that flower. Place offsets in rich light soil. Certain bulbs, such as lilies, can be propagated by removing individual scales from the dormant bulb and placing them in a bag of damp moss. After a few months the scale will develop into a small bulb (a bulbil), which can be potted as if it were a large seed and grown on. Certain lilies (tiger lilies, for instance) produce bulbils in their leaf axils (where the bulb leaf joins the stem) that can also be propagated. Examples of bulbs are tulips, onions and lilies.

Corm This is similar to a bulb and often confused with one. Structurally, however, a corm is different, consisting of a stem that is swollen as a food store. It is shorter and broader than a bulb. The leaves of the stem are modified as thin dry membranes that enclose the corm and protect it against injury and drying. Examples of corms are crocus and gladiolus. The procedure for propagating these is the same as for taking offsets from bulbs.

Rhizome This is a stem that grows horizontally near the soil surface. A rhizome usually stores food, but, as it grows, it develops buds along its length. Rhizomes can be cut into sections with at least one eye or bud. Plants propagated in this way include iris.

Runner This is a stem that arises from a crown bud and creeps over the ground. The plantlet that forms at the tip is easily rooted and forms a new plant. Plants with runners include strawberries and spider plants.

Tuber This is a swollen underground stem or root that stores food. Tuberous plants, such as potatoes and dahlias, can be dug up and the tubers separated. Each section must have a segment of the crown that contains at least one eye or bud.

PROPAGATING TUBERS

1 *Take a sharp knife and cut the tuber (in this case a begonia tuber) through the middle so that each part has a shoot.*

2 *Dust the open cuts with a fungicide such as sulphur or Bordeaux mixture. Prepare two small pots with moist potting mix.*

3 *Plant both halves so that they sit firmly on top of the potting mix. Keep the potting mix moist and plant on when new growth appears.*

ROOT CUTTINGS

To produce a new plant from a root cutting, there must be a shoot bud present or it must be possible for the cutting to form one. The ability of root cuttings to form these buds depends on the time of year. The dormant (resting) season is usually the best time to take root cuttings and it is best to take them from newer root growth.

Make cuttings 3–10cm (1¼–4in) long from roots that are 1–1.5cm (⅜–½in) in diameter. Ensure the roots are from the chosen plant and not neighbouring plants. Cuttings are best taken during the winter, when roots have large carbohydrate supplies, but they may also be taken throughout the growing season. Cut straight through the end of the root closest to the stem. Cut the other end on a slant.

This will help you to remember which end is the top (the straight cut) and which is the bottom (the diagonal cut).

Store cuttings from dormant roots for three weeks in moist rooting medium at 5°C (41°F). After this, remove from storage and plant upright in the growing medium. Keep moist and warm in a bright location until the plant has grown large enough to pot on or plant out. This will, of course, vary depending upon the vigour of the plant and slow-growing plants may be best potted up and grown on for a season before finally planting out the following spring.

If root cuttings are taken during active growth, miss out the period of storage and place the cuttings directly in the rooting medium. Phlox and euphorbias are propagated from root cuttings.

STEM CUTTINGS AND LAYERING

Many trees, shrubs and herbaceous plants are propagated from stem cuttings. A root system must be formed on a stem either before or after the stem is removed. Roots can be formed on stems in two ways: by layering and by taking stem cuttings. With layering, the stem is allowed to produce roots before it is cut from the parent plant.

Stem cuttings form roots after the stem is removed. The main difficulty with stem cuttings is keeping the stems alive while they form new roots. Some plant stems root better when the wood is soft and actively growing, others root best from mature wood. Cuttings taken from plants that are actively growing are called softwood cuttings, while those taken after the wood is mature are known as hardwood cuttings.

TAKING ROOT CUTTINGS

1 *Dig up a small section of root from a suitable species with thick fleshy roots. The section must either have a shoot bud or be capable of forming one – in which case the cutting should be taken in the dormant season – if it is to be successful.*

2 *Remove as much of the soil as possible from the root cutting before slicing off the small side roots. Using a sharp knife, remove these as well as dead and damaged portions and any side shoots to leave a section of healthy root.*

3 *Cut the remaining sections of the root into small pieces, approximately 5cm (2in) in length, cutting the bottom end at an angle. Insert the root cutting into propagation potting mix, with the angled end pointing down.*

TAKING HARDWOOD CUTTINGS

1 *Select healthy, blemish-free pieces of wood about the thickness of a pencil. Cut each of these into sections about 20–25cm (8–10in) long, angling the top cut.*

2 *Stand the cut stems in a jar of water until you are ready to plant them out. Ideally, stand the jar in a cool moist place out of direct sunlight.*

3 *Dig a narrow trench that is deep enough for the cuttings. About 2.5–5cm (1–2in) should emerge above ground. The length of the row will depend on the number of cuttings.*

4 *Loosely fill the trench to about two-thirds full with sharp sand or fine grit. This is essential as it will allow the passage of air around the bases and prevent rotting off. It will also encourage rooting.*

5 *Insert the cuttings about 10–15cm (4–6in) apart, making sure that the angled cut is uppermost. If you place any cuttings in upside down – i.e. with the buds facing downward – rooting will not occur.*

6 *Gently firm the soil, making sure that the cuttings are firm but that the soil surface is not over-compacted. Leave the cuttings for the whole of the growing season before lifting and planting out next winter.*

TAKING STEM TIP CUTTINGS

1 *Take cuttings from the tips of the stems and put them in a plastic bag. The length of the cuttings will vary, depending on the subject, but take about 10cm (4in).*

2 *Trim the cuttings to just below a leaf joint and then remove most of the leaves and side shoots, leaving just two at the top. This will help to prevent stem rot.*

3 *Place up to twelve cuttings in a pot of potting mix that is specially formulated for cuttings or a 50:50 mixture of sharp sand and peat substitute such as coir or leaf mould mix.*

4 *Water well, and cover with the cut-off base of a soft-drinks bottle, a perfect substitute for a propagator. A heated propagator will speed up the rooting process. Place several pots in the same unit.*

Layering is a useful way of increasing some shrubs and climbers that cannot readily be propagated from cuttings. Simple layering is a method of getting a growing shoot to produce roots while it is still attached to the "parent" plant. There are several variations on the technique, and the one you use will depend on the plant and the type of growth it produces.

Softwood cuttings are taken from first-year branches that have not yet become woody. Flowering shrubs are often propagated by softwood cuttings. Late spring and early summer are the best times for success with this method. Take cuttings 5–10cm (2–4in) long. Larger cuttings produce larger plants sooner, but they are prone to more rapid water loss. Make cuts slightly below a leaf node. Remove any leaves on the lower section and insert them into potting mix, making sure that no leaves are touching each other or the potting mix. Remove any cuttings immediately from the tray or pot if they die or appear diseased. Pot healthy cuttings up promptly once they recommence growth following rooting.

Hardwood cuttings are taken once the tissue becomes woody and the plant is dormant. Cuttings can be taken two weeks after leaf fall and before bud burst. Select healthy wood that was produced the previous summer. The wood should be about pencil thickness and cut into sections of approximately 20–25cm (8–10in). Several cuttings can be made from the same branch of some shrubs.

To take hardwood cuttings, make basal cuts just below a node, and upper cuts slightly above a bud. The upper cut should be slanted and the lower cut straight, so that a cutting is less likely to be inserted into the potting mix upside down. Once inserted all the tops of the cuttings should be slanted cuts. Bury cuttings vertically in moist sandy topsoil or sand.

The cuttings should not freeze, but must remain cool. In spring, remove the cuttings from storage and plant in a hotbed or other protected site with exposure to morning sun or filtered light. Leave 2.5–5cm (1–2in) of cutting above ground. Keep cuttings moist until a root system forms. Transplant the cuttings the following spring while they are still dormant.

LAYERING SHRUBS

1 *Choose a stem that will reach the ground without breaking and prepare the soil beneath it. In most cases, the native soil will be satisfactory, but if it is heavy clay, add some potting mix to improve its texture.*

2 *Trim off any side shoots or leaves. Dig a shallow hole and bend the shoot down into it.*

3 *To help hold the shoot in place, peg it down with a piece of bent wire.*

4 *Fill in the hole and cover it with a stone. In many cases, the stone will be sufficient to hold the layer in place and a peg will not be required. The stone will also help to keep the area beneath it moist.*

5 *It may take several months or even years for shrubs that are hard to propagate to layer but, eventually, new shoots will appear and the layer will have rooted. Sever it from its parent and pot it up into a container.*

6 *If the roots are well developed, transfer the layer directly to its new site.*

SIMPLE DIVISION

1 *Water the plant that is to be divided during the previous day. Carefully dig up a clump of the plant using a spade, in this case a Michaelmas daisy (Aster novi-belgii).*

2 *Insert two garden forks back-to-back into the plant and lever apart by pushing the handles together. Keep on dividing until the pieces are of the required size.*

3 *The pieces of the plant can then be replanted in the bed, but dig over the soil first, removing any weeds and adding some well-rotted organic material.*

4 *Alternatively, small pieces of the plant can be potted up individually. After watering, place these in a closed cold frame for a few days before hardening off.*

DIVISION

Division is the cutting or breaking up of a crown or clump of suckers into segments. Each segment must have a bud and some roots to propagate successfully. These segments are replanted and grow into new plants identical to the parent. Most perennials should be lifted and divided when they become overgrown and begin to lose vigour. Vigorous growth in most perennials occurs on the outer segments of the clump. Old growth in the centre of the clump is discarded.

Carefully dig up the plant, loosening the roots and lifting it from the soil. Split apart the main clump with two spades or forks, or chop with a shovel or large knife if the clump is firmly massed. It is advisable to divide autumn-flowering perennials in spring, while those that flower in spring and summer are best divided in autumn.

GRAFTING AND BUDDING

Grafting and budding involve inserting or attaching a part of one plant on to another so that both parts continue to grow. In grafting, you attach a short twig from a desirable variety with two or more buds (called a scion) to a seedling. This seedling is called the stock and forms the root system for the new plant, while the scion becomes the top growth. Budding involves inserting the bud from a desirable variety into a cut or slit in the bark of the stock. The bud develops into the whole top of the plant. You must match scions and buds with stocks according to their ability to grow together.

CHIP BUDDING

1 *Select good bud wood that is free from blemishes and obvious damage, pests or diseases. If you are doing this in the summer, then you must first remove the leaves.*

2 *Remove the bud using a very sharp, flat-edged knife. Cut out the bud with a thin shaving of the wood below the bark and leave a "V" shape at the base.*

3 *Prepare the stock plant by cutting a "church window" shaped notch from the stem that is the same thickness as the chipped bud and leave a small notch cut into the base.*

4 *Place the bud into the notch, fitting the "V"-shaped base into the notch at the base of the "window cut".*

5 *Make sure that the bud fits snugly, with the edges of the bud-wood in contact with the edge of the "window" notch.*

6 *Secure the graft firmly with grafting tape to ensure that the join does not dry out. The graft will usually take in about 4–6 weeks in the summer but winter grafts can take longer.*

THE GREENHOUSE ENVIRONMENT

Greenhouses provide an environment in which levels of light and shade, temperature and moisture, and protection from the elements can be closely controlled and monitored. You can propagate plants to grow outside, protect tender plants from frosts and grow certain crops out of season. A basic understanding of the ways that the greenhouse environment can be controlled will help you on your way to a bumper harvest.

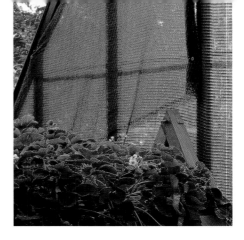

Above: *Shading helps to keep temperatures down in the summer and also protects the plants from sun scorch.*

LIGHT INTENSITY

Natural light has all the right wavelengths that plants need to function and grow successfully. Light intensities vary considerably during the year and gardeners often try to compensate for this by giving extra light to the plant. The quality of this light must be correct for the growth of plants, and light bulbs used to supplement natural light must be of a suitable daylight quality. Natural winter light intensity is often insufficient for certain crops. Conversely, summer light levels, especially when combined with elevated temperatures, can cause problems for other crops. Balanced growth requires good greenhouse design and proper planning for the light requirements of the crop. As a general rule, the ridge that runs along the middle of your greenhouse (if yours is a traditional "A"-shaped one) should always be orientated so that it runs east to west.

LIGHT READINGS WITH A METER

These should be taken inside the greenhouse and then compared with an outside reading. The difference between the two readings will indicate the percentage of available light transmitted into the greenhouse. A good tip here for those without a professional light meter is to use the automatic aperture reading on an SLR camera or a photographic light meter. It will not give actual figures, but will indicate to a certain extent just how much of the available light is getting through.

ADDITIONAL LIGHTING

Supplementary lighting can be used to "top-up" existing daylight, especially in winter. You should always buy bulbs that give a full spectrum of light (the same quality as daylight – often sold or described as "grow lights"). Almost all bulbs for household use are short of the particular light wavelengths that plants need to produce food and grow successfully. Grow lights tend to use a lot of electricity and it may be cheaper to provide additional light for just a part of the greenhouse, suspending the lights above a crop that really needs the light. Grow lights are available as bulbs or strip lights and can sometimes be bought as special enclosed units.

SHADING

This controls temperature and light. Shading is usually put in place in order to reduce summer temperatures (if they are excessive) or to protect young plants and shade-loving ones from very intense sunlight. Blinds, netting or white shade paint can all be effective.

TEMPERATURE

Almost all plants like a fall in night-time temperature of about 4–6°C (7–10°F) below that in the day. Many commonly grown species have a relatively wide range of tolerances, but most grow best between about 16–24°C (60–76°F). All plants have maximum and minimum temperature tolerances that should never be exceeded.

You can take an average temperature reading inside the greenhouse using a maximum and minimum thermometer. Compare it with one taken outside. You should note, however, that more than just the outside temperature influences that of a greenhouse. The action of the sun, even on a relatively cold day, can result in temperatures being much higher inside than out. Wind is also a factor to consider that can cause a chilling effect far below the temperature average, rapidly cooling the glass and air nearby.

HEATING SYSTEMS

Most heaters depend upon a hotbox or burner. These work by heating the air directly. They are more generally used

Above: *Some automated systems measure air temperature, and then turn on heat and open vents as necessary.*

Above: *A maximum/minimum thermometer is an essential tool in helping you to judge the conditions in your greenhouse.*

Left: *Even a relatively small greenhouse can vastly increase the range of plants that you can grow in your garden.*

CHECKING THE CONDITIONS

The greenhouse microclimate differs from the garden chiefly because the light intensity is lower, the temperature is higher and air turbulence is less. How you modify the environment largely depends on what you intend to grow. Winter salad crops need some additional heat, particularly on cold winter nights. Slightly tender, overwintering perennials may not need any heat unless the temperature drops very low. You must know what the environment will be even on cold winter nights. The only really accurate way to assess the suitability of an environment for plant growth is to take regular readings. Many devices exist to monitor the internal conditions within protected structures. These include thermostats for heating and automatic ventilators, although a seemingly endless array of humidification, automatic shading and watering devices are now available for small greenhouses.

GREENHOUSE HYGIENE

Practising good hygiene is important in maintaining the health of the plants. Dead leaves and debris left lying about can harbour pests and diseases, as can badly affected plants if they are not removed promptly. Once a year, thoroughly clean all surfaces, including glass and glazing bars, with hot soapy water. This will pay dividends during the growing season by reducing the number of annually re-occurring pests and diseases. Where plants are grown in open borders, rotate crops or replace the soil with fresh topsoil every two or three years.

where there is no need to provide heat on a regular basis – in cold greenhouses, for example, or in polytunnels used for raising early hardy stock. Some enterprising gardeners link hot water pipes to their domestic heating systems to provide heating for the greenhouse. The disadvantage here is that the heat tends to be applied at times to suit the household but not the plants within the greenhouse.

INSULATION

It is possible to insulate a greenhouse by providing additional layers within the structure to trap air. Bubble-wrap plastic is a popular method as it is easy to place in position and allows for the transmission of light. Such methods always reduce the amount of light transmitted, but will save upon heating costs. In addition to this, careful siting of the greenhouse can help to reduce the chilling effects of high winds.

HUMIDITY

Most plants thrive in about 40 to 60 per cent humidity. Plants that are grouped together often set up their own small microclimate where the humidity is higher in the immediate vicinity. Much of the humidity requirement for a plant depends upon where it comes from. Rainforest plants often need 85 per cent or more humidity, whereas cacti need as little as 15 per cent (in cultivation). The humidity is also affected by other factors, notably temperature. Warm air can hold much more moisture than cooler air.

The need to increase humidity rises during the hotter months when it is harder to keep down the temperature in protected structures. Increasing the humidity also helps to slow down the water loss from leaves and may also help to prevent wilting or scorch.

Humidity should be raised by damping down (spraying a hose on hard surfaces, paths or under benches) on hot dry days. If there are only certain plants, such as young seedlings, that require elevated humidity, then these are best covered with a thin layer of clear plastic.

AIR CIRCULATION

All plants need a constant supply of clean fresh air around them in order to grow healthily. Outdoors, normal wind movements would supply this, but in a greenhouse you will need to make provision for this.

Ventilators help control temperature and air flow. Roof vents should normally occupy the equivalent of 15 per cent of the floor space in order to be fully effective. They are normally a single structure that opens "window fashion" with a safety catch to keep them open to the required width. As with greenhouse design in general, there are many designs, most being simple variations on a theme. Side ventilators are also occasionally seen in some greenhouses. These are usually arranged in a "louvre type" fashion, with several overlapping strips that can be opened or closed with a small lever.

Above: *Bubble-wrap plastic is an ideal material with which to insulate the greenhouse in the winter.*

GREENHOUSE CULTIVATION

In a greenhouse you can hasten the arrival of spring by forcing hyacinths, tulips, azaleas and a whole variety of spring crops. You can also lengthen summer, with roses that bloom far into the autumn, and brighten winter with carnations, camellias and rare tropical flowers. You may also harvest tomatoes in mid-winter and vegetables or greens at any time of the year.

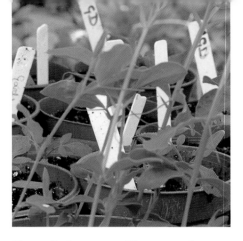

Above: *Early crops and flowers can be raised in pots ready for planting out when the weather is warmer.*

METHODS OF GROWING

Think carefully about how you plan to use your greenhouse and what plants you would like to grow there. The true art of greenhouse gardening lies in using every available area of space. This will involve planning the layout of the growing areas in the greenhouse and making a cropping plan to ensure that you not only use all of the available space, but also every "time space" within the growing calendar.

GROWING IN OPEN GROUND

Many greenhouse plants will grow well in open soil borders. The soil can be prepared in a similar way to that used for borders outside. Remember that much of what benefits outdoor soil (digging and adding organic matter) is also good for indoor soil. The advantage is that the system is sustainable over a long period and can even be serviced as a small raised bed system to help maintain steady soil temperatures. Taller crops, such as tomatoes, are particularly well suited to growing in open borders in the greenhouse, but a whole

range of both ornamentals and edible crops can also be grown in this way. Remember that if you intend to grow certain crops indoors – salad crops, tomatoes, legumes or cucumbers, for example – then you may need to rotate these, or in smaller spaces avoid growing them in open ground every second or third year. This is done for the same reasons that outdoor crops are rotated.

Above: *Staging can provide extra space in the greenhouse as well as a comfortable surface on which to work.*

Left: *You can grow crops in soil beds as well as in pots in the greenhouse.*

GROWING IN POTS ON STAGING

Staging is essentially a shelf or shelves on which plants in pots are arranged. It enables the gardener to work at a comfortable height and is particularly useful for those who wish to raise seedlings and propagate plants. The area beneath the staging is somewhat shaded but by no means wasted as it can be used for overwintering dormant plants, growing ferns and other shade-lovers, and for some forms of propagation (lilies propagated from scales, for instance). It also provides the perfect place for propagators and can easily be adapted to become a propagating tent.

USING GROW BAGS

Grow bags offer a good alternative to open beds in smaller greenhouses, where space is limited and no open beds exist. These can be purchased or you can easily make your own by filling a large plastic potting-mix bag with a mixture of garden compost and a little grit. Each bag will support four tomato plants and even greater numbers of smaller plants. Grow bags are ideal for raising sweet peas (*Lathyrus odoratus*) for use on patios or roof gardens where the rich deep soil in which they thrive is unavailable. They can equally be used to raise garden peas or beans.

GROWING CLIMBING PLANTS

The last dimension in the greenhouse is the vertical one, ultimately to the roof. Lean-to greenhouses are especially useful for this, their back walls being well suited for growing such things as vines or kiwi. Even freestanding "apex" houses (those shaped like an "A" with a central ridge) can be used to raise climbing crops, such as cucumbers or melons, to say nothing of the thousands of delightful and colourful ornamental climbers that thrive in the greenhouse.

A YEARLY GREENHOUSE CROPPING PLAN

The plan shown below is a sample of how a greenhouse can be used to be productive all year round. The essential point is that you plan what you want to grow. Once you have decided on this it is a relatively simple matter to make your greenhouse a productive space.

GREENHOUSE TASK	MID-WINTER	LATE WINTER	EARLY SPRING	MID-SPRING
Edible crops	Sow seeds for early crops. Interplant with radishes. Sow early cabbage and cauliflower in pots. Bring strawberries in from frames. Top-dress vines and fruiting climbers.	Sow broad beans. Pot on early vegetable seedlings. Reduce young shoots of vines to one to two per spur and raise lowered rods back to the greenhouse side.	Sow the seeds of Brussels sprouts. Sow indoor tomato seed and make sowings of calendula, tagetes or similar in order to encourage beneficials and pollinators. Prick out seedlings.	Sow seed of outdoor tomatoes, celery, celeriac, melons and cucumbers. Harden off early vegetable plants. Tie new growth from vine rods on to wires. Remove side shoots of early tomatoes.
Ornamentals	Take cuttings of plants such as chrysanthemums. Bring bulb pots in for forcing. Pot on autumn-sown sweet peas into "long" pots.	Start off dahlia cuttings. Cut back and re-pot fuchsias and pelargoniums. Sow sweet peas (*Lathyrus odoratus*). Pot up cuttings of herbaceous plants. Sow herbaceous seed and begin sowing bedding plants.	Harden off early sweet peas. Pot up cuttings and sow seed of half-hardy annuals. Take cuttings. Prick out seedlings. Pot up summer bedding tubers and corms.	Finish sowing half-hardy bedding. Pot up cuttings and prick out seedlings. Make up summer tubs and hanging baskets for growing on.
General	Wash glass panes of greenhouse and frames. Keep conditions on the dry side. Be vigilant for winter pests and diseases. Provide heat as necessary.	Keep an eye on ventilation. Watch for pests and diseases. Keep conditions on the dry side. Remove dead or dying material from plants. Provide heat as necessary and ventilate.	Damp down on hot days and ventilate. Watch for pests and diseases. Begin to feed plants as growth increases. Dig, manure and top-dress borders ready for planting.	Damp down at least twice daily when hot and ventilate. Continue to watch for pests and diseases. Dig borders and manure if you have not already done so.

GREENHOUSE TASK	LATE SPRING	EARLY SUMMER	MID-SUMMER	LATE SUMMER
Edible crops	Plant greenhouse tomatoes into prepared borders or large pots of loam-based potting mix. Interplant with calendula and tagetes to encourage bees into the crop. Prick out celery and celeriac cuttings.	Thin grape trusses using vine scissors. Thin fruit if necessary on peaches growing under glass. Pick tomatoes regularly as they ripen. Pinch out and tie in melons and cucumbers as they reach their intended size.	Hand pollinate melons and cucumbers. Perform last thinning on grape trusses. Feed tomatoes with dried blood to develop uppermost trusses.	Remove lower leaves of tomatoes as fruit ripens. Support melons, removing leaves that shade the fruit. Harvest cucumbers. Sow seeds of winter leaf crops and companion plants.
Ornamentals	Harden off bedding plants. Place winter-flowering cyclamen in shade and allow to partially dry out.	Take cuttings of deciduous shrubs. Propagate houseplants. Sow seeds of spring bedding plants in frames.	Take cuttings of evergreen shrubs and deciduous species. Propagate houseplants. Sow seeds of biennials in frames. Re-start rested cyclamen corms.	Take cuttings of pelargoniums and fuchsias to act as "mother plants" for cuttings the next season.
General	Provide shade over sensitive crops. Feed plants regularly with a liquid "tea". Watch for pests and diseases and introduce biological control.	Water regularly. Continue potting on developing cuttings and seedlings of all plants.	Water regularly (twice daily in hot weather) and damp down two or three times daily to maintain humidity.	Continue potting on developing cuttings and seedlings. Continue to watch for pests and diseases and introduce biological control if necessary.

GREENHOUSE TASK	EARLY AUTUMN	MID-AUTUMN	LATE AUTUMN	EARLY WINTER
Edible crops	Cut melons as soon as they are ripe. Clear tomatoes as they finish.	Plant up winter leaf and salad crops, interplanting these with an appropriate companion planting.	Lift crowns of rhubarb for forcing and leave them on the surface for a week.	Sow seed of early onion varieties. Lift further crowns of rhubarb for forcing. Prune peach trees that are growing under glass.
Ornamentals	Take last semi-ripe cuttings and softwood cuttings.	Harden off spring bedding plants ready for planting.	Move bulbs for forcing into a frame to encourage top growth. Lift and pot up lily-of-the-valley for spring display.	Bring in bulbs for forced flowers. Stool back "mother" plants for early cuttings.
General	Decrease watering as days shorten. Pot on developing cuttings and seedlings of all plants. Remove shading and provide gentle heat on cold nights.	Pot on any remaining cuttings and seedlings. Pick over plants on a regular basis in order to remove dead or dying material. Provide gentle heat on cold nights.	Keep conditions on the dry side. Be vigilant for winter pests and diseases, as plants become more stressed due to low light levels. Provide heat as necessary.	Repair any damage to glass panes immediately it is noticed. Order seed for the coming season if you have not done so already.

COLD FRAMES AND CLOCHES

Individual and multiple plant protectors are useful for covering the transplants or seedlings of warm-weather vegetables or flowers that are set out ahead of the normal planting season. These usually take the form of low plastic tunnels, cloches or individual bell jars. The colder the area in which you live, the greater their usefulness because they effectively extend the length of the normal growing season.

Above: *This is a sturdy brick cold frame with a soil bed for growing winter and early spring vegetables.*

COLD FRAMES

These enable you to sow summer flowers and vegetables some weeks before outdoor planting and may even allow for an extra crop within a season. They are relatively inexpensive, simple structures, providing a favourable environment for growing cool-weather crops in the very early spring, the autumn and even into the winter.

Cold frames have no outside energy requirements, relying on the sun as a source of heat. They collect heat when the sun's rays penetrate the light (the top cover) which is made from plastic, glass or fibreglass. The ideal location for a cold frame is facing the direction of the sun with a slight slope to ensure good drainage and maximum solar absorption. A sheltered spot against a wall or hedge is best. Sink the frame into the ground to provide extra protection, using the earth for insulation. Put a walkway to the front and adequate space behind the frame to help when removing the light.

Designs for cold frames vary. For example, some contain barrels that are painted black and filled with water. These absorb heat during the day and release it at night. Some cold frames are built with a very high back and a steep glass slope. Others are insulated very well and may also include moveable insulation. A simple method of providing insulation is to use sacks filled with leaves over the top of the frame and bales of straw or hay stacked against the sides at night in order to protect against freezing.

There is no standard-sized cold frame. The inside depth of the frame should be determined by the height of the plants that you plan to grow. Spring annuals, perennial seedlings or low over-wintering stock may need as little as a 30cm (12in) backboard and a 20cm (8in) front board. Potted plants may need a 38cm (15in) front board and a 45cm (18in) back board. A standard glass frame light is usually about 1 x 1.8m (3 x

6ft). Do not make the structure too wide for weeding and harvesting; a width of 1.2–1.5m (4–5ft) is convenient to reach across.

Cold frames are useful for hardening-off seedlings that were started indoors or in a greenhouse. This hardening-off period is important because seedlings can suffer serious setbacks if they are moved directly from the warmth and protection of the greenhouse to the garden. It is also possible to start cool-weather crops in the cold frame and either grow them to maturity or transplant them in the garden. Cold frames may also be useful for rooting the cuttings of deciduous and evergreen shrubs and trees, and the softwood cuttings of chrysanthemums, geraniums and fuchsias during the warmer months. Ventilation is most critical in late winter, early spring, and early autumn on clear, sunny days when temperatures may rise above 45°C (113°F). The light should be raised partially to prevent the build-up of extreme temperatures inside the frame. Lower or replace the light early each day in order to conserve some heat for the evening.

In summer, extreme heat and intensive sunlight can damage plants. You can avoid this by shading with a lath (a slatted wooden frame) or old bamboo window blinds. Water plants early so that they dry before dark; this helps to reduce disease problems.

CLOCHES

Traditionally a bell-shaped glass cover, a cloche is a moveable structure that serves as a mini-greenhouse. Cloches can be used to protect transplanted tender plants from spring frosts. They also help to warm up the soil for crops sown directly in the soil.

Left: *When the seedlings are fully acclimatized and ready to be planted out, the lights or lids can be left off altogether.*

Above: *A rigid plastic cloche is easy to use. The sections butt up against each other and can be pegged into the soil. Endpieces are also available.*

Above: *Glass bell jars are simple cloches for covering one plant. They are expensive, but large plastic jars make a good, if not as attractive, alternative.*

The traditional or European cloche is usually built in 60cm (24in) sections that vary in height from 20–60cm (8–24in) and 40–65cm (16–26in) in width. It is made of four panes of glass held together with heavy galvanized wire fittings. It has a handle for ease in carrying and for operating the ventilation system. Several cloches placed end to end make a miniature greenhouse.

Plastic bottles with the bottoms cut out can provide protection for small individual plants. These will last a season or two, but will become brittle over time. Flexible fibreglass sheets held in an inverted "U"-shape by stiff wire hoops or small wooden stakes can be used to cover rows of plants.

A tunnel-like plant protector can be made with a 1.5m (5ft) strip of plastic or fleece laid over 1.8m (6ft) wire hoops placed 1m (3ft) apart. Elastic tiedowns over the top near each hoop will hold the plastic.

Temporary cloches can also be made by arching black, semi-rigid, plastic piping over the row or bed and sticking it into the ground on each side. Lay clear plastic over the arches. If the beds are enclosed with wood, attach brackets to the inside edges of the boxes or sink short pieces of pipe with a larger inside diameter along the sides to hold the arches. The arches can be used to support fleece or shade cloth to ward off both frost and bright sunlight. When this

cloche is no longer needed, simply remove the plastic sheet and pipe ribs and store them until the following season.

THE BOTTLE RADIATOR

In areas prone to late air frosts, this simple method can protect outdoor crops such as bush tomatoes. Fill a glass or plastic bottle with water and place it next to the plant. The sunlight will warm the water in the bottle, which will in turn release a gentle heat at night. This is sufficient to prevent cold shock to the plant and will ensure good growth and cropping. It can also be used in conjunction with a fleece covering to enhance the warming effect.

Left: *Old-fashioned cloches are particularly good for decorative vegetable gardens. However, they are also very expensive.*

Far left: *Upturned, clear plastic bottles with the bottoms cut out are ideal for using as mini-cloches, protecting individual plants. This is also an environmentally friendly technique.*

PLANT HEALTH

The main concern for new organic gardeners is that their plants will be attacked by pests and diseases. There is an array of techniques to control these undesirables, although the organic gardener must first learn to recognize signs of distress. However, you are unlikely to experience more than a handful of the problems described, all of which are relatively easy to solve. Pests, for example, are eaten by creatures known as beneficials and so the ecology of the garden, once stabilized, will be enough to keep most problems at bay. There is always a technique to control more persistent problems and so ensure the health of your plants.

Left: *A scarecrow is a traditional way of protecting your crops from marauding birds. It can also be decorative and amusing.*

Above: *Companion plants such as these marigolds can provide welcome colour in the kitchen garden.*

Above: *Brightly coloured flowers can encourage a variety of beneficial insects into your garden.*

Above: *Decorative planting in the vegetable plot can provide additional colour and interest.*

WHY PLANTS GET SICK

Plants are prone to numerous ailments, some of which can be a serious threat to their survival. Pests and diseases are only one of the potential pitfalls that you will meet during a normal growing season. A basic knowledge of the other main factors that can affect plant health are all you will need to help your garden to flourish. While the sight of your plants suffering can be alarming, there are, in general, only a few potential health threats that you are likely to encounter.

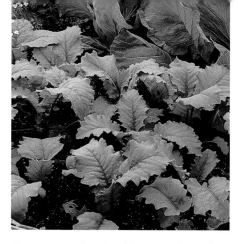

Above: *Large blocks of the same type of plant are easy for pests to locate and are therefore prone to attack.*

FROST

This can cause serious problems and is actually more critical than average minimum temperatures. Most harmful are unexpected frosts that can cause severe damage even to hardy subjects, especially when they may have produced "soft" new growth.

While warm air rises, cold air will settle and collect in hollows and depressions. Cold air is laden with water vapour and is therefore heavier. Any valley or low-lying area is, therefore, a potential frost pocket. Cold air will accumulate in a depression and then back up the sloping sides as the build-up increases. Any barrier, such as a hedge or a wall, will obstruct the passage of the cold air and a frost pocket will form. Any plants growing in the vicinity will be exposed to the frost and may be damaged by it.

When the soil is frozen, water is no longer available to the plant and shallow-rooted plants are not able to access any water to replace that which they are losing through transpiration. The plant will dehydrate and the foliage will brown and shrivel. Ground frosts may also cause the soil to "heave" and plants will be lifted out of the ground.

Alternate freezing and thawing is often more damaging to the plant than the initial frost itself, especially for tender or half-hardy subjects such as bedding plants. Severe frost can split the bark on woody subjects and may also distort leaves.

The damage caused by frost is directly related to its duration. A temperature of -4°C (25°F) for one hour may cause little or no damage, while the same temperature for four hours may be disastrous.

WATERLOGGING AND DROUGHT

The build-up of water in the soil, particularly where this occurs over a prolonged period of time, can be highly detrimental to the health of your plants. This is of greatest concern with plants that are not adapted to such waterlogged conditions. As a result, the roots of the plants will suffer and probably die from asphyxiation.

Water shortage or drought only tends to occur during the summer months when temperatures and light intensity are at their peak. The most obvious sign of the effects of water shortage on a plant is when it wilts and loses its turgidity. Water shortage also causes plant functions to slow down dramatically and prolonged drought can result in permanent cell damage.

WIND

The effects of wind damage to plants, especially woody trees and shrubs, are sometimes only too obvious. Wind often worsens extremes of temperature and drought. In severe cases of wind damage, trees can be broken and shrubs uprooted. The stronger the wind, the more damage is likely to occur.

LIGHT IMBALANCES

A plant's growth is always directed towards the available light. Plants growing in shade often become drawn and etiolated. Conversely, strong sunlight damages plants by scorching the foliage. To prevent such problems it is best to select plants that will grow well in the prevailing site conditions.

NUTRIENT IMBALANCES

Plants exhibit varying symptoms to a nutrient imbalance depending, in general, upon the severity of the problem. Symptoms of deficiency may include stunted growth, discoloured leaves (including mottling and interveinal coloration), the premature death of leaves and parts of the plant, twisted and distorted growth and poor root growth and development.

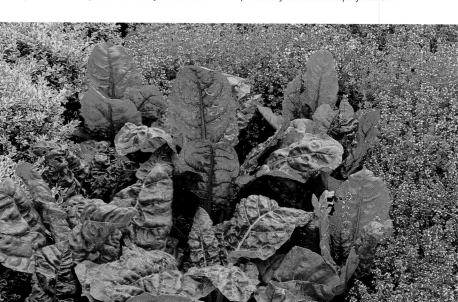

Left: *Planting crops among companion plants will make it more difficult for pests to locate them.*

Right: *A healthy, flourishing border, which is free of pests and diseases, is the ultimate aim of all organic gardeners.*

The symptoms are usually noticed first on the shoot tips, although problems may appear on any part of the plant and in different stages of growth. Determining a cause may involve an analysis of the soil.

Any nutrient can be toxic to the plant if it is present in sufficiently high amounts or is out of balance with other elements in the growing medium.

POLLUTION

Specific symptoms of pollution may include leaves turning brown at the tips and margins, leaf discoloration or premature leaf fall. Growth may also be stunted.

Soil pollutant damage can be very severe and rapid in its effects on a plant and its growth. Common problems that you may encounter include extreme soil acidity or alkalinity, chemical toxicity, salt toxicity or pesticide residues. Of these, only soil acidity is relatively easy to cure. If serious pollution is suspected, then this requires specialist help. Such situations, however, are thankfully rare.

PESTS AND DISEASES

It is important to bear in mind that a certain level of pest and disease invasion is normal even on healthy crops. However, it is also true to say that healthy vigorous plants are more resistant to serious attack than plants that are growing under stress. The best form of pest and disease control is obviously prevention. You will need to be able to find and recognize a range of pests and diseases in order to prevent outbreaks of them in your garden and, if necessary, take prompt action.

Left: *Healthy plants are often the result of careful selection according to the site conditions.*

Right: *It is very important to recognize potential problems before your plants suffer too much damage.*

PREVENTING PROBLEMS

Organic gardening is about working with nature to create an environment in which plants can withstand attack from pests and diseases, without you resorting to the use of harmful insecticides. If plants become infested with pests or diseases, they may fail to give a good display and crop yields can suffer. Prevention is better than cure, and a keen eye and regular checks will help you to anticipate and prevent the worst of any potential problems.

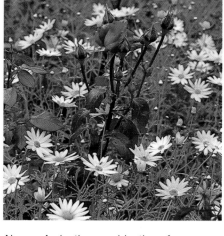

Above: *A planting combination of roses and daisies will help to attract beneficial predators to the garden.*

GOOD CULTURAL PRACTICE AND HYGIENE

Many pests and diseases can survive without a susceptible host even under the most unfavourable conditions. Myriad plant diseases survive from one growing season to the next on plant debris, in the soil, on seeds or on alternate hosts (some pests and diseases affect different plant species at different times of the year e.g. peach-potato aphid). This means it is vital to remove and properly dispose of any infected plant materials. It is also important for the organic gardener to be aware of the diseases that can threaten an individual crop and recognize the conditions in which these potential threats to plant health can thrive.

GROW DISEASE-RESISTANT CULTIVARS

Plant varieties and cultivars were mostly chosen for other reasons than their disease-resistant qualities. Often they become so commonly grown that their diseases become widespread. Many plants have disease-resistant strains or cultivars, but this does not necessarily guarantee that they will be immune to a disease. However, they will be better able to resist the worst of its ravages.

Above: *Place straw under growing strawberries in order to protect them from rot and soil-dwelling pests.*

Above: *The regular washing down of the glass panes in a greenhouse can reduce the build-up of disease-causing organisms.*

Right: *Regular deadheading of old or damaged blooms will help to reduce the spread of some fungal diseases.*

AVOID PLANT STRESS

A plant that is stressed – by drought or an unfavourable temperature, for example – will be predisposed to pest or disease attack. Plants that are not subjected to higher levels of stress than they can cope with will remain healthy and better able to deal with potential attackers.

Stressed plants often show signs of physical disorders (e.g. being tall, drawn and pale due to lack of light). These can be due to the weather, being wrongly sited, nutrient imbalance or the presence of a toxic substance in the air or soil. Physically stressed plants may become sicker than if a pest- or disease-causing organism actually had invaded them. Stress can kill a plant if the problem is not quickly remedied.

RIGHT PLANT, RIGHT PLACE

Plants all have their preferred locations and the occurrence or lack of a particular environmental factor or factors will ultimately determine whether a plant will prosper in the position in which it has been

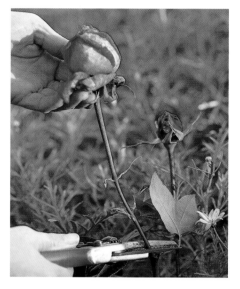

planted. Ferns, for example, need a cool moist site. Placing one in a hot sunny site will lead to its death as it struggles to keep its moisture. Plants that become stressed will neither grow as well, nor be as disease-resistant, as they would otherwise. Choosing an appropriate site in the first place will at least help to ensure the initial health of your plants and will render them more able to resist other potential threats to their health.

RECOGNIZING THE PROBLEM

Organic gardeners who understand pest life-cycles and behaviour are better able to determine when control will be most effective. Insects living in your garden are all part of nature's complex ecosystems and food chains. Less than one per cent of species that you are likely to encounter are considered pests. Since few insects are actually harmful, organic gardeners must learn which are pests, which are beneficials, and which ones will have no effect on the garden whatsoever.

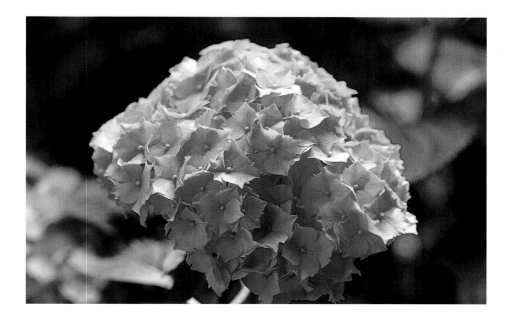

Despite the fact that they are not always popular, insects play an important role in our gardens. Beneficial insects, such as bees, are necessary in the organic garden to pollinate fruit and some vegetable crops. Others, such as springtails, also help to break down dead plant tissue, while wasps and ground beetles capture and eat other pest insects and are called predators. Wasps and midges have larvae that attack pests by living inside their bodies and are called parasitoids. Organic gardeners must learn to cherish this "willing army" of helpers in their gardens.

PEST AND DISEASE CYCLES

Often gardeners believe that their plants have been attacked overnight. This may be true in the case of damping-off disease or with larger pests such as rabbits. More often, however, much has occurred before the symptoms are actually visible.

The pathogen (the pest- or disease-causing organism) must be introduced (inoculated) to the host plant. Most pathogens either move by themselves (as with most pests) or must be carried to the host plant (as with the vast majority of diseases). Rain, wind, insects, birds and people usually spread plant diseases.

Splashing rain carries spores of apple scab fungus from infected apple leaves to uninfected leaves. Wind blows fungal spores from plant to plant, while aphids and whiteflies transmit many common plant diseases. Believe it or not, smokers can transmit tobacco mosaic virus from a cigarette to tomato plants.

Once the pathogen has been transferred to the host plant, it begins to multiply, change or grow into a form that can then enter the host. In many fungal diseases, the pathogen arrives on the plant as a spore, which must germinate before it can begin to grow and invade the plant. Once the fungal spore germinates, it sends out thread-like tubes called hyphae. These penetrate the plant through wounds or natural pores in the outer skin of leaves, stems and roots. The roots of bedding plants that have been damaged during transplanting are a common entry point for root-rotting fungi. A single aphid that lands on a plant can give birth to a clone every twelve hours and can eventually form a small thriving colony within a few days, leaving the gardener with the impression that it suddenly appeared.

Once established, pests or diseases can grow or increase in number and begin damaging plant tissue. As they consume nutrients or plant tissue, evidence of the

damage to the plant begins to appear. Symptoms may be seen on any plant parts and include mottling, dwarfing, distortion, discoloration, wilting, shrivelling or holes and notching in the margins of leaves. The first signs of pest infestation may not appear until well after the insect has laid its eggs and disappeared.

Seeds or cuttings from infected plants will also transmit disease. Certified organic seed guarantees that at the time of sale the seeds are free of all diseases. Always try to obtain disease-free stock as this should guarantee that the plant is not infected and will not introduce disease into your garden. This is particularly important with plants such as roses as well as crop plants like raspberries and other small fruits.

Pest insects and mites may carry diseases that infect plants. Organic gardeners use the term "pest management" rather than pest control or pest eradication. It is impossible to eradicate pests from your garden completely. The best option is to try to keep pest numbers low in order to minimize the damage that they can cause in your garden.

ADOPT AN INTEGRATED STRATEGY

Organic gardeners must learn how to use a range of pest management techniques, such as introducing beneficial predators into their gardens (often referred to as biological controls), making gardens less attractive to harmful pests, and encouraging conditions in the garden that favour beneficial predators of all types (cultural controls).

PLANT PESTS

Pests can be described as those creatures that harm your garden plants and, if left unchecked, they can quickly cause a great deal of damage. There is a huge army of these pests, but most organic gardeners are unlikely to encounter the vast majority of them. A basic knowledge of the commonest types that occur in domestic gardens is all that you should need to be familiar with in order to protect your plants and guarantee their health and successful growth.

Above: *Pests may well be present before symptoms appear. Close examination may reveal them before the plants start to suffer.*

HOW CAN YOU TELL IF A PEST IS A PROBLEM OR NOT?

Deciding whether a pest is a problem or not is very much a matter of opinion. Commercial growers assess the importance of a pest in terms of their financial losses. Domestic organic gardeners, however, tend to grow fewer plants or crops and mainly grow these for their beauty or for the pleasure of eating home-grown produce. The final decision as to the importance of a pest will rely upon the circumstances and experience of individual gardeners. All organic gardeners must be willing to accept a certain number of pests in their garden as these form part of the intricate food webs that result in natural control. If there are no pests, then the animals that eat them will disappear and open the door to future, potentially serious, pest outbreaks.

RECOGNIZING PESTS

It is important that you are able to accurately identify a pest that has been attacking your plants so that you can take the appropriate action. Just because an insect is seen walking on an affected plant does not mean that it is the one causing the damage. The only real way to control pests

involves getting to know them. Many pests produce characteristic symptoms that make it possible to diagnose the cause with relative certainty. Some have a wide range of host plants, and symptoms may not always be as conspicuous on all affected plants. Close examination – perhaps with a hand lens – may be necessary for the final diagnosis. With careful observation and experience, it is possible to keep one step ahead of the pests in your garden.

CONTROL OPTIONS

It is important to control pests before they become a problem. A single black bean aphid (*Aphis fabae*) that lands on a broad bean at the start of the summer could theoretically give rise to 2,000,000,000,000,000 aphids by the start of the autumn. This would be about a million tons of aphids. Numbers such as this are impossible but it does go to show that early control is essential. Quantities such as those quoted in the aphid example cannot occur as the food supply would run out before this can happen. In addition, a whole host of predators eat them. In just a few days, however, pests can cause considerable damage and quick action is

needed if you are to save your plants. Organic gardeners must employ a full range of control measures to ensure their plants survive this seasonal invasion, including cultural practices (crop rotation, good hygiene and encouraging biodiversity), physical controls (hand picking, traps, repellents and barriers) and biological control (using other animals that naturally eat pests). These are covered more extensively later in this section but for now it is important to stress that pests can only really be controlled by an integrated strategy that uses a variety of techniques.

CAN PESTS BE TOLERATED?

It is worth pointing out that we tend to be unduly concerned with pests damaging our plants. Supermarkets have conditioned us to expect blemish-free produce. We need to judge the overall health of a plant rather than react when we see a pest. If there were no pests in the garden, then there would be no predators. Step back and look at the whole picture and remember that everything, even pests, has its place in nature. They all add to the interest and diversity that is the most unique quality of an organic garden.

Above: *Birds can be serious pests in the garden. Here, large bites have been taken out of a brassica.*

Above: *Rabbits can devastate a garden overnight, leaving nothing but chewed off stumps as a result of their visit.*

Above: *Although fascinating to watch, squirrels are a garden pest and are closely related to rats.*

COMMON PESTS

There is a seemingly endless array of garden creatures that are waiting to devour and attack your garden plants. The most common pests are almost worldwide in their distribution, but they can be controlled relatively easily. It can be discouraging to see how many potential pests may attack your garden, but it is important to bear in mind that you will only encounter a handful of these in your gardening career.

PEST	PLANTS AT RISK	TREATMENT
Ants and termites	Ants are not really pests, but they "farm" aphids for sticky sugar. Termites can attack some woody species.	Few organic treatments, but baits based on borax are useful. Use a herbal spray of essential oil (citronella and lavender) or lukewarm water as a repellent.
Aphids	Most cultivated plants growing in the open, under glass or indoors.	Encourage beneficial insects to feed on them. Organic insecticidal soap can also be useful, particularly if the aphids are being "farmed" by ants.
Birds	Some birds will attack fruit and brassicas as well as brightly coloured flowers, including blossom.	Bird scarers may be employed as a deterrent and netting will also provide cover for individual crops and plants.
Cabbage root fly	The small maggots grow and develop on and within the roots of the developing cabbage plant.	Place a collar around newly planted seedlings, sinking it into the ground to prevent the newly hatched maggot from reaching the plant roots.
Carrot fly	These root-feeding maggots feed on carrots.	Try companion planting and avoid large monocultures of carrots. Erect plastic or fleece barriers, about 45–50cm (18–20in) high and 2–3m (6½–10ft) apart.
Caterpillars	Many different species of plant, especially those in the cabbage family.	Birds and other predators will reduce populations. Biological control, using a bacterial agent, and pesticides such as derris. Hand-pick off individual plants.
Chafers	Raspberries, strawberries, potatoes, lettuce, young trees, lawns and some herbaceous perennials.	Keep the ground weed-free, and well cultivated in order to reduce the number of bugs. Roll lawns in late spring.
Deer	Browse on garden plants. Male deer rub their antlers against trees, causing damage to the bark.	Notoriously difficult to control, often best kept out by fencing. Repellents are available, based upon formulae such as bear or even lion droppings.
Fruit flies	Troublesome on softer fruits in warm conditions, especially tomatoes.	Cover the fruit with a small piece of rag. Paper bags are also good to use, but can be difficult to get around a truss of tomatoes.
Gall mites and wasps	These pests affect a wide range of trees and shrubs, especially oak trees.	Generally not problematic or life-threatening. They are a good indicator of healthy biodiversity in a garden.
Leaf hoppers	There are many different types, affecting a wide range of plant species.	Difficult to control. Remove dead leaves to reduce overwintering eggs and nymphs. Encourage predators such as lacewings.
Leaf miners	There are many hundreds of species that all have their preferred host species.	Hand-picking of severely affected leaves. Biological controls exist but the problem is rarely serious enough to warrant their artificial introduction.
Leather-jackets	Can be a nuisance, especially of turf grass. They feed on roots just below the soil surface.	Can be difficult to control. Damp sacking over the soil can lure them up to the surface where they can be hand-picked or left for birds to eat.

PEST	PLANTS AT RISK	TREATMENT
Mealy bugs	Suck the sap of many species and produce a sticky honeydew that supports the growth of sooty moulds.	Biological controls are available. Cultural control is more difficult and involves drenching with an organic soap solution and then rinsing.
Mites	A common pest of many plants, especially those growing in hot dry conditions.	Biological controls are available. For a cultural control, improve humidity or spray foliage with an organic soap solution and then rinse.
Moles	Damage roots by lifting small newly planted trees. Tunnel under lawns, making them a serious pest.	Best controlled by trapping or using repellents. Sonic repellent devices are rarely effective. Removing one mole can simply "open the door" to another.
Nematodes (eelworms)	A few species cause disease-like symptoms. A problem when the same plants are grown in the same place.	Regular crop rotations can help to reduce damage. If numbers build up or plants become badly affected, avoid growing the affected species.
Rabbits and hares, squirrels, voles and mice	Rabbits gnaw shoots. Mice and voles eat small bulbs and corms in winter. They all ring-bark young trees.	They may be trapped or a variety of repellents are available. Tree and shrub shelters are useful against voles and mice as is fencing for rabbits and hares.
Sawflies	Developing larvae eat plant tissue. Fruit sawflies are notorious. Slugworm sawfly attack ornamentals.	Control slugworm by applying insecticidal soap. Control fruit sawfly larvae with derris. Both these treatments reduce numbers of beneficial insect predators.
Scale insects	Several species, some of which have specific host plants.	A cultural control consists of swabbing woody stems with a strong organic soap solution or pruning and removing affected parts.
Sciarid fly (fungus gnat)	Tiny flies that feed on soil fungus. The larvae attack the roots of young plants in water-logged potting mix.	Control by preventing the potting mix becoming too wet, although biological controls of nematodes are also available.
Slugs and snails	Common pests of a wide variety of plants. Snails, in particular, cause damage and defoliation of plants.	Often difficult to control although they can be caught in traps containing beer. A variety of barriers and deterrents are also available.
Thrips	Small insects suck the sap of soft foliage and attack flowers. Rarely a problem outside in cooler climates.	Remove seriously damaged foliage. Several natural predators (usually mites) are available for use against thrips.
Weevils	Larvae attack roots, stems or flowers and fruit of a range of plants. Adults feed on affected plants.	Wet acidic composts favour ground-living types such as vine weevil. Biological control possible with parasitic nematodes if temperatures sufficiently high.
Whiteflies	A greenhouse pest in cooler climates that may occur outside in warmer areas.	Biological controls are available but the best option can be to avoid growing susceptible species.
Woodlice (pill bugs)	Usually a pest indoors of crops like cucumbers. May chew through young seedlings.	Often more of an indication of poor hygiene than a problem in itself. A sign that you must clean up the greenhouse.

PLANT DISEASES

The early detection of plant disease can help to halt the widespread infestation of your crop. Try to establish a routine of regularly checking your plants and crops. Look closely for any telltale signs, using a hand lens if necessary. Remember that the first or most obvious symptom may not always be the only one or even the most important. Always check to see if there are other symptoms to ensure that you get the full picture before making your final diagnosis.

Above: *Modern rose varieties are highly susceptible to diseases such as blackspot and mildew.*

RECOGNIZING PLANT DISEASES

Vigilance is the key to success in controlling plant disease. Carefully inspect leaves, stems, roots, flowers and fruits for any sign of disease. You may even find it useful to cut open a branch or stem to look for problems such as discoloration of the tissue, which may explain leaf or stem wilting and sudden wilting of a section of or a whole plant.

Stand back and look at the overall picture. Consider the whole environment. This will include the weather, soil, the stage of development of the plant (and any pathogens present), cultural practices and the condition of other plants in the area. All of this information can help to indicate what may be wrong with the plant. Remember that a plant growing in the wrong location may be stressed.

Try to determine when the symptoms became apparent. The onset of a problem may be due to a cultural practice, the seasonal appearance of a disease or insect, or a weather-related event. Remember that long-term stress is slow to appear, taking a year or more at times.

Try to determine whether the problem is spreading, as this may indicate that it is a disease. Check whether plants of other species have been affected, as diseases are usually (but not always) species-specific. Problems caused by environmental factors do not spread, although the symptoms may become more severe.

You must know what the plant should look like in order to be able to recognize any abnormalities. Reading up a little on the species that you are growing in your garden can help you to make a more accurate diagnosis of the problem.

Remember that there is usually no single cause of a disease infestation. The primary cause may be associated with cultural or environmental conditions. And just as there is probably no single cause, there is usually no single symptom.

When you are attempting to diagnose the cause of plant illness, always inspect symptoms that appear on parts that are still alive (or at least partially alive). Dead plants are often invaded by secondary infestations of decomposer fungi, which may hide the original problem. If possible, make an examination of the entire plant, including roots, although this may not be possible for large specimens such as trees.

CONTROL OPTIONS

Ultimately, where a serious disease is suspected, it may be advisable to avoid growing susceptible species altogether, or, in the case of fruit and vegetables, to rotate the crop as part of a regular cycle. Make notes that provide details on disease occurrence (the type of disease and when it appeared), the plants affected, the weather and environmental conditions in your garden each year. By doing this you can better anticipate what problems are likely to occur in your garden during the growing season.

Finally, remember that even the best gardeners lose plants to disease. This is only serious when large numbers of plants are affected. A diverse garden will contain other highlights, and diseases will claim only a fraction of the planting.

Left: *Although a plant may be in obvious distress, closer examination may be needed to properly determine the cause.*

Right: *Disease-causing organisms can enter a plant each time it is cut or pruned.*

COMMON DISEASES

There are all kinds of diseases that can affect your plants. Most of these are mercifully rare, but every garden will suffer from its share of diseases during the growing season. Most of these conditions are relatively easy to deal with, but a correct diagnosis is essential. As always, it is preferable to try to prevent these diseases taking hold and spreading in the first place rather than treating them when they occur.

DISEASE		PLANTS AT RISK AND THE SYMPTOMS	TREATMENT
Bacterial canker		Many trees and shrubs. Reduces vigour and the rate of growth of the affected plant. Branches become girdled and die back. A sticky secretion will ooze from cracks or welts in the bark.	Difficult to control once a plant is infected. Confine the problem to one specimen by cleaning pruning tools between cuts and before moving on to another specimen of the same type.
Blackspot		A common fungal disease of roses, which is most prevalent on modern hybrid tea and floribunda types. Black spots appear, primarily on the leaves and sometimes on the stems as well.	Prune bush roses into a goblet shape. Use disease-resistant cultivars. Dust affected plants with sulphur early and intermittently throughout the growing season.
Bracket fungus		This disease can affect all types of tree. Bracket fungi are the fruiting bodies of fungi that either parasitize healthy heart wood or, more commonly, decay heart wood that is already dead.	Many affected trees live for many years and need only be felled if they present a risk of collapse.
Common scab of apple		A bacterial disease that causes the formation of large (albeit harmless) scabs on the surface of the apples. Commonly encountered in damp weather and on trees with crowded branches.	Rake up and dispose of affected leaves. Prune out cracked or scabby shoots to remove places for the fungus to overwinter.
Coral spot		A common fungus affecting many woody plant species. Appears as pink or bright red, raised pustules on wood that is showing signs of dieback.	Prune out infected tissue and destroy it. Regular "hygienic pruning" can help to prevent it taking hold in the first place.
Downy mildew		A group of fungal diseases that affects a wide range of plants. Appears as a white coating over leaves that display distended growth, browning and wilting. Thrives in warm moist conditions.	Dust with sulphur or spray with Bordeaux mixture to form a protective barrier against the spores. Note that these are both easily washed off by watering or rain.
Fireblight		Attacks plants of the Rosaceae family, notably apples, pears, plums, cherries, pyracanthas, cotoneasters and roses. The affected plant dies back rapidly from the branch tip.	Remove and destroy all affected material, cutting back to at least 50cm (20in) below the point of infection. Best to remove diseased plants, replacing them with a non-susceptible tree or shrub.
Fungal canker		Affects many woody plants. The bark tissue begins to peel and flake away around the affected tissue in concentric rings.	Prune out the affected material, about 15cm (6in) below the point of infection, and burn it. Clean tools with disinfectant between cuts and especially between pruning individual plants.
Honey fungus		A soil-dwelling fungus that parasitizes the roots of woody plants. Leaves tend to discolour and wilt and fail to develop in the spring. Ultimately, this can weaken and kill the plant.	Difficult to control organically. It may be best to grow herbaceous plants in affected areas for two to three years before attempting to replant woody plants there.
Mosaic virus		This group of viruses affects a very large number of species and is characterized by an irregular, angular mottling or streaking of the leaves.	Winged insects that feed on plants, then migrate to another, can rapidly spread the virus. Control the pests themselves where possible.
Phytophthora		A soil-borne fungal disease that affects many species of woody plants, particularly conifers. Branches die back, often very quickly. Serious infection may cause death for a large proportion of the root system and severe dieback of top growth.	There is no cure for this condition and the removal of badly affected plants may be the only answer. The disease is often restricted to damp or heavy soils, although prolonged wet weather can result in outbreaks.
Powdery mildew		Affects many plant species, with asters being especially prone. The leaves become covered with white powdery patches that may distort growth or even cause leaf drop in severe cases. Thrives in warm, humid or wet conditions.	Sulphur and Bordeaux mixture can provide protection, but these are easily washed off in wet conditions. Avoid growing susceptible species if conditions favour the spread of the disease.
Rust		A common fungal disease affecting many species. Characterized by rusty coloured patches or spots, known as pustules, on leaves. Tissue around the pustules yellows and dies, and this, in turn, may distort growth or cause leaf drop in severe cases.	Commonly seen on soils rich in nitrogen. It may have a noticeable effect on seasonal crops or those grown for their leaves. Bordeaux mixture can reduce its spread but it is difficult to control completely. Avoid susceptible crops and varieties if the problem is persistent.
Silverleaf		Affects both fruiting and ornamental species of *Prunus*. The leaves on some branches gain a silvery sheen, gradually dying back a year or two later. A purple fungal growth appears on the dead tissue.	The affected wood should be pruned out below the point of infection and disposed of in late summer after fruit has set. Badly infected specimens should be removed completely and disposed of, preferably by burning.
Stem rot		Attacks trees and larger woody plants. Stems and branches gradually become hollow.	Smaller trees or shrubs may be much more seriously affected and may be best removed if their condition deteriorates too much.

PLANT DISORDERS

Many external factors can affect garden plants. Weather seldom does what we want it to – there is either too little or too much rain or it is too cold or too hot. If you combine these climatic disappointments with other factors that can affect your plants, such as pollution or nutrient deficiencies, you will see why these difficult conditions can produce a number of disease-like symptoms. They can all put severe stress on an ornamental plant or crop and so precipitate attack from living organisms.

Above: *Nutrient deficiencies can cause discoloration of the leaves. This plant is short of magnesium.*

RECOGNIZING DISORDERS

Plants can be susceptible to a long list of outside forces. Extremes of weather, nutrient deficiencies and physical damage can all take their toll on the health and vigour of a plant. Other environmental factors, such as too much or too little water or pollutants in the soil, can also encourage disease-like symptoms.

Soil pollution can be caused by nutrient deficiency, misapplied fertilizer (resulting in too much nutrient and, therefore, toxicity), spilt lawnmower fuel (perhaps due to careless filling) or buried inert material. Airborne pollution can be more insidious and more difficult to determine or detect.

Weather events such as high winds or frost may go unnoticed if you are not there to witness them. A huge storm will leave evidence in its wake. The effect of a sharp early morning frost, however, or a steady drying wind on a sunny afternoon may not show the damage caused until several days have passed. Often frost occurs in the hours just before daybreak and quickly disappears to leave a fine sunny morning.

Disease can result from a combination of factors, affecting growing conditions and actual disease-causing organisms. Plants may initially be placed under stress – by high winds or frost, for example – making them vulnerable to attack by living agents. For instance, drought may damage roots, which in turn renders them more liable to infection by fungal diseases.

It is important to determine whether the distress that your plant is suffering is the result of a pathogen or due to a problem in the environment. In order to work out which of these is responsible, look to see if the occurrence of ill health is random or uniform in terms of its distribution. As a general rule of thumb, randomly distributed symptoms on injured plants are usually caused by a living factor, such as infectious diseases or a pest. In addition to this, infestations, particularly those caused by diseases, tend to radiate out from central points. Uniform patterns are generally associated with non-living or non-infectious agents such as poisons, fertilizers, environmental stress or mechanical damage.

Above: *Drought is a common cause of stress in potted plants, damaging both roots and shoots.*

CONTROL OPTIONS

If the cause of the problem is physical, you will need to find out whether it is due to a recurring environmental factor inherent in the site, such as constant buffeting by strong winds, or whether it is caused by "one-off" events such as unseasonable frosts or contamination from a careless neighbour's weedkiller spray. Some factors can be removed, such as polluted soil, and windbreaks can be planted and fleece draped over tender specimens on cold nights. If plants continue to be affected, it could be that the plant is in the wrong place and you may have to try it elsewhere.

Left: *Plants sometimes show unusual growth patterns in response to environmental conditions. Here, the growth of a tree has been affected by the wind.*

COMMON DISORDERS

Disorders are the result of either an imbalance of essential nutrients or of a range of stresses that are caused by adverse or difficult environmental conditions. Many of the disorders and conditions described here can resemble diseases. This means that is very important for you to diagnose the cause of the distress in the plant before taking any remedial action. A plant disorder will call for a different response to a plant disease.

CONDITION		PROBABLE CAUSE	TREATMENT
Bare patches or areas of poor plant establishment		The patchy establishment of cover crops or turf can be due to soil compaction or underground obstructions. Soil can easily become compacted if it is walked on a lot, particularly when it is wet. Buried obstructions such as rubble can also cause similar growth distortions.	Remove all buried rubble prior to planting or replanting. Relieve compaction by cultivating and replant if required.
Blackening of leaf tips		Usually the result of overwatering, particularly with container-grown plants. The waterlogged soil or potting mix forces oxygen out of the soil, thereby suffocating the roots which suffer a form of drought-stress.	Do not water until the soil or potting mix dries out a little. Check to see if plants need watering before doing so.
Etiolation		Sun-loving plants kept in low light conditions quickly become starved and will be significantly weakened. If kept in these conditions for any length of time, the plant will eventually die.	Choose specimens that are appropriate for the light levels in the garden.
Leaf blackening		Frost damage on buds and leaves in early spring, even to hardy specimens, is usually noticed on new growth that has not yet become acclimatized. It is the sudden shock that often causes the problem, not the actual temperature itself.	Cover slightly tender plants with fleece in the winter. Lightly spray plants with water in the evening to help protect against late frosts.
Leaf scorch		High winds and bright sunlight, especially on shade-loving species. Some plants can also be damaged by watering in bright sunlight, by providing too little or too much water or by applying too much fertilizer to the soil. Hail can also cause leaf spotting or holes.	Water in the evening. Choose wind-resistant species, if appropriate. Apply fertilizer at recommended rates. Do not over- or under-water plants.
Mechanical or physical damage		High winds, which are especially damaging to deciduous woody plants in full leaf. Herbaceous plants can easily break if not adequately staked, as may newly planted trees and shrubs. Snow can snap the branches of conifers and evergreens. Visiting animals can also flatten or snap garden plants.	Stake plants firmly and ensure that animals are excluded from areas where plants could be damaged.
Nutrient deficiency		A lack of or too much of a particular nutrient. Nutrients can also become in short supply if other nutrients are present in large amounts.	Deficiencies are best treated with the application of fertilizer or choose plants that are adapted to deal with the site conditions.
Poisoned ground		Leaked fuel or lubricants used in construction work can leave the ground contaminated. This is usually more of a problem in gardens attached to modern houses. Underground gas pipes can leak, flooding the ground with gas that is lethal to plant roots. Other chemical spillages could come from machinery such as a lawnmower.	Remove all affected soil and replace with fresh topsoil. If pipes are leaking, make sure that they are fixed before replacing soil. Fill lawnmowers with fuel over a plastic sheet.
Root girdling		This can cause instability and the collapse of larger trees and shrubs. Tree and shrub roots become woody following the first year's growth and, if these are constrained in round pots, they tend to grow in spirals.	Try to use bare-rooted stock whenever possible. Tease out roots from the rootball immediately prior to planting.
Wilting		A normal response in many plants to either a lack of water or high temperatures, and not necessarily a cause for great concern. Ligularias habitually wilt on hot summer afternoons, even when planted in wet ground, only to "pick up" and show no ill effects later.	Treatment may not always be necessary. Check the soil first to see if it is dry. If not, wait until the evening to see if the plant shows any signs of improvement.

BENEFICIAL PREDATORS

A thriving population of natural predators and parasites can significantly help to keep pest populations down. The organic gardener must strive to create and maintain an environment in which these welcome visitors to the garden or greenhouse can prosper. Above all, this means avoiding pesticides, which can wipe out beneficial predators and so upset the natural balance in the garden or greenhouse.

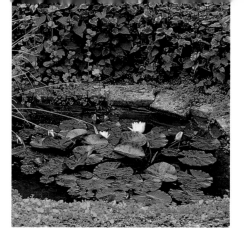

Above: *Creating a diverse range of habitats, including a pond, in your garden will encourage beneficial predators.*

BIOLOGICAL CONTROLS

Nearly every species of plant-feeding insect has another insect that is its predator or parasite. Some pests, such as aphids, are eaten by ladybirds (ladybugs), hoverflies and midge larvae, parasitized by wasps and infested by fungal diseases. Large pest populations are a food larder for many "natural enemies", including carnivorous animals, parasites and diseases.

Biological methods of control use these natural enemies of pest insects to keep their populations under control. It is like having an army of insects and other creatures doing the work for you. Biological controls can be encouraged into the garden by creating a suitable habitat. Ironically, this means that the pests must be present first. They must also be present in sufficient numbers to support a viable population of the beneficial predator. This can be a complex area and the easiest way is to encourage the conditions that will favour a balanced food web to develop. Purchasing beneficials is only generally recommended for use in greenhouses although a few (particularly microbes) are suitable for use outdoors.

CREATING SUITABLE HABITATS

The easiest way to achieve this is to get a mixture of habitats. The more variety your garden has, the more biodiversity it will support. Ponds, long grass, log piles, and food plants for animals with varied tastes all encourage a stable garden ecosystem where pests are kept at relatively low levels.

Many birds and bats eat insects. Bats need a roosting site, so place a purpose-made bat box on the shady side of a tree. Position the box at least 3m (10ft) high with a clear airspace in front. Night-scented flowers encourage the moths that bats feed upon. This is the key. The predators must be able to live in your garden or they will go and find a more suitable habitat elsewhere.

The longer you garden organically, the more balance will appear in your garden. This is simply because your garden ecosystem begins to stabilize and diversify over time.

BENEFICIAL INSECTS

Predators (those that devour pests directly) and parasitic insects (those whose young hatch inside and devour pests) are often termed "beneficials". Predators include lacewings and wasps. Parasitic insects

Above: *Log piles encourage beneficial predators such as beetles to colonize and take shelter in your garden.*

(more correctly termed parasitoids) are less well known than predators, but equally effective. They lay their eggs in a pest species. When the eggs hatch, the larvae feed on the pest insect, killing it. The majority of these insects are tiny wasps, although some flies and mites also fall under this category. Learning to recognize beneficial insects is crucial if you want to avoid killing your army of garden helpers.

Above: *Biological controls are a successful way to fight pests. They are mainly used in greenhouses, but others are now becoming available for the open garden. The control insects are released, here from a sachet, in order to attact the pests.*

BENEFICIAL PREDATORS IN THE GARDEN

There are many beneficial predators that will willingly take up residence in your garden and help to control populations of pests in a natural way.

- Anthocorid bug or red kneed capsid
- Bats
- Birds (robin, blue tit and thrush)
- Centipedes
- Earwigs
- Frogs, toads and newts
- Ground beetle

- Harvestman
- Hedgehogs
- Hoverflies
- Lacewings (adult or larva)
- Ladybirds (ladybugs)
- Mites e.g. *Phytoseiulus*
- Nematodes e.g. *Heterorhabditis*

- Parasitic wasps (*Encarsia* or *Aphidoletes*)
- Slow worm
- Spider on web or wolf spider
- Tachinid flies
- Wasps (solitary and social)

BIOLOGICAL CONTROLS IN THE GREENHOUSE OR GARDEN

The application of biological controls in the greenhouse or garden involves using predatory insects or other beneficial animals to control commonly occurring pests. Many pests are only a problem because their natural predators are missing from the garden. Introducing a biological control usually results in the rapid control of the pest.

NAME	PREFERRED TEMPERATURE RANGE	WHAT THEY CONTROL
Amblyseus cucumeris (predatory mite)	25°C (77°F)	The nymphal forms and adults consume large quantities of immature thrips.
Aphidoletes aphidimyza (predatory midge larva)	21°C (70°F); needs 80%+ humidity	Tiny mosquito-like midge larvae that control substantial populations of more than 60 species of aphids.
Cryptolaemus montrouzieri (predatory beetle)	20–25°C (68–77°F); needs 70%+ humidity	This ladybird is effective in controlling mealybugs on houseplants and in greenhouses.
Encarsia formosa (parasitic wasp)	18–25°C (64–77°F)	Minute, flying parasitic wasps, which lay their eggs inside whitefly scales (the pupa stage) and eat them in two to four weeks.
Heterorhabditis megidis (parasitic nematode)	Minimum soil temperature of 14°C (57°F). If temperature drops below 20°C (68°F), they become less effective.	Patrol the soil to a depth of about 18cm (7in) and quickly take care of the slow-moving grubs, like vine weevil grubs and chafers. Very effective in pots and containers. Soil must be moist.
Metaphycus helvolus (parasitic wasp)	20–30°C (68–86°F)	These tiny, black and yellow wasps are effective against several soft-scale species, including brown scale. The females lay their eggs under the body of first- and second-stage scales. The grubs feed on scales and develop into adults within two weeks. Adults also provide control by feeding on non-parasitized scales. *Metaphycus* are most effective in semi-tropical conditions.
Phasmarhabditis hermaphrodita (parasitic nematode)	Minimum soil temperature of 5°C (40°F)	Useful for slug control. Should be applied during the early growing stages of vulnerable plants. Needs moist soil.
Phytoseiulus persimilis (predatory mite)	Use once temperature is regularly above 15°C (60°F). Best at 18–25°C (64–77°F); needs 60%+ humidity	Predator mites, slightly larger than the two-spotted mites (also known as red spider mites) upon which they feed.
Steinernema feltiae (parasitic nematode)	Minimum temperature of 10°C (50°F), although they remain effective when the soil temperature drops below this.	Aggressive predators used to control fungus gnats, mushroom flies and leatherjackets. They can be used on lawns as well as in flower and vegetable gardens, fields, orchards and greenhouses.

Above: *Ladybirds (ladybugs) are just one of the many beneficial insects that will help to keep garden pests in check.*

MICROBES

Bacteria, fungi, viruses, protozoans and parasitic nematodes are microorganisms that attack insects. These microscopic hordes are generally effective against very specific pests and present little risk to humans and the environment. Many organic gardeners may well be familiar with a popularly known, microbial-based insecticide known as Bt or *Bacillus thuringiensis*. This commonly available product, which is used to kill many different kinds of moth and butterfly larvae, is a bacterium. It produces a toxin that kills specific caterpillars. The larval pest usually dies within four to seven days. There are many strains of Bt, each type controlling specific pests.

Parasitic nematodes are also very effective against certain pests that live in the soil. However, the nematodes require moist conditions in order to survive and their temperature requirements further limit their use to greenhouses in many cases.

Despite their potential, very few fungi, viruses and protozoa are commercially available because these living organisms are difficult to raise, store and apply. The best way to encourage these willing and tiny helpers into your garden is to maintain a healthy soil that is rich and diverse in terms of the life it contains.

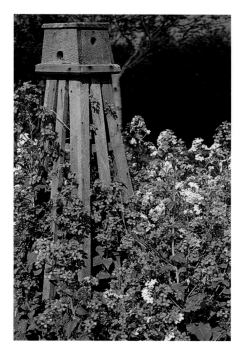

Above: *Providing convenient shelter, such as this lacewing hotel, for beneficial insects can help to increase their numbers.*

OTHER CONTROL METHODS

There are many ways of dealing with the different pests that appear in the garden. Some of these methods have been tried and tested for generations, others are individual to the gardener and are often the result of a happy accident. As an organic gardener, you must learn to use as many different tricks as possible to manage the pests in your garden and to protect your plants.

Above: *Companion plants such as these marigolds confuse or deter pests that would otherwise attack garden plants.*

GOOD GARDENING PRACTICE

The selection and culture of plants can reduce the potential for pests and diseases. Cultural practices are methods the organic gardener can use to change environmental factors that affect plants and their pest populations. It is essential, therefore, that gardeners know the cultural or growing requirements of each plant. Providing the correct conditions results in a vigorous plant that is less likely to be attacked by pests and diseases and can tolerate some damage.

ASSESSING THE DAMAGE

When problems do arise, you must decide whether a pest is causing enough damage to warrant control. In other words, you will

Left: *Slugs and snails are notorious garden pests that are easily kept at bay using a water trap.*

Above: *Compact discs are an unusual and amusing way of scaring away marauding birds from your crops.*

need to assess how far the problem can be tolerated before action is necessary. Some form of pest damage is inevitable with any crop, but you will need to establish limits. To do this, you will need to take into consideration the amount of damage that can be tolerated, the numbers of an individual pest that can cause significant damage and the plants' stage of development. The health and vigour of the plant can also have a direct bearing on when or if you need to take action. A few holes on a leaf may not require control, but, if most of the leaf has been eaten, the plant may die.

TAKING ACTION

Monitor your plants to determine when action is necessary. A thorough inspection of the plant allows you to identify a problem before major damage occurs. You should also inspect the plant's entire environment for clues to the problem. Observing and keeping records of weather conditions, for example, can help provide clues to growth patterns and problems.

TYPES OF CONTROL

Control options can be arranged by their mode of action and their impact on the environment. These methods of control can be grouped from least to highest impact: cultural and mechanical controls and "permitted" chemical controls (soaps, oils and botanical insecticides).

Cultural control includes hand removal of larger pests, the use of screens, barriers, and traps, freezing and crushing. These methods generally have little or no negative effect on the environment and are particularly suitable for smaller gardens.

COMPANION PLANTING

This is commonly used to protect plants from pest attack. The theory is that the companion plants – flowers growing next to a food crop, for example – disrupt the searching pattern of the pests looking for host plants. They literally smell these hosts but become confused with the more diverse planting style. Separating rows of cabbages, broccoli or other brassicas with rows of onions has always been a popular combination, possibly because the onion's strong scent confuses cabbage pests. Tomato plants also grow well next to cabbages and seem to deter caterpillars while growing leeks near carrots repels carrot flies.

SCREENS AND BARRIERS

Any material that is fine enough to keep pests out can be used as a barrier. A variety of screens of different mesh sizes can keep out large insects, birds and rabbits, but they can also prevent pollinating insects from reaching a plant, resulting in lack of fruit. Cardboard and metal collars will prevent cutworms from reaching young transplants. Sticky bands placed on tree trunks trap beetles and soil-hibernating pests. Copper strips are available for slug control. These supposedly react with the slugs' slime to shock them. Sharp particles, such as crushed eggshells, are also used to control slugs.

TRAPS

Certain insect pests can be monitored by using traps. Sticky coloured traps, pheromone traps and pitfall traps (like beer traps for slugs) can all be used to monitor the occurrence of some pests. Whiteflies and aphids are attracted to bright yellow, and this colour is used for sticky cards upon which they become trapped.

You may want to apply a control and then enclose the plants in netting to keep further infestation from occurring – perhaps putting up netting and then releasing predators.

Traps usually serve as a monitoring system, warning of the presence or increase in undesirable pest numbers. Traps can also be useful in timing control measures by showing the presence of migrating or emerging adults. The control measure can then be introduced at the best time to control the particular pest. Codling moth traps for use in orchards are a good example of this. They are sometimes used to control numbers, but most types are limited in their real effectiveness. Yellow, sticky traps attract whiteflies, aphids, thrips, leafhoppers and other small flying insects. Traps that use pheromones or attractive scents to tantalize adult insects are best used as a way to check presence and numbers. Pitfall traps can be cups or jars placed into the ground filled with yeast and water or beer to trap slugs.

WATER

A jet of water from a hose washes aphids, spider mites and other small insects from plant foliage. This must be done frequently since it does not kill insects or eggs and it does not prevent some insects from crawling back on to plants.

INSECTICIDAL SOAPS

These are made from the salts of fatty acids. Fatty acids are components of the fats and oils found in plants and animals. These soaps should not be confused with ordinary cleaning soaps. Insecticidal soaps kill only what they touch and are effective against soft-bodied pests such as aphids, thrips, crawler stage scales, whiteflies, leafhoppers and mites. Insecticidal soaps may cause burning on some plants, particularly those with hairy leaves. Test

Above: *Birds can be dissuaded from attacking your plants by stretching string and shiny foil over the crops.*

insecticidal soap on a single leaf if you are unsure – burning will usually occur within 24 hours.

BOTANICAL INSECTICIDES

Derived from plants, botanical insecticides include pyrethrum, citrus oil extracts and the extract of the neem tree. They act rapidly to stop feeding by insects, although they may not kill the pest for hours or days. There are also disadvantages to the use of botanicals. They must be applied frequently, may be difficult to obtain, and, although generally less toxic than many pesticides, they are still toxic and may harm other beneficial garden residents.

Above: *Sticky traps are another form of pest control in greenhouses. Here, pheromones attract pests to the trap where they get stuck. Other traps consist of sheets of plastic covered with a non-drying glue.*

Above: *Horticultural fleece, which is stretched over developing young plants, can provide a physical barrier against smaller pests such as flying insects.*

TRAPS, BARRIERS AND DETERRENTS

The prevention of pest and disease attacks is an essential part of organic gardening. Plants that are infected by pests or diseases are weaker specimens that are difficult to treat and never quite recover their former vigour. Many garden pests can be trapped or kept at bay using relatively inexpensive materials and sometimes recycled household items. Put the barriers in place when the plants are young and always ensure that pests are not trapped inside the barrier.

CONTROL METHOD	HOW IT WORKS
Beer traps and deterrents (granules, copper strips and greasebands)	Traps are effective ways of both controlling pests, such as slugs, and finding out which ones you actually have. Deterrents are physical barriers over which the pest cannot or will not pass. There are many types and their effectiveness can vary.
Bug nets in the greenhouse	Greenhouse vents are problematic in terms of pest control in that they allow both pests in and purchased biological controls out. Bug nets are put in place to avoid this happening.
Fleece on frames	Frames covered in horticultural fleece can be used over outdoor crops to help keep pests out and control the temperature.
Fleece stretched over a crop	Fleece can be used to create a favourable microclimate around young plants. It also acts as a barrier to airborne pests. On the downside, however, it can also keep out airborne predators from pests that overwinter in the soil.
Fruit nets over fruit	Fruit nets are especially useful for summer soft fruit crops that can quickly be devastated by birds.
Individual cloches	Cloches can act as barriers to a wide variety of airborne pests. Any pests that are sealed into this environment may, however, find the perfect environment within which to thrive.
Mesh cages for trees	Mesh cages are usually used to keep rabbits and hares at bay. They are usually simple constructions formed from three or more stakes driven into the ground with chicken wire (or similar) attached to them.
Rabbit fencing	A continuous barrier to prevent rabbits entering areas where plants are growing. The base of the wire should be buried below ground level to prevent the rabbits burrowing a passage beneath it.
Bird scarers (e.g. scarecrows)	Bird scarers have the drawback of a limited lifespan before the birds learn that they are not a real threat. They can, of course, be changed and most bird scarers are only needed on a seasonal basis.
String or wire netting stretched over seedlings (e.g. peas)	Aerial barriers can protect against bird attack. They may only be needed for the duration of the crop's life or even less.
Traps (sticky, coloured traps used in the greenhouse)	Sticky traps can provide a certain degree of control against the flying adults of insect pests. However, they are not as effective as they are sometimes thought to be and are, in fact, of more use for showing whether a particular pest is present or not, thereby allowing appropriate control measures to be put in place.
Traps (pheromone)	Pheromone traps are used to detect the presence of insects. The pheromones attract members of the opposite sex and the appearance of the target species allows you to begin looking for and controlling the young that cause the damage.
Tree guards (spiral)	Spiral guards are useful for protecting the bark of newly planted trees from rabbits and hares, especially in winter and early spring. These guards expand as the tree develops, but they are best removed completely after about a year.
Tree shelter	These protect newly planted trees from vertebrate pests and from the worst rigours of the environment by providing a favourable microclimate around them. They naturally degrade under the action of sunlight, but are best removed after two to three years.
Twiggy branches over plants	Arched over young plants, these can be an effective deterrent to pests such as birds and cats. They do not prevent the migration of beneficial predators to the plants.

Above: *Slugs and snails can be caught in a trap that is filled with stale beer, or water that has been mixed with yeast.*

Above: *Ring tunnels that are covered in a fine mesh will prevent flying insects from attacking your crops.*

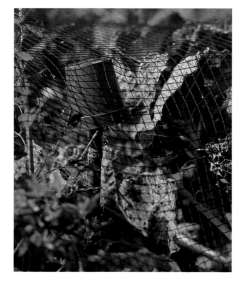

Above: *Plastic netting, stretched over the crop and carefully secured, provides an effective barrier against birds.*

Above: *Old plastic bottles make an ideal barrier to protect young plants from pests. These are cheaper than traditional cloches.*

Above: *Chicken wire, stretched over young plants, will prevent birds from reaching and eating them.*

ORGANIC PESTICIDES

While most pesticides are not used in organic gardens, some naturally occurring substances can be used to protect your plants from pests and diseases. The pesticides which you are allowed to use in an organic garden should only be applied when necessary and not on a regular basis.

ORGANIC PESTICIDE	HOW IT WORKS
Bacillus thuringiensis	These are bacterial spores that produce a toxic protein that is useful against caterpillars but will not cause any harm to beneficials. *Bacillus thuringiensis* works quickly, paralysing the caterpillar and so preventing any further damage, although it quickly degrades in sunlight and needs frequent re-application throughout the growing season.
Bordeaux mixture	A compound containing copper and sulphur used to control various fungal diseases including apple scab and potato blight. It is harmful to fish and livestock, and frequent use can lead to a build up of copper in the soil that can be harmful to worms.
Derris	A chemical extracted from the roots of the derris and longocarpus plants. It is useful against a variety of insects including aphids, caterpillars, sawflies and plant-eating beetles. It can prove harmful to beneficials, although it is not a threat to bees.
Insecticidal soap	This is not soap, like the domestic washing soap, but is made from the salts of fatty acids, extracted from plant material. It can be effective against a wide variety of insect pests, although it can damage sensitive plant species.
Plant oils	Their effectiveness varies but most depend upon coming into contact with the pest itself and suffocating it, although some, like neem tree oil, do appear to have insecticidal properties.
Pyrethrum	This organic pesticide is extracted from the flower-heads of *Chrysanthemum cinerariifolium* and is especially effective in controlling aphids. However, it does not persist for long and can also cause harm to beneficial insects.
Sulphur	An effective fungicide against a variety of plant fungi, including powdery mildew, greymould and blackspot. Sulphur can also prove harmful to predatory mites and can cause damage to certain sensitive species.

Above: *Tree shelters and quills protect trees from rabbits and voles, and also provide an ideal growing environment for the tree.*

Above: *Scarecrows are an attractive method of deterring birds and occasionally large pests away from your vegetable garden. They should be moved around the garden and redressed so that the birds do not get too accustomed to them.*

THE ORNAMENTAL GARDEN

Unlike the more fleeting nature of crops in the kitchen garden, the plants in the ornamental garden are usually permanent, which means that a stable ecology may be set up very easily. In fact, lawns, shrubs, trees and flower beds can all be adapted to organic culture. The ornamental garden needs flair and imagination, not only in its design and construction, but also in the types of materials it uses; there is little point in creating an organic garden with materials treated with toxic chemicals and wood that was logged from a tropical rainforest.

Left: *A flower garden in the height of summer provides colour and a natural food source for garden insects.*

Above: *Flowers are like fuel stations for insects, providing them with nectar in return for pollination.*

Above: *There is an absolutely staggering range of flower forms in nature, many of which are highly ornamental.*

Above: *Careful selection by gardeners has led to the development of many large and showy varieties of flower.*

THE GARDEN FRAMEWORK

It would be a great shame if we spent a lot of time and effort creating an organic garden, only to find that we had done so at the expense of another habitat or the wider environment. A truly organic approach to gardening should extend beyond the way we grow the plants and maintain the beds and borders to include all the elements of the garden, from the hardscaping materials to the furniture.

Above: *A natural dry-stone wall – assembled without mortar – can quickly become colonized with showy flowers.*

ECOLOGICALLY SOUND MATERIALS

Pictures of logged rainforests, eroded soils and drought-ravaged landscapes are all too familiar. So familiar, in fact, that we run the risk of becoming immune to their shocking truth. Many habitats around the world face increasing pressure from human activities. While there is often little we can do as individuals, we can at least try not to contribute to the demise of such habitats. Rainforests, the source of much of the wood used for garden furniture, are often clear felled, resulting in the loss of much of the biodiversity that they contain.

For this reason, it is important that we use ecologically sound materials. Numerous suppliers claim that they offer ecologically sound products, gathered from sustainable sources. You should check the ecological credentials of the items you buy wherever possible. Buying materials from local sources can help. Always ask who the supplier is, where the materials come from and how their extraction impacts upon the environment. Rocks for alpine gardens, wood for posts and fences, mulch material and potting mixes can all be detrimental to the environment if not carefully sourced.

It is also worth finding out what chemical treatments the material has undergone. Some wood is treated with preservative that may leach out into the soil given time. Potting mixes that are purchased may also contain chemical additives.

Even when products are environmentally sound, it is always worth finding out if the same material (or one that is sufficiently similar) is available from a local source. Transporting materials over great distances, particularly those that are bulky or heavy, involves the use of a considerable amount of fossil fuel. One of the cornerstones of sustainability is to think globally while acting locally. It may even be possible to see the products being made if you do buy from local sources.

Ultimately, of course, the closest source is that which you produce yourself in your own garden. Any organic gardener should, therefore, aim to be as self-sufficient as possible.

PLANTS SUITABLE FOR COPPICING

Most broadleaved trees can be used for coppicing, although some are more suitable than others as the rate of growth varies so widely.

In general, most conifers are not suitable for coppicing because they do not readily re-grow from a stump.

PLANT SPECIES	SITE	POTENTIAL USES
Wattle (*Acacia*)	Warm dry situations with good drainage. Especially tolerant of low fertility.	Hurdles and barriers (wattlework). Excellent in warmer climates where other weaving species will not prosper.
Gum (*Eucalyptus*)	Hot dry situations especially where soil is well drained and seasonally dry.	Durable fence posts, stakes and young ornamental growth.
Willow (*Salix*)	Tolerant of wet situations and heavy soils. The roots are notoriously aggressive and may damage nearby drains or foundations.	Weaving work, building and fencing. In a small garden, dogwood is a good substitute for weaving work.
Hazel (*Corylus avellana*)	Any garden soil with good drainage and a pH over 6.5. Tolerates frost, shade, and exposure.	Wattle work, weaving, pea and bean sticks.
Sweet chestnut (*Castanea sativa*)	Light, slightly moist, acid garden soils. Protect from frost and exposure.	Wattlework and fence construction.
Dogwood (*Cornus*)	Most garden soils but dislikes exposure and can sucker aggressively.	Red, orange or lime-green shoots suitable for basketry and other fine rustic weaving work.
Elder (*Sambucus*)	An adaptable species that will thrive in a variety of situations.	Twigs are useful for a number of garden projects and the berries and flowers can be used to make wines and cordials.
Honeysuckle (*Lonicera*)	Likes most soils and thrives with the roots in shade and the topgrowth in full sun.	Stems are a traditional basketry material.

USING RECYCLED MATERIALS

Recycling plays an important role in the organic garden. Waste materials from the kitchen and garden are added to the compost heap; plastic bottles can become mini cloches; and old carpet makes a useful protective cover. Old building materials, such as bricks, slabs, quarried stone and wooden railway sleepers (ties), can all be re-used in the garden.

SUSTAINABLE DESIGN

The more self-sustaining your garden is the better. Gardens that rely heavily upon recycled material – compost, leaf mould and pea sticks, for example – produced within their own confines are naturally self-sustaining. Some external input will always be needed but the garden's long-term success is assured. In short, you will have a sustainable organic garden.

BIO-ENGINEERING YOUR PLOT

This term describes the use of living material to construct the garden framework. It ensures that you make the most of the natural capabilities of some plant species, such as willow, that have been used for centuries for building and fencing. Other examples include using grass for stabilizing soil on slopes or woody plants for hedging. Living barriers do not rot and are self-sustaining.

WILLOW WEAVING

1 *Willow comes in various lengths. The shorter lengths are finest and suited for fine-quality work. This 2.1m (7ft) bundle of "weavers" is the best length for fencing. Thicker uprights are also needed to form the vertical columns to weave around.*

2 *Place the uprights in the ground about 10–20cm (4–8in) apart, ensuring that they are firmly secured. Use a metal spike to make the holes if the ground is hard. The stakes at each end must be the largest and need to be firmly secured.*

3 *Groups of four weavers are used together. Place two in the first gap (between the uprights) and the second pair in the next gap along. Take the back pair of weavers in front of the vertical upright, behind the next upright and to the front again.*

4 *Pick up the other set of weavers and do the same again. Add more weavers as they become thinner and slot these into the uprights to anchor them in. This will give the cross-over effect to the previous weavers.*

5 *Use successive groups of four weavers and continue to weave. Work from the front in order to ensure that the willow fence is neatly finished. Cut off any stubs as you progress.*

6 *At the end of the panel, wrap all four weavers round the post and begin weaving in the other direction. Ensure the weave is tight here and avoid making joins in the weave on the end posts.*

7 *The panels can be solid and used to form a garden boundary. They may also contain spaces, as shown, and act as dividers, while not obstructing the view beyond.*

8 *The finished willow fence will last for many years, especially if it is adorned with climbers such as ivy. Willow fencing encourages wildlife as well as making an attractive feature.*

ORNAMENTAL LAWNS

In spite of the growth in popularity of hard surfaces, such as decking and paving, a well-tended ornamental lawn is still regarded by many as the quintessential feature of a beautiful garden. The lawn provides a safe surface on which children can play as well as an area for relaxing. In the organic garden, the lawn also provides a unique habitat for a wide range of wildlife. There is no reason why you should not have a fully organic lawn that looks pleasing while also contributing to the garden's diversity.

Above: *A well-manicured lawn is the result of regular care and maintenance. Mowing stripes in the lawn is a finishing touch.*

WHAT MAKES A GOOD LAWN?

Some gardeners believe that a good lawn is the product of time, patience and effort, which is true of highly manicured lawns. Others believe that an attractive, but low-maintenance, lawn is the ideal. Neither of these lawns is an impossible dream in the organic garden, but consider whether a lawn can withstand the wear and tear it is likely to receive in a small garden. In this case, it might be better to consider an alternative such as paving or gravel.

You should also consider how much time you are willing to spend maintaining the lawn. Short, highly ornamental lawns need more regular maintenance than longer grass areas, but all lawn areas require some degree of maintenance.

CAN I HAVE AN ORGANIC LAWN?

Lawns, like any community of plants, can be grown quite successfully the organic way. The key to success lies in keeping the grass plants healthy. Lawn grasses are naturally very resilient and competitive plants, well able to withstand a great deal of abuse when they are healthy. Provided they get sufficient light, water, nutrients, air and space, you will be rewarded with an attractive lawn.

CARING FOR AN ORGANIC LAWN

Each grass plant occupies just enough space to grow and closely "knits in" with its neighbours. The taller the plants grow, the lower the number of plants in any one space becomes. As they grow taller, their needs increase and the most competitive plants win. Regular cutting results in a dense coverage with short green leaves and a high number of plants in a given area. The more regularly you cut grass, the more vigorously it grows. Irregular cutting means fewer plants in the area. Less frequent removal of the green material at the top of the plants makes the leaf bases white or yellow and also results in a patchy lawn.

A lawn that is cut regularly will be greener and more attractive than one that is cut more infrequently. In addition, short-cut lawns are an ideal habitat for many garden creatures, particularly birds such as starlings and thrushes. Short grass can even be flower-rich and benefit bees and butterflies.

However, tall grasses favour visiting wildlife and can become an attractive feature in their own right, but they are not ideal for sitting out or for children to play on.

CHOOSING GRASS PLANTS

Once you know what sort of lawn you want, then you must choose the right grass species for your site and what you want to use it for. Some grass species, such as ryegrass, are hardwearing, while others, like the fescues, are drought-tolerant and need less mowing. Trying to grow the wrong grass species for your garden environment will only work if you go to great lengths to tend it and, even then, it will probably be extremely susceptible to damage. Heavy clay soil that becomes wet in winter will not support a close-mown community of fescues, but would be ideal for a ryegrass and bent mixture.

TYPES OF LAWN GRASSES

The grasses below, if present in seed mixes or turf, should prosper in the given conditions. Common names of grasses, while frequently used, are not the same in all countries and the Latin names are given as a definitive reference.

Coarse-leaved species
Large-leaved timothy (*Phleum pratense*)
Meadow grass (*Poa pratensis*)
Perennial ryegrass (*Lolium perenne*)
Rough-stalked meadow grass (*Poa trivialis*)
Small-leaved timothy (*Phleum bertolonii*)
Tall fescue (*Festuca arundinacea*)
Wavy hair grass (*Deschampsia flexuosa*)

Drought-tolerant species
Chewing's fescue (*Festuca commutata*)
Hard fescue (*Festuca longifolia*)
Meadow grass (*Poa pratensis*)
Red fescue (*Festuca rubra*)
Sheep's fescue (*Festuca tenuifolia*)
Slender creeping red fescue (*F. rubra litoralis*)

Fine-leaved species
Browntop bent (*Agrostis tenuis*)
Chewing's fescue (*Festuca commutata*)
Hard fescue (*Festuca longifolia*)

Red fescue (*Festuca rubra*)
Sheep's fescue (*Festuca tenuifolia*)
Slender creeping red fescue
(*F. rubra litoralis*)

Shade-tolerant species
Chewing's fescue (*Festuca commutata*)
Hard fescue (*Festuca longifolia*)
Red fescue (*Festuca rubra*)
Wavy hair grass (*Deschampsia flexuosa*)

Species for damp conditions
Large-leaved timothy (*Phleum pratense*)
Rough-stalked meadow grass (*Poa trivialis*)
Small-leaved timothy (*Phleum bertolonii*)

Wear-tolerant species
Browntop bent (*Agrostis tenuis*)
Hard fescue (*Festuca longifolia*)
Sheep's fescue (*Festuca tenuifolia*)
Tall fescue (*Festuca arundinacea*)

HOW TO SOW A NEW LAWN

1 Dig the ground thoroughly, removing deep-rooted perennial weeds. Rake the soil level. Use pegs marked with lines drawn 5cm (2in) down from the top as a guide, having checked with a spirit (carpenter's) level on a straightedge that the pegs are level.

2 Allow the soil to settle for a week or so, and then consolidate it further by treading it evenly in order to remove large air pockets. The best method by which to do this is to shuffle your feet methodically over the whole area, first in one direction, then at right angles.

3 Rake the consolidated soil in order to produce a fine, crumbly structure that is suitable for sowing seeds. If you can, leave the area for a couple of weeks to allow any weed seeds to germinate. Hoe off the weed seedlings and leave them to die before you apply the grass seed.

4 Use string to divide the area into clearly demarcated strips. The strips should be approximately a metre (yard) wide. Divide the strips into squares with bamboo canes or stakes. Move the canes along the strips as you sow.

5 Use a small container that holds enough seed for a square metre (yard). Make a mark on it if the amount only partly fills the container. Scatter the seeds as evenly as possible with a sweeping motion of the hand.

6 Hire or buy a calibrated granular fertilizer spreader to sow large areas quickly. Check the delivery rates over sheets of paper first and adjust the spreader until the correct amount is being applied per square metre (yard).

HOW TO LAY A LAWN WITH TURFS

1 Dig and consolidate the soil as for seed. There is no need to leave it for a few weeks to allow weed seeds to germinate; the turf will prevent them from sprouting. Start by laying the turf along a straightedge.

2 Stand on a plank while you lay the next row, as this will distribute your weight. Stagger the joints between rows to create a bond like brickwork. Turf in a long roll will have fewer joints, but these should not align.

3 Tamp down each row of turf to eliminate air pockets with the head of a rake, then roll the plank forwards to lay the next row. Brush sandy soil, or a mixture of peat substitute and sand, into the joints to bind the turfs.

LAWN MAINTENANCE

A rich green lawn is coveted by many gardeners, but a certain amount of maintenance is needed to achieve this. The secret of a healthy and attractive lawn lies in adopting a regular routine. Applying systematic care will also make the lawn relatively easy to maintain. Mowing is the most important and frequent operation carried out, but other practices, including watering, feeding, aerating and top-dressing, will also need to be done to keep your lawn in good condition.

Above: *Mowing will help to keep your lawn both green and healthy but it must be done frequently for the best results.*

MOWING

Where mowing is concerned there is a simple rule that you should always remember. The more grass that you remove by mowing, the more rapid its regrowth will be. The cutting height should be higher during late autumn, winter and early spring when little growth is taking place, but may be lowered in the warmer growing season. Raising the cutting height can also alleviate drought-stress and can help lawns stay green during hot dry summers. As a general rule, you should never remove more than a third of the leaf at any one mowing (unless of course you are cutting down an area left deliberately long for wildlife).

Grass can produce 2–3mm (½–⅛in) of growth over a 24-hour period in ideal conditions. The single most important factor is that you should mow regularly. Mowing will need to be less frequent when growth is slow, as in periods of dry or cool weather. Remember that lawns may need cutting in mild periods during the winter.

LAWN CLIPPINGS

Grass clippings contain up to 3% nitrogen, 0.7% phosphorus and 2% potassium by dry weight. Returning clippings directly to the grass surface during mowing promotes the recycling of nutrients and "feeds" the lawn. Clippings also add organic matter to the soil, which will retain water, thus making the lawn more drought-resistant and helping to conserve water. On the downside, grass clippings can make turf more susceptible to disease and soil-borne pests and lead to a build up of "thatch" (a mat of partially decomposed grass leaves above the soil surface). Grass clippings should always be removed if they are excessively thick and will restrict future growth. This is especially true if the grass has not been cut regularly enough.

CONTROLLING THATCH

Thatch is the general term used to describe the layers of organic fibrous material found in turf. It is a perfectly natural component of turf and is desirable to a certain extent because it increases resilience to wear and drought tolerance. Too much thatch, however, can cause an increase in disease, localized dry spots, leaf yellowing, proneness to scalping (during mowing) and a soft spongy surface. It may also affect the tolerance of grass plants to heat, cold and drought.

Top-dressing and avoiding the over-application of nitrogen can help to reduce the build up of thatch, as can liming on acidic soils. Thatch can also be physically removed. This activity is commonly referred to as scarification but is also known as vertical mowing, power-raking or de-thatching. Scarification not only removes thatch, but also removes or controls moss and creeping weeds. It can also help air and

---

TURF PROBLEMS

Numerous problems periodically affect turf. The organic approach emphasizes the importance of maintaining strong healthy grass and removing the causes of ill health.

Organic control of turf diseases
- Maintain a vigorous growing sward.
- Control moisture to avoid humid surface conditions, e.g. by brushing.
- Ensure free movement of air.
- Regular aeration treatments.
- Reduce thatch.
- Box off clippings where possible.
- Avoid excessive nitrogen combined with cool conditions (in autumn).
- Avoid lime where possible (test water and top-dressings for lime).
- Adopt a balanced fertilizer regime.
- Sterilize loams and top-dressings.

Organic control of turf weeds
- Aerate to improve surface drainage and enhance grass vigour.
- Hand-dig persistent weeds.
- Mow and collect clippings regularly.
- Scarify the lawn surface.
- Remove earthworm casts.

Above: *Grass clippings, leaves and other debris form a thatch at the base of grasses which can stifle them. Remove it with a spring-tine rake. Raking also removes moss.*

Above: *In autumn, rake fallen leaves into piles and scoop them up with a pair of boards. Choose a still day when the leaves are dry to make the job pleasant.*

water to enter the soil. Scarification must only be carried out when the grass is actively growing.

TURF AERATION

Aeration, put simply, means allowing air to get into the soil. In a lawn, it can improve surface drainage, improve soil air supply and relieve compaction. It also makes the lawn more drought-resistant because of improved, deeper grass root growth. Thatch will be reduced due to the increased microbial activity that is the result of better-aerated soil. Improved drainage leads to a warmer soil that will stimulate root growth and will help release unwanted chemicals and gases from the soil.

You should aerate the turf when the soil is moist, but not wet because it will then damage the soil structure. Aerating the lawn when it is too dry can be difficult if the soil is hard. Small areas can be done by hand, with the traditional garden fork proving very effective for relieving localized compaction.

ROLLING THE LAWN

Rolling a lawn gives a smooth, flat and level surface, but it is frequently overdone and invariably leads to soil compaction, loss of structure, poor drainage, poor aeration and reduced root growth. It is important never to roll a lawn when it is wet.

TOP-DRESSING MATERIALS

Numerous materials can be used as bulky top-dressing and each has its own benefits for both soil and grass plants.

Charcoal Sometimes used to improve surface drainage and ventilation.

Garden compost and leaf mould Improves the moisture-holding capacity of a rootzone while being relatively sterile. Often best used in mixtures. Homemade compost should be left for sufficient time to decay. Rich in trace elements.

Sand Porous and compaction-resistant, sand is used as a component for most top-dressing mixes and on its own.

Topsoil Used in "composts" for top-dressing and on its own for fine-turf areas if it contains sufficient sand.

AERATING THE LAWN

1 *Poor grass growth could be because the soil is poorly drained. You can aerate the lawn by pushing the prongs of a fork into the ground.*

2 *Gently brush a soil improver, such as sharp sand or a mixture of soil and sand, into the holes made by the fork.*

TOP-DRESSING THE LAWN

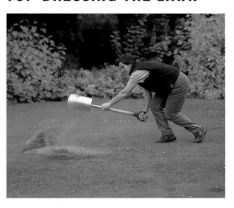

1 *Scatter dry topsoil or top-dressing mix evenly over the surface of the lawn using a shovel. As you throw the shovel outwards in a wide arc, twist it through 180° by rotating the handle. This will help you to spread the mix evenly.*

2 *Using either the flat side of a rake or a stiff broom or besom, work the top-dressing into the surface with short, even strokes. Only apply a top-dressing when the grass is actively growing.*

BRUSHING

Brushing scatters worm casts, grass clippings and other debris on the surface. It also disperses dew and "dries" the surface of the lawn, making it easier to obtain a clean cut with the mower. Frequent brushing can also act as a mild scarifier, lifting the grass blades ready for mowing. Brushing is also used to "work in" bulky top-dressing into the turf surface. A stiff broom or a besom is the most commonly used tool for brushing turf.

TOP-DRESSING

This is the application of a bulky material to the surface of the lawn and usually has no or only minor nutritional value. It is carried

out to help level the surface or to improve the nature of the soil. It may also help to reduce the build up of thatch. Top-dressing should be applied when both it and the surface are dry. It must be thoroughly incorporated into the turf using a brush or besom. Top-dress during the growing season so that the grass has a chance to grow through it and never apply so much that it smothers the grass.

Top-dressing is easier to work into the sward if the area has been mown and scarified first. If it is being carried out as part of autumn renovation work you can mow the area closer than normal. Make sure that you use the same type of material each time you apply top-dressing.

FERTILIZING YOUR LAWN

Organic fertilizers are applied to turf to ensure that there are sufficient nutrients available for healthy, sustained grass growth. The nutrient reserve within the soil is continually being diminished by plant uptake and removal of clippings. Nitrogen is the most important nutrient as it has the most effect upon growth and development. In most situations only nitrogen and potassium will need supplementing by fertilizer application. Most soils have adequate reserves of phosphorus and micronutrients. Organic fertilizers are available as pre-formulated dressings, although fine fertilizers such as fish, blood and bone are quite suitable for early-season application.

Soluble forms of fertilizer (compost teas or worm liquid for instance) should never be applied when grass is not actively growing. The first application of fertilizer in the spring helps to boost grass growth and recovery

Above: *Feed lawns using an organic fertilizer mix formulated for the season: spring and summer feeds have more nitrogen than autumn ones.*

HOW TO REMOVE WEEDS

1 *Use a special weeding tool or knife to prise out weeds. Push the tool in next to the plant and lever out as you pull. Even deep-rooted plants can be removed like this.*

2 *Make any necessary lawn repairs. If you have had to lift a lot of weeds growing close together, leaving a bare patch in your lawn, sprinkle grass seeds over the area.*

from winter and quickly improves the appearance of the turf for summer. Closely cut lawns need regular applications every four to six weeks through the growing season. Fertilizer dressing for use in late summer must be low in nitrogen, as an excess will invariably lead to soft growth that is prone to frost damage.

Apply lawn fertilizer evenly over the area to ensure uniform turf grass growth. Poor distribution may lead to scorching in areas that receive too much fertilizer. The best time to apply fertilizer is during a dry interval in a showery weather period when rainfall will wash it into the sward. Water the lawn if there is no rain for 24 hours.

WATERING LAWNS

Grass becomes dormant during prolonged dry weather. This may lead to invasion by weed species, but the main concern of

most gardeners is that the lawn keeps its colour. Raising the height of cut may reduce this problem, but, in prolonged dry periods, the only real solution is to water. Well-aerated lawns often allow the quickest entry of moisture and lose less water to evaporation. Hand watering may be feasible for smaller areas, but it can be time-consuming. If you live in a drought-prone area, the best option is to choose drought-resistant species.

TURF GRASS DISEASES

Fungi cause the majority of diseases. The best way of controlling diseases is to keep the grass growing strongly by choosing the right species for the conditions and ensuring that the lawn is well maintained. Not all turf and soil fungi are harmful, however. Many are beneficial, aiding the decomposition of plant materials and organic matter and so releasing nutrients.

HOW TO CREATE A MOWING EDGE

1 *An edge of bricks or paving slabs prevents flowers smothering the lawn. Mark out the area to be lifted, using the paving as a guide. To keep the edge straight, use a half-moon edger. Lift the grass by slicing it with a spade.*

2 *Remove enough soil to allow for the depth of the slab or brick and a few blobs of mortar. Make a firm base by compacting gravel or a mixture of sand and gravel. Use a plank of wood to make sure it is level.*

3 *Bed the edging on mortar for stability. As it will not be taking a heavy weight, just press the slabs on to blobs of mortar and tap level. Lay the slabs evenly and flush with, or very slightly below, the lawn. Check levels.*

REPAIRING A LAWN

1 *Lift the area of damaged turf using a large shovel to beyond the point of wear or damage.*

2 *Cultivate the soil beneath in order to remove compaction or, alternatively, remove all the contaminated soil.*

3 *Add a layer of new, good-quality topsoil using the shovel.*

4 *Lightly firm down the topsoil with the back of a rake.*

5 *Sow grass seed over the newly added soil and gently rake in the seed.*

6 *Water in the seed and keep the patch moist until the new grass is established.*

REMOVING MOSS

Moss readily establishes on areas where grass growth is weak. Moss growth is favoured by a moist surface, mowing too close, surface compaction, shade, low soil fertility and excessive pH. Removing moss is palliative and moss soon returns unless the health of the grass is restored. The best solution is to find the cause and remedy it.

LAWN REPAIRS

There are two methods for repairing turf areas: seeding and turfing. Turf has an instant effect, but seeding is more economical over larger areas. Grass established from seed is usually more hard-wearing.

Repairing with turves Mark out the area and use a half moon and turfing iron or a spade to remove the worn/damaged area of turf. Fork over the soil to relieve surface compaction and add a suitable pre-seeding fertilizer. Firm the area by treading. Rake to obtain a tilth. Lay new turves on prepared soil, ensuring all joints are staggered and leaving the turves about 6mm (¼in) proud of the surrounding area to allow for future soil settlement. Top-dress and ensure the area is irrigated when necessary.

Repairing with seed Mark out the affected area and break up the soil by forking. Rake to produce a suitable tilth and "top up" soil levels if need be. Consolidate the surface by treading and apply a suitable pre-seeding fertilizer. Rake to a tilth and sow the seed in two (or more) directions. Rake in the seed, ensuring the area is level with the surrounding turf. Firm by rolling, if required.
Overseeding This method is used to thicken an existing lawn. Seed is scattered over the lawn, where the seed will then germinate, grow and fill-in the turf surface. Overseeding can be done by hand, broadcasting and scratching in the seed. When overseeding grassy areas, lower seed rates are used than those for new lawns. When soil conditions are dry, ensure that the seed is covered and in contact with the soil underneath. Keep the soil moist until the seed germinates and establishes.
Repairing damaged edges Mark out and lift an area of turf around the damaged edge. Fork over the soil in order to prepare a tilth and relieve surface compaction. Incorporate a suitable pre-seeding fertilizer and firm the area by treading. Rake to obtain a suitable tilth. Re-lay the turf with the damaged edge

innermost. Top-dress the newly laid turves, working the top-dressing into the joints. Pay particular attention to the damaged zone. The top-dressing should ideally have a small quantity of seed mixed into it. Alternatively, the area may be overseeded once the turf is laid and top-dressing applied. Ensure the area is irrigated when necessary.

Above: *Insert a half-moon edging tool into the soil. Lever forwards to form a gulley with one vertical side against the lawn and one curved side against the border.*

WOODY PLANTS

Woody plants maintain permanent living structures above ground. They are unique in that their stems repeatedly thicken and strengthen, as is easily seen in the familiar growth rings in wood. Woody plants take many forms: they can be small ground-hugging shrubs or forest giants, and both the largest and oldest living things on our planet today are woody plants. They are the backbone of many gardens, providing height and structure as well as a feeling of permanence.

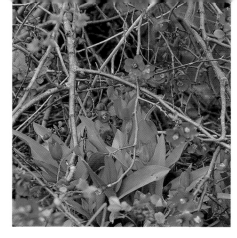

Above: *Woody plants, such as this flowering quince (Chaenomeles), often have very decorative and colourful flowers.*

BUYING WOODY PLANTS

Woody plants may be bought bare-rooted or rootballed, or in containers. All plants should be vigorous, healthy and suitable for the site conditions and intended use. Check that bare-rooted specimens are properly wrapped so as to prevent their roots drying out and ensure that trees and shrubs are free from any obvious pest or disease.

PREPARING THE GROUND

Organic matter is best incorporated across the whole area as a mulch after planting. This encourages the development of a healthy root system. Apply across the whole site during digging if the soil is sandy.

Adding fertilizer is only generally recommended when analysis reveals the soil to be deficient in particular nutrients. Woody plants set up mutually beneficial relationships with soil fungi and gain much of their nutrients as a result of natural nutrient cycles. Often, the best floral displays occur on soils of low fertility, making fertilizer unnecessary.

The key to woody plant growth usually lies in applying organic mulch on an annual basis. Leaf mould is arguably the best substance to use, but well-rotted compost or manure is almost equally useful. An application of bonemeal or similar organic base dressing before mulch is applied can prove to be beneficial when shrubs are newly planted.

PLANTING OUT BARE-ROOTED OR ROOTBALLED TREES

The soil should ideally be moist and friable, not frozen or excessively dry or waterlogged. Bare-rooted or root-balled specimens are usually planted during the dormant season. For deciduous broad-leaved species, this is in winter. An early planting results in better establishment in the following season, and often makes the

PLANTING A SHRUB

2 *If the soil has not been recently prepared, fork it over, removing any weeds. Add a slow-release fertilizer, such as bonemeal, wearing rubber or vinyl gloves if required, and fork this in.*

4 *Remove the plant from its pot, taking care not to disturb the rootball. If it is in a plastic bag, cut away the bag rather than trying to pull it off. Place the shrub in the hole and draw the earth around it. Firm the soil down with the heel of your boot and water in well.*

1 *Never plant a shrub that is stressed. Before you start planting, check that the plant has been watered. If not, give it a thorough soaking, preferably the night before planting. If this is not possible, ensure that the shrub is watered at least an hour before you plant. This allows the water to be absorbed thoroughly by the potting mix and will help the plant to establish.*

3 *Dig a hole wider than the rootball. Put the plant in the hole and check it is deep enough by placing a stick across the top of the pot. It should align with the top of the soil. Adjust the depth of the hole accordingly.*

5 *Finally, mulch all around the shrub, covering the soil with an 8–10cm (3–4in) layer of bark or a similar material. This will not only help to preserve moisture but will also help to prevent any weed seeds from germinating.*

PLANTING A CLIMBER

1 *Dig over the proposed site, loosening the soil and removing any weeds. If the ground has not recently been prepared, work some well-rotted organic material into the soil to improve soil texture and fertility.*

2 *Add a general or specialist shrub fertilizer, if necessary, to the soil at the dose recommended on the packet. Work into the soil around the planting area with a fork. A slow-release organic fertilizer is best.*

3 *Water the plant in the pot. Dig a hole that is much wider than the rootball. The hole should be at least 30cm (12in) from the wall or fence. The free-standing canes will be angled towards the wall or fence.*

4 *Stand the plant in its hole and place a cane across the hole to check that it is at the same level. Take the plant from the pot or cut the bag away. Holding the plant steady, fill in the soil. Firm as you go with your hands.*

5 *Train the stems up individual canes. Tie in with string or plastic ties. Even twining plants or plants with tendrils will need this help. Spread them out, so that they will ultimately cover the whole of their support.*

6 *Water the climber thoroughly. Put a layer of mulch around the plant to help preserve the moisture and prevent weed growth. Do not pile mulch up against the stems of the climber, however.*

---

plants more resistant to spring drought. Evergreen specimens establish more readily if planted during early autumn or late spring in conditions in which enough moisture is available for rapid root growth.

Mark out the positions of the plants and dig each pit, allowing ample space to accommodate the roots, rootball or container size. This is usually a quarter to half the diameter again of the rootball. Take care not to smear the sides of a pit dug in heavy soil as this will effectively cause it to fill up with water during the wetter months, resulting in root dieback, subsequent shoot dieback and in extreme cases, the death of the whole plant.

Remove protection from the roots and place the tree into the hole. Prune any damaged tissue with a sharp knife or secateurs (hand pruners). Position the plant in the pit with roots well spread. Where

trees require staking, the stake should be hammered into the ground before planting the tree to avoid damaging the roots. Position the stake on the side from which the wind most commonly blows.

PLANTING OUT CONTAINER-GROWN PLANTS

Container-grown specimens may be planted throughout the year, provided that the ground is sufficiently moist and adequate water supplies are available and used to irrigate the newly planted area. Other site-related stresses, such as high wind and hot conditions, may also have to be minimized where plants are planted outside of the optimum winter period. Preparation of the planting pit, and staking, are the same as for bare-rooted or rootballed trees, but the positioning of the rootball and treatment of the roots differs

slightly. Remove the tree from the container and lightly shake out the rootball over the hole of excavated soil. Check the root collar area for girdling roots. These are roots that spiral around and may eventually damage the developing stem. Where present sever these cleanly with a knife and remove carefully out of the rootball. Tease out the lower roots using a fork. Place the rootball in the hole so that the roots are spread out and the surface of the potting mix is level with the ground. Tease out the circling roots at the edges of the rootball with a fork or by hand especially where plants are pot bound. Fill in and firm, staking where required.

Immediately after planting, remove any damaged, diseased or untidy growth. Do not remove excessive amounts of top growth, however, as this will reduce the plant's ability to produce food.

STAKING TREES AND SHRUBS

Large shrubs and trees larger than about 1.2m (4ft) may require staking. Low stakes are now recommended as they allow the top growth to move in a circular motion. This motion encourages rapid lower-stem thickening and the development of fibrous root systems that are essential for quick establishment and support of the plant.

PROTECTING NEWLY PLANTED SPECIMENS

Plants unused to cold or hot drying winds may suffer from drought stress. Cold drying winds may damage foliage, buds and branch tips, as well as the bark of thin-barked tree species unused to such exposure. Tree shelters protect trees from adverse conditions, providing an extremely suitable environment for the rapid growth and development of the tree. They are also useful in protecting plants from voles, rabbits and sometimes deer attack. They are usually designed to last three to five years before the material starts to degrade under the action of sunlight. Shrub shelters are similar in most respects to those for trees but are generally shorter.

STAKING A STANDARD ROSE

1 For a standard shrub, make sure you use a strong stake. It should be of a rot-resistant wood. Firmly place the stake in the planting hole, knocking it into the soil so that it cannot move.

2 Plant the shrub, pushing the rootball up against the stake, so that the stem and stake are approximately 8–10cm (3–4in) apart.

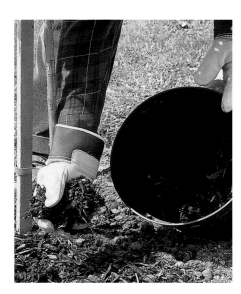

3 Firm the soil down around the plant with the heel of your boot.

4 Although you can use string, a proper rose or tree tie provides the best support. Fix the lower one 15cm (6in) above the soil.

5 Fix the second tie near to the top of the stake, but just below the head of the standard shrub.

6 Water the ground around the plant thoroughly and mulch with chipped bark or a similar material.

Spiral guards, designed to protect larger trees from rabbits, can act as tree shelters for smaller plants. When used on larger trees, they are designed to expand as the stem diameter increases, thereby not constricting growth. Open-mesh guards, which are mesh rolls supported with two or more canes or stakes, provide alternative rabbit protection.

Re-firm roots of all newly planted trees and shrubs after wind or frost, using the heel of your boot, to exclude air pockets around the roots.

Irrigation should only be applied on very dry soils during the first year of establishment. Water is best applied only when absolutely necessary using a sprinkler to thoroughly drench the soil.

All shrub and tree bases should be kept weed-free during the first year. Mulching may help to achieve this, but some hand weeding may be necessary.

RENOVATING OLDER SHRUBS

Shrubs that become overgrown look unsightly and will often have a poor display of flowers. Many shrubs can, however, be rejuvenated by pruning. In certain cases the pruning programme can be staggered over a period of two or more years. Deciduous species, such as lilacs (*Syringa*), may be pruned after flowering, or more commonly during the dormant season. Evergreen shrubs, such as *Viburnum tinus*, are best treated in mid-spring. Remove all weak spindly growth and any badly placed branches or crossing stems. Remove stems to leave a balanced framework by cutting them back to around 30–45cm (12–18in), depending on the species and its vigour. Mulch using leaf mould or compost to 5–10cm (2–4in) in depth. Ensure that the plant is never short of water in the summer.

The following season the shrub will have produced a mass of new shoots. These should be thinned as necessary. After renovation, all shrubs should be pruned according to their normal requirements.

RENOVATING HEDGES

If hedges become overgrown or too wide through neglect or incorrect maintenance, they may respond to drastic pruning methods. The method is similar to that which is carried out on shrubs. Instead of cutting hard back to the base, however, only one side of the hedge is pruned back hard to the main stems of the hedge plants.

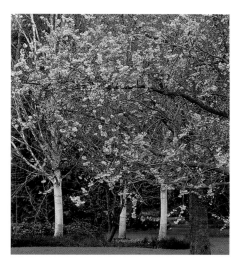

One side of the hedge is left alone so there is enough foliage area left to stimulate new growth and recovery on the pruned side. This can also prove useful in providing cover for wildlife, especially nesting birds.

The process is repeated on the other side of the hedge the following year or, perhaps, two years later. Evergreen subjects (but not conifers) should be pruned in this way during early to mid-spring and deciduous subjects when they are dormant in late winter.

Left: *Flowering trees such as these cherries (Prunus) can provide a welcome and refreshing splash of spring-time colour.*

Feed using an organic mulch, such as farmyard manure, and water during the following season to ensure that the hedge survives such drastic pruning. This technique can be very successful for many evergreen plants as well as most deciduous plants.

RENOVATING WOODY CLIMBERS

Climbers that have not been pruned or trained properly often degenerate into a tangled mass of woody stems which look unsightly and give poor foliar or floral displays. Hard pruning will often rejuvenate the plant. In most cases, the plant will tolerate close pruning in early spring to within 30–60cm (12–24in) of the ground or its main framework of branches. Plants in poor health may not survive this treatment, in which case you may need to carry out the work over a period of two or more years.

Water the base of the plant well and apply bulky organic material. New growth must be trained and pruned according to the species. New growth can initially be trained as if it were a newly planted climber.

PROVIDING PROTECTION

1 *Many shrubs need some winter protection. This shrub is in a pot but the same principles can be applied to free-standing shrubs. Insert a number of canes around the plant. Cut a piece of horticultural fleece, hessian (burlap) or bubble plastic to size, allowing room for overlap. Wrap around the plant, using a double layer for very tender plants.*

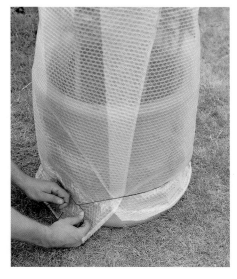

2 *Tie the protective cover around the pot or lightly around the shrub if it is in the ground. Horticultural fleece can be tied at the top because moisture can penetrate, but, if you are using bubble plastic, then leave it open for ventilation and watering.*

FLOWERS FOR BEDS AND BORDERS

Flowers are an essential part of the ornamental garden and there can be few sights that can rival a flower border at the height of summer. Understanding the lifecycles and horticultural needs of these plants is essential if you are to use them to their best effect in flower beds and borders. This section looks at planting and caring for herbaceous perennials, bulbs and annuals.

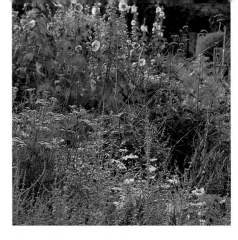

Above: *Few sights in the ornamental garden can rival that of a flower border in full bloom in mid-summer.*

HERBACEOUS PLANTS

The strict definition of a herbaceous plant is one that dies down to or near to ground level each year in order to avoid harsh and extreme weather conditions. In the garden this includes herbaceous perennials as well as grasses – which may not actually die down but never exceed a certain height – and bulbs.

Herbaceous perennials are non-woody plants that live for more than one year. They usually grow, flower and set seed before dying down to ground level in the autumn. They remain there until the next season when the cycle begins again. Herbaceous perennials may form sizeable clumps which are best divided every three to five years to maintain vigour and promote flowering.

Ornamental grasses contrast superbly with broad-leaved plants and narrow-leaved forms and are ideally suited for creating "dry" gardens.

The maintenance requirements for the vast majority of these plants are the same and they form the backbone of the ornamental garden by providing colour which, if planned properly, may benefit the garden all year round.

Planting out Herbaceous plants may be planted in either autumn or spring. The advantage of autumn planting is usually noticed on drier soils as the plants establish and are potentially more drought resistant. Those planted on heavier soils may benefit from spring planting, as heavy soils may be wet and cold – conditions that may cause the newly planted specimen to rot. Grasses are planted in the same way as "true" herbaceous plants. Bulb planting is different and is dealt with separately.

Pot-grown specimens should be watered at least an hour before planting. The ground should be dug and manured before being levelled ready for planting.

A base dressing of bonemeal or fish, blood and bone may also be applied. Plant only when the soil is moist, but not waterlogged or frozen. Dig a pit larger than the rootball and ensure that the plant is well firmed, taking care not to compact the soil when it is returned around the rootball. Care should be taken immediately after to ensure that slugs and snails do not damage the crowns. Set traps and barriers around them to avoid this.

Thinning Removing weak shoots allows the plant to divert its energy into the remaining shoots, which will be sturdier and produce larger flowers. Thinning is carried out when the plant has reached one-quarter to one third of its eventual height and is useful for plants such as as delphiniums, phlox and Michaelmas daisies.

Stopping This is the removal of the growing tip of a stem in order to encourage the side shoots to develop. The tips may be

---

HOW TO PLANT PERENNIALS

1 *Always prepare the soil first. Dig it deeply, remove weeds, and incorporate a fertilizer and well-rotted compost if the soil is impoverished. Most perennials are sold in pots, so arrange them to create pleasing associations.*

2 *Water thoroughly at least an hour before knocking the plant from its pot, then dig a hole. If the rootball is congested, tease out a few roots first. Work methodically from the back of the border or from one end.*

3 *Carefully firm the soil around the roots with the heel of your boot. This helps to remove any large pockets of air.*

4 *It is important that you always remember to water thoroughly after planting and keep the new plants well watered in dry weather for the first few months.*

pinched out when the plant has attained a third of its ultimate height. This encourages the buds on the leaf axils to develop and leads to more flowers being produced, although these will be smaller than if the one terminal bud had been allowed to flower. This technique is successful for a range of plants including *Helenium*, *Rudbeckia*, *Dahlia* and *Chrysanthemum*.

Dead-heading Unless the plant produces decorative seed heads or seed is to be collected for propagation purposes, it is often best to remove all flowers as they begin to fade. Further side shoots will then often develop and the flowering period will be extended. Notable exceptions to this are those plants that produce seed heads that are valuable food sources for overwintering birds. Examples of this include teasels, *Echinops* and many of the ornamental grasses.

Cutting back Some shrubby perennials (often referred to as sub-shrubs), such as *Chrysanthemum*, *Phygelius* and *Penstemon*, benefit from being pruned annually in early spring. This is especially true of sub-shrubs that are somewhat tender. The older twiggy and unproductive growth is cut hard back in order to promote the growth of new shoots that will flower in summer and autumn.

Feeding Few perennials require more than an annual fertilizer application if initial soil preparation has been thorough and included the addition of bulky organic matter. An organic fertilizer, such as bonemeal or fish, blood and bone, may be added to the soil in spring, preferably after rain.

Above: *When dead-heading, snip off the flowers cleanly where they join the stem. Cut back to the first set of leaves if a whole head of flowers has to be removed.*

CUTTING BACK

1 *Some herbaceous plants remain green throughout winter. Cut back to sound growth, removing dead and leggy material.*

2 *Here, the old stems have been cut off so that they are level with the emerging growth, so as not to damage it.*

Bulky organic material, such as leaf mould or compost, applied in spring before shoot growth is also beneficial. Care must be taken not to apply this too thickly and not to cover the crowns of plants resting at the soil surface as these may rot off.

Renovating Herbaceous perennial plants should be lifted, divided and replanted every three to five years. Some fast-growing and vigorous plants, such as *Ajuga* and *Stachys*, may need to be divided every year. Herbaceous plants can become woody towards the centre and may lose vigour.

Lifting the plants for dividing will not only rejuvenate them but also allows for other border maintenance operations to be carried out. The site can be cleared of any weeds and organic matter such as compost or manure dug into the border. The process of division is beneficial to the whole border. In addition, it keeps the plant healthy and will prevent the over-vigorous growth of fast-growing species. Lifting and dividing is normally done while the plants are dormant in late autumn or early spring.

Transplanting Most perennials can be transplanted relatively easily. This should be done during the dormant season, which is usually in autumn or early spring. Some plants dislike cold wet conditions and these should be moved once the soil has warmed sufficiently to encourage growth. This is particularly true for any plants that are not fully hardy. Some plants that are relatively long-lived, such as peonies, resent being disturbed and will take two or more years to establish again after transplanting.

Plant replacement If possible, all planted areas should be designed to contain plants that have similar life spans and respond to rejuvenation techniques. Some species are relatively short lived and will die out before others within a bed. It is possible to rejuvenate beds on a set cycle, say every three to four years, and avoid gaps appearing in the periods between.

Plant losses can occur in severe winters when those that are normally regarded as hardy are exposed to very low temperatures. Half-hardy or tender perennials are even more susceptible. Some perennials are probably best lifted and stored over winter until the worst weather has passed, when they can be planted out again.

Above: *Lightly dig over the soil around the plants, removing any weeds. Avoid digging around plants such as asters which have shallow roots.*

ANNUALS AND BIENNIALS

As the name suggests, annuals are plants that grow, set seed and die, completing their lifecycle within one growing season. Some garden annuals may actually be perennials in nature, but are treated as annuals for ease of cultivation. Many half-hardy and summer bedding annuals fall into this category. Almost all spend a maximum of one calendar year in the ground before dying off.

Biennials are similar to annuals as they flower once and die, but differ in that they grow and establish in the first season before resting in a similar manner to herbaceous perennials over winter. They grow, flower and die the following season. Some plants that are grown as biennials (especially as bedding) are perennials. They are treated as biennials, however, because they tend to weaken during their second year and are therefore better re-started in order to maintain vigorous plants.

Annuals are used as displays in their own right or as small groupings of colour among more established plantings. Groups of annuals strategically placed together in, for example, containers can have a greater

PLANTING ANNUALS

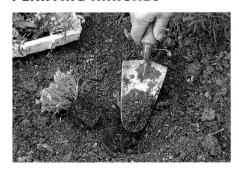

1 *Remove the plants from the pack. If they are attached to each other, try not to tear off too many roots when removing. Dig a hole wider and slightly deeper than the rootball.*

2 *Fill in the hole around the plant with soil and gently firm down with your hands. Water the plant with a watering can fitted with a fine rose.*

visual impact than if they were spread throughout the garden. Many annuals, especially those with composite flower heads, attract beneficial insect species into the garden and some are used as companion planting for vegetable crops. Annuals can also be a useful infill in new borders as they are easily removed or thinned out later when the perennials have grown and become established.

Planting annuals, biennials and tender perennials Hardy annuals can be sown *in situ* and then thinned. Some may self-seed freely through borders. If annuals are to be grown in pots or trays prior to planting, the planting is much the same as for herbaceous plants. Always ensure that the risk of frost has passed before planting out tender specimens and that these plants are acclimatized thoroughly beforehand.

SPLITTING CONGESTED PLANTS

1 *Some perennials need splitting every few years to keep them flourishing. In spring, lift the whole of the clump from the ground.*

2 *Clean the ground thoroughly, removing any weeds, particularly perennial ones that have appeared since the border was last dug.*

3 *Incorporate some well-rotted organic material such as farmyard manure in order to rejuvenate the soil.*

4 *Remove the earth from the plant and divide. Use the new growth around the edge, and discard the woody centre.*

5 *Replant some of the divisions, making certain that the roots are well spread out. Firm them in and then water.*

6 *Keep the plants watered until they have re-established themselves. They will soon fill out the gaps in the border.*

SOWING SEED IN OPEN GROUND

1 *Dig over the ground and break it down into a fine tilth using a rake. Do not work the soil when wet or it will become compacted.*

2 *Using a garden line as a guide, draw out a shallow drill. Use the corner of a hoe, a stick or a trowel.*

3 *If the soil is very dry, water the drill using a watering can and leave to drain. It should not be muddy for sowing.*

4 *Identify the row with a clearly labelled marker. This is important because when the row is backfilled it will be impossible to see where the seed is until it germinates.*

5 *Sow the seed thinly by hand along the length of the drill. Sowing thinly will reduce the amount of thinning that is required at a later stage.*

6 *Rake the soil back over the drill and lightly tamp it down with the back of the rake. When the seedlings emerge, thin them out in order to prevent overcrowding.*

Many hardy annuals thrive in poorer soils, and are undemanding and easy to grow. Dry banks are ideal for a whole range of species including poppies and nasturtiums, both of which flower more abundantly on slightly poorer soils.

The only "pruning" required for annual plants is dead-heading to promote new shoot and flower development, or stopping to promote side shoot development and multiple flower production as opposed to large single flowers.

BULBS, CORMS AND TUBERS

These rest below the surface and are modified buds, stems or roots. They emerge, often for only a short time to grow and flower, before retreating back down underground to escape harsh weather conditions.

Planting and maintenance Bulbs, corms and tubers can be lifted during their dormant period and transported and stored easily. Generally speaking, bulbs are planted in a hole that has been dug to about two to three times their length deep. Bulbs have a base plate, which is where the

roots appear. This must always be placed in the hole roots down and should be in contact with the soil in the base of the hole. Placing fine sand in the base will ensure this. The top of the bulb (the neck) should

Above: *The rule is that bulbs should be planted at a depth of three times their own size. Exceptions include nerines, crinums and some lilies, which prefer to be planted with the top of the bulb at soil level.*

always point upwards. Fill the hole firmly once the bulb is in the hole. After this the bulbs need little care and attention, although tall varieties may need staking and all should be dead-headed after flowering.

Above: *Dig a large hole, according to the requirements of the individual bulbs or corms. These gladioli corms are placed, base down and nose up, about 10cm (4in) apart. Gladioli corms need to be lifted in autumn.*

BEDS AND BORDERS

Whether you are creating a flower border from scratch or updating an existing design, there are a number of important factors that you will need to consider before you start planting the scheme. Begin by looking very carefully at the site and its conditions. This initial planning and preparation will help you in your choice of plants. Hardiness and suitability to the soil type, as well as the aspect of the site, are also factors that will determine which plants will thrive.

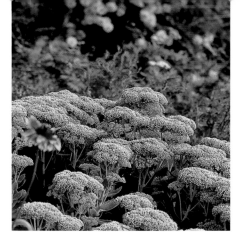

Above: *Flowers are not only decorative, but will also encourage pollinators and other insects into your garden.*

PLANNING AND SITING

Ideally, the bed or border should be positioned in a sunny site away from the shade of trees or buildings unless you intend to plant a border with shade-loving species. A hedge, wall or fence can provide valuable protection for your plants, and will create a warm microclimate for more tender plants. A sheltered spot will also extend the planting season. These structures may also provide a backdrop for climbers.

When you begin planning the border, ask yourself what you hope to achieve. Borders that are to be viewed from a distance will benefit from larger groupings of each plant type. Larger specimens can also appear very striking from further away. These can be used as character plants and provide a recurring theme through your border.

Borders may have a particular theme. They may be planted with fruiting shrubs, plants to create a "tropical" look or fragrant plants such as philadelphus and lavender for rich summer fragrance. Colour also provides interesting themes. A golden border of yellow flowers in association with plants that have variegated or yellow leaves is striking. Remember that you can leave gaps in the planting for seasonal features

Above: *Combining strong colours such as orange and blue can produce striking planting associations.*

such as bedding plants and bulbs. Decide what look you would like to achieve before buying any plants.

SEASONAL CONSIDERATIONS

Ask yourself when you want the border to look its best. Perhaps you would like a bright display of bulbs in spring followed by a colourful selection of annuals and bedding plants in summer. Alternatively, you may want to plan for a bed or border that provides year-round interest, in which case you will need to consider a selection of hardy shrubs or perennials that are appropriate for your garden conditions.

Make a list of all the plants that you would like to include and when they will look their best. Many plants have more than one season. For example, shrubs such as *Viburnum opulus* flower in early summer and have bright red berries in autumn. If you intend to use winter-stem shrubs such as *Cornus alba*, then choose varieties with interesting foliage, such as the golden form 'Aurea'.

Left: *Herbaceous borders are easy to create and maintain, and can provide year-round interest if they are properly planned.*

COLOUR CONTRASTS

Once you have your list of desired plants, consider their colours. Contrasting colours can look effective. Try plants that have blue, purple or pink flowers, and choose as many examples of these as you can find with bronze foliage. A much brighter combination would call for hot vibrant colours such as yellow, orange and red.

Cottage gardens throw all caution to the wind, including a riot of contrasting and clashing colours to provide unexpected and beautiful combinations of hue and form. Alternatively, you might prefer a monochrome scheme, using flowers of one colour – white or cream, say, offset by a display of green foliage.

FOLIAR AND TEXTURAL EFFECTS

Placing plants with contrasting foliage next to each other can create great interest in a border. This is also true where evergreens are used in conjunction with winter-stem colour. *Cornus sibirica*, for example, has striking red stems in winter and is best shown off against a carpet of weed-suppressing variegated ivy. Textural contrasts can also be striking. For example, the bold leaf forms of plants such as *Rheum* contrast well with the more feathery forms of astilbes and *Aruncus* in summer.

THREE-DIMENSIONAL STRUCTURE

When you plan out a border on paper, it can sometimes be difficult to envisage just how it will look when it is established and growing. In order to get a better idea of the final result, it can be helpful to draw a sketch relief of the border. This should always be done as a projection into the future, based upon the lifespan of the plant. This will be the following year in the case of herbaceous plants but may be five years or more in the case of shrub beds.

PLANTING OUT A PERENNIAL BED

1 *If the bed was dug in the autumn, winter weather should have broken down the soil. In spring, rake over the soil and remove any weeds that have reappeared.*

2 *Although well-rotted organic material should have been added at the time of digging, a sprinkling of bonemeal will ensure the plants get off to a good start.*

3 *Draw a grid on a plan and then mark out a scaled-up version on the bed, using sand or potting mix. Alternatively, use string between canes to mark out the plan.*

4 *Using your planting plan and grid as a guide, lay out the plants, still in their pots, on the ground. Stand back, try to envisage the border as it will be, and make any necessary adjustments.*

5 *Dig a hole and, with the plant still in its pot, check that the depth and width is right. Adjust if necessary. Remove the plant from the pot and place in the planting hole. Fill in the hole with soil and then firm the plant in.*

6 *When the bed is completely planted, water in all the plants. They should be kept watered until they have become established, especially throughout dry periods.*

7 *Go over the border with a fork, or use a rake if there is room. This will loosen any compacted areas, as well as level the soil.*

8 *Cover the soil between the plants with a layer of mulch like composted bark to keep weeds down and preserve moisture.*

9 *Mark each plant with a label. The finished border should need little attention, apart from removing the odd weed.*

PLANTING GROUPS

When designing and planning your border, always remember to set out and plant the herbaceous plants in groups of three, five, seven or nine. In this way, you can create a more natural and informal effect because this approach does not show the rigid lines or geometric shapes that often appear when you plant even numbers of plants.

Larger planting groups than this need not adhere to this number rule because an overall random effect is created by the shape of the drift alone. Larger shrubs, such as *Deutzia* or *Buddleja*, can make stand-alone specimens. Smaller shrubs, such as rosemary or potentillas, may well have greater impact if they are positioned in groups.

CREATING BORDERS WITH HERBACEOUS PLANTS

The popularity of herbaceous plants has meant that they are used in a wide variety of different situations in the garden. However, they are primarily used in the herbaceous border where they can be shown to great effect. Three important categories of this kind of border are usually recognized.

One-sided borders These were extremely popular in Victorian and Edwardian gardens and are the very essence of the English "gardenesque" style. The design usually involves creating a border along one side of a pathway, with the plants arranged in order of ascending height from the path edge. The border is usually positioned in front of a solid backdrop beyond which the eye cannot see.

The backdrop may be living, such as a hedge, or man-made, taking the form of a wall or fence. These beds, while pretty, are often limited by their lack of perspective. The relative proximity of the backdrop often draws attention away from the nearer plants and destroys any illusion of distance. This drawback can be rectified by planting mainly red-flowered plants at one end of the border, gradually changing to blue-flowered plants at the other end. This makes the border seem longer than it actually is. Such schemes are only really effective, however, in borders that are 10m (35ft) or more in length.

Island beds These differ from one-sided borders in that the plants can be viewed from all sides by walking around the whole bed. This kind of planting does not have a backdrop and relies, therefore, on the strategic placement of groups of large plants in the centre of the feature. Island borders allow the onlooker to view the plants from a number of different angles, thus enhancing the interest of the border as a whole.

Mixed borders These designs use many types of plant, including trees, shrubs, herbaceous plants, annuals and bulbs. In a mixed border, one group of plants should complement and enhance the other. For example, the trees provide the shelter and backdrop for the shrubs and flowers in a woodland garden. Rock gardens can also be regarded as mixed borders, with a rich (if diminutive) array of dwarf trees, creeping shrubs and ground-hugging herbaceous plants and bulbs.

ROSE BEDS

A well-tended, healthy and pest-free rose bed has long been, and indeed continues to be, the desire of many gardeners. However, roses can be at risk from pests and diseases. This risk is increased when too many roses are grown in one bed. Most modern cultivars are also too highly bred to resist the range of diseases that can affect them, having been chosen for flower size rather than disease immunity. Choose old-fashioned varieties or modern cultivars that offer resistance to disease.

Most rose pests are common garden pests that are easily controlled by natural predators. The trick with roses is to indulge them with plenty of colourful companion planting, especially daisy-type plants – *Argyranthemum* is ideal – which will encourage those beneficial insects into your garden. It can yield wonderful results and makes the bed even more colourful. Old-fashioned roses need less work in general than modern cultivars and are often more suitable for pollinating insects like bees.

GROUNDCOVER PLANTING

This is a way of exploiting the competitive abilities of plants that grow by spreading sideways and smothering their neighbours. An obvious example of a plant type that is good for this is turf grass, but many herbaceous and shrubby species are also able to fulfil this function. These include conifers, roses, heathers, and both broadleaved evergreens and deciduous

---

A PARTLY SHADED BORDER

A shady spot in the garden can provide the right growing conditions for a dazzling array of flowers. This mixed border in heavy shade is shown in summer to late autumn.

1 *Aconitum napellus* (poisonous)
2 *Digitalis purpurea* (poisonous)
3 *Anemone sylvestris*
4 *Hyacinthoides non-scripta*
5 *Astilbe* 'Aphrodite'
6 *Primula bulleyana*
7 *Aconitum napellus vulgare* 'Albidum' (poisonous)
8 *Cardiocrinum giganteum*
9 *Lilium regale*
10 *Convallaria majalis*
11 *Primula vialii*
12 *Anemone nemorosa*
13 *Digitalis purpurea* var. *alba* (poisonous)
14 *Campanula alliariifolia*
15 *Aquilegia vulgaris stellata* 'Nora Barlow'
16 *Aster novi-belgii*
17 *Digitalis ferruginea* (poisonous)
18 *Galax urceolata*
19 *Primula japonica* 'Millers' Crimson'
20 *Acer*
21 *Mahonia* 'Charity'
22 *Cotinus coggygria*

3m (10ft)

27m (90ft)

plants. Their main characteristic is a close, compact and low-growing form that suppresses the underlying weeds. The same effect can, of course, be achieved by planting closely. This method is especially useful with herbaceous plants that grow up quickly and suppress the weeds below. No groundcover will suppress all weeds, however, and you may have to weed among them while they become established.

There are numerous groundcover roses available that offer a colourful carpet of flowers. If you opt for roses as a groundcover, you should be aware that some are covered with thorns and it can be difficult to weed between them. Mulching the bed following planting can help to suppress weeds until the plants achieve full cover. All groundcover can take two to three years (or more) to become fully established and so should be considered as a long-term, labour-saving feature.

BORDER MAINTENANCE

It is possible to plan a border to be low maintenance, but there is no such thing as a maintenance-free border. Decide how much time you can spend caring for the

TIDYING UP

1 *Some edging plants spread out over the grass, possibly killing it or creating bald patches, as has this poached egg plant (*Limnanthes douglasii*).*

2 *If the plant is an annual and has finished flowering, it can be removed. Otherwise, just cut back the part that is encroaching on the grass.*

border and choose your plants accordingly. A close planting, particularly one that uses ground-covering shrubs or closely planted herbaceous plants, will certainly cut down on the weeding as can mulching the border regularly. Any border will need at least one seasonal tidy up in late winter. Shrub beds are also best mulched at this time before bulbs and other flowers have fully emerged. Choose shrubs that will grow into the space

available and avoid very vigorous varieties or ones that need pruning on a regular basis. Even large herbaceous borders need not be too difficult to maintain. Delay your winter clear up for as long as possible and choose species that do not need staking. Do not worry if the plants grow among each other, it will just add to the effect. The less labour a border needs, the less disturbance there will be to the wildlife it contains.

A SPRING BORDER FOR AN OPEN, SUNNY SITE

A sunny spot can provide the ideal conditions for a wide range of showy blooms in the early part of the year. The plants in this border prefer a neutral to slightly alkaline soil.

1 *Lupinus* 'The Page'
2 *Aster novi-belgii* 'Fellowship'
3 *Lobelia* 'Bees Flame'
4 *Heuchera micrantha* 'Palace Purple'
5 *Aquilegia skinneri*
6 *Primula* 'Gold Lace'
7 *Aquilegia chrysantha* 'Yellow Queen'
8 *Lupinus arboreus* 'Mauve Queen'
9 *Iris* 'Blue Eyed Brunette'
10 *Heuchera* 'Leuchtkäfer'
11 *Campanula latifolia* 'Brantwood' (deep blue) and *C. latifolia* 'Gloaming' (light blue)
12 *Iris chrysographes*
13 *Sidalcea* 'Party Girl'
14 *Physostegia virginiana* 'Vivid'
15 *Geranium macrorrhizum* 'Ingwersen's Variety'

1.8m (6ft)

8m (26ft)

CONTAINERS

These are an attractive feature in any garden and are very useful when there is no soil at all for planting, as is the case with patios and roof gardens. They are also easy to maintain. There are many types of container available, which means that you can create a theme of your own choice: Mediterranean or perhaps lush and tropical in style. You can also plant up seasonal containers to create different effects through the year or you can change the style from year to year.

Above: *A wooden barrel makes an attractive container in which to grow a profusion of plants.*

TYPES OF CONTAINER

Always choose containers that fit in with the general garden style and with each other. Terracotta and wooden planters are easy to fit into almost any garden scheme, but shiny metal containers may be more difficult to place. Hanging baskets usually take the form of a basket of wire, but they can also be made of wicker. This is lined with a permeable material such as wool, hay, coir matting or even conifer cuttings. You can buy purpose-made lining material which is made from recycled materials or you can make your own. Hanging baskets are an excellent way of covering a wall or post and can even increase the growing space in your greenhouse. They are best planted with a selection of trailing plants (placed around the edge of the basket) and upright types (placed in the centre). They are extremely prone to drying out and should be watered at least once a day and even twice in hot dry conditions. Window boxes should be treated in a similar way to hanging baskets.

The size of a container will influence the kind of plant that you can grow. Any container must be at least 15–20cm (6–8in) deep, although most plants will be happier in a deeper one than this. Be wary of putting a small plant in a very large pot, as this can lead to very wet potting mix that the plant will not want to root into. Large pots with arrangements of several plants are ideal and much easier to look after than several smaller pots.

MATERIALS AND FINISHES

Containers are available in a range of different materials and finishes. Glass fibre and resin containers are extremely strong and lightweight but they tend to be expensive because they are hand-made. They are available as extremely realistic stone-look containers, but can also be found in almost any other finish, including wood and glazed ceramic. Plastic containers are very cheap, lightweight and often last a long time. The finish on some may be poor, but they are very easy to paint and customize. Metal containers are available as pots, "manger-style" window boxes or hanging baskets. There are many different designs and the best quality ones have a properly lacquered finish.

PLANTING A CONTAINER

1 *The materials you need include a suitable container, your choice of plants (in this case, the central plant is a striking cordyline), some stones to place at the bottom of the container for drainage and potting mix.*

2 *Cover the bottom of the container with small stones or some pieces of tile or pottery, so that water can drain freely from the container.*

3 *Partly fill the container with a good-quality potting mix.*

Above: *Hanging baskets can help to provide colour and interest at eye-level throughout the year.*

Above: *Using a watering can is one of the easiest ways to keep the soil moist. It allows you to deliver the right amount of water.*

Above: *You can create a stunning display with a range of different containers, including an old wheelbarrow.*

Stone and terracotta pots offset the shades of flowers and foliage beautifully. The main problem with terracotta is that it is water permeable and requires more frequent watering than plastic, resin or metal pots. Both stone and terracotta containers can be very heavy, so plant them up *in situ*. Look out for frost-resistant types that will not crack in winter. Glazed ceramic pots need less watering than plain terracotta pots, and can be chosen in almost any colour to suit the theme of the garden.

Wooden or wicker planters have a very natural look and can easily be home-made. Oak, cedar and chestnut are the best woods

to use because they do not need preservative and planed wood – of any type – can easily be painted. Wicker is an excellent material for making hanging baskets, while wood can be used for window boxes. Wicker or wooden planters benefit from being lined with plastic or a non-permeable paint. The paint can be plastic resin or bitumen based, but make sure that it does not contain fungicides or preservative. Alternatively, plastic sheeting can be stapled firmly inside the pot. Wooden and wicker pots should be raised off the ground slightly to prevent the base rotting. There are many different designs,

ranging from half-barrels to wheelbarrows. However, take care with wooden items for outdoor use because many of them have been chemically treated. A wide variety of recycled objects can be used as containers. An old boot, bucket or watering can, painted if you wish, can all be used.

DRAINAGE

All containers must have drainage holes in the base. To ensure that the potting mix drains freely, place a layer of gravel – about 4cm (1½in) deep for most pots – over the base of the pot before putting in the mix. Terracotta and stone pots may need as

4 *Scoop out a hole in the potting mix and insert the plant, positioning it so that the top of the rootball will be level with the surface of the potting mix.*

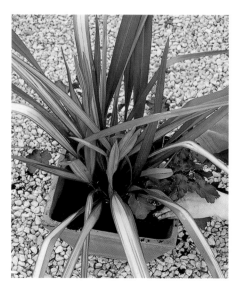

5 *Place any extra plants around the edge of the main plant. Add more potting mix in order to fill in any gaps, and firm down. Water the container thoroughly.*

6 *The plants will soon grow away and fill out the container to create a stunning year-round feature.*

much as one-fifth of their total depth filled with gravel to help protect them from frost damage. Standing pots on bricks or purpose-made "feet" also helps them to drain freely.

ORGANIC POTTING MIX

The best potting mixes contain sufficient air space to allow the roots to breathe, while retaining enough water and nutrients to support plant growth. Potting mix must also be heavy enough to support the weight of the top growth of the plant if it is to remain upright. You can buy a general-purpose potting mix, although some gardeners prefer to mix their own.

Potting mix can be loam-based or soilless. Loam-based potting mix is a "heavy-weighted" mix that provides good anchorage for tall or heavy specimens. It

also holds on well to nutrients. It is ideal for plants that will stay in containers for several years or more as it will not degrade or become structureless.

Soilless potting mixes do not contain loam. They have the advantage of being free-draining and relatively lightweight, although some grit or sand is usually added to give them weight. Coir-based potting mixes are made with a natural fibre that is a by-product of the coconut-growing trade. It has been hailed as a peat substitute and is equally good in containers. However, it is expensive and can be difficult to re-wet once dry. Composted fine bark is cheap and readily available. There have been some advances in its use in recent years and it has even been suggested that bark-based potting mix increases a plant's resistance to pest and disease attack.

MAKING ORGANIC POTTING MIX

You can make your own potting mix with ingredients such as well-rotted compost, leaf mould and worm compost; loamy garden soil; and clean, coarse sand or fine grit. The organic matter and loam should be thoroughly sieved. A slow-acting, balanced fertilizer may also be added along with ground limestone to bring the mixture's pH to around 6.5 which is suitable for the majority of plants. Containers for seasonal displays such as bedding will not need loam.

PLANTS FOR CONTAINERS

Fruit, herbs and even vegetables can all be grown in containers, as well as a wide range of ornamental plants. A flowering shrub such as an azalea can act as a focal point and enliven a shadier part of the garden. Pots of fresh herbs and salad crops can provide a welcome addition to summer meals and a window box can even be used as a miniature wildlife garden. Seasonal bedding can transform a patio into a riot of colour and be changed regularly to reflect the seasons. Containers also enable you to grow a range of plants that would not otherwise grow in your soil. For example, if your garden soil is alkaline, you can still enjoy the spring and summer delights of acid-loving rhododendrons, blue poppies (*Meconopsis*) and Himalayan primulas.

PLANTING A HANGING BASKET

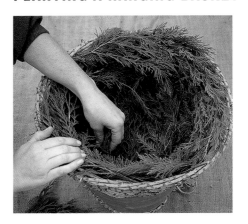

1 Line the hanging basket with a suitable organic material. Conifer branches are an ideal material, as is shown here.

2 Fill the lined basket with a suitable soilless organic potting mix to about one-third of its depth.

3 Position the plants first to see how they will look. Fill in the spaces between the plants with more potting mix.

4 Any gaps between the plants can be filled with small bulbs or bedding in order to provide a riot of spring colour.

CARE AND MAINTENANCE

There are a number of tasks that you will need to perform in order to keep your container plants in peak condition.

Watering Knowing when and how much water a plant needs is one of the most important aspects of container gardening. Often a look at the surface of the potting mix may give the impression that it is dry. If you dig down with your finger, however, you quickly discover moist potting mix. If the mix feels wet, then do not water it.

Feeding Container plants need more fertilizer than plants grown in the open garden because frequent watering washes out the nutrients. For the best results, start feeding container plants six to eight weeks after planting. Use a liquid tea, worm liquid or a purchased soluble food such as seaweed extract or liquid manure every two to three weeks. Apply fish emulsion or garden compost once or twice a season to add trace elements to the mix. Do not add more than the recommended rate of any fertilizer as too much can harm plant roots.

PLANTING A WINDOW BOX

1 *Assemble all the necessary materials. These include the window box, crocks, a good organic potting mix and the plants. If the box is light, assemble it on the ground. If not, then assemble it in position.*

2 *Holes in the bottom are essential to allow good drainage. Stop the potting mix from being washed out by placing crocks over these. If very good drainage is needed, then a layer of gravel can also be added.*

3 *Partially fill the box with potting mix, gently tapping the sides to make sure that no air gaps remain. Never over-firm soilless potting mixes as they will become waterlogged and airless, and the plants will suffer.*

4 *Place the plants in position and check these positions before finally planting. Make sure that they are planted in the potting mix at the same depth that they were in their pots or trays. Plant them fairly close for an instant effect.*

5 *A selection of bulbs makes a useful additional display for the window box. The bulbs can be planted in among the main plants and are best planted in groups of three so that they give a fuller display. Water the basket once it is planted.*

6 *Window boxes that are planted for seasonal display will quickly use up all the available nutrients. This is less of a problem with baskets planted for winter interest, such as this, but summer boxes will need regular feeding.*

Monitoring plant health Containers are best placed where they will receive maximum sunlight and good ventilation. During periods of high temperatures and bright sunshine, many containers may benefit from shade during the hottest part of the day. Shelter plants from severe rain, hail and wind storms. Also watch out for and control insect pests.

Pinch pruning When young, the growth of many ornamentals is readily shaped by the pinching out of young shoots. Many specimens treated in this way yield impressive results. This pinching out, or stopping as it is sometimes called, stimulates the development of side shoots and, if carried out regularly, results in dense bushy growth. The selective use of this method of pruning allows for considerable freedom in the shaping of plants.

MAKING ORGANIC POTTING MIX

Mixing your own organic potting mix is relatively easy. You can use a combination of a variety of materials, including loam, leaf mould, garden compost and worm compost.

INGREDIENTS	RATIO BY VOLUME	ADDITIONAL INFORMATION
Loam : Leaf mould : Garden compost	1 : 1 : 1	A basic mix that is well drained, fertile and suited for longer-term plantings.
Leaf mould : Worm compost	3 : 1	Very nutrient rich. Add extra grit for better drainage. Best for short-term pots of vegetables, herbs and flowers.
Loam : Manure : Leaf mould	3 : 1 : 1	A rich mix for heavy feeding plants such as pot-grown tomatoes and peppers.
Leaf mould : Loam	1 : 1	Ideal for long-term plantings such as trees and shrubs. Use acidic loam for lime-haters.
Loam : Leaf mould or Coir	1 : 1	Enrich with 225g (8oz) seaweed meal; 110g (4oz) bonemeal; 85g (3oz) hoof and horn; 55g (2oz) ground limestone per 30 litres (63 pints) base potting mix.

THE WILDLIFE GARDEN

Wildlife gardening involves providing food, shelter and a habitat for creatures as well as relying on native plants that are suited to the climate and soils in the locality. A single plant species may directly and indirectly serve species of insects, invertebrates, fungi, and other organisms, which in turn become a meal for larger wildlife such as birds. In time you will have a functioning ecosystem on your doorstep. In fact, creating a garden of this kind can help break up the "grass desert" responsible for reducing the variety of birds, insects and other wildlife.

Left: *Wildlife gardens use plants, such as this fennel* (Foeniculum vulgare), *for their ability to attract insects.*

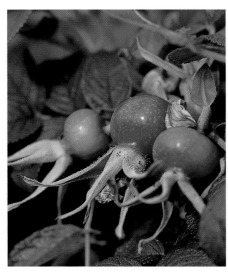

Above: *Garden wildlife can be both pretty and, in the case of ladybirds (ladybugs), useful for controlling aphids.*

Above: *Flowers such as sweet peas* (Lathyrus odoratus) *encourage pollinators and beneficial insects into your garden.*

Above: *Colourful fruits such as these rosehips provide much-needed food for garden wildlife such as birds.*

WHAT IS A WILDLIFE GARDEN?

The organic garden can provide a welcome refuge for a wide range of wildlife, from birds and butterflies to creatures such as frogs and hedgehogs. The basic requirements for any visitor to the garden are food, water and shelter. You may also want to consider organizing some, or all, of your planting schemes around species that will attract a diversity of fascinating wildlife.

Above: *Wildlife gardens such as this grassland area can be attractive as well as providing useful habitats.*

WHAT ARE THE BENEFITS OF A WILDLIFE GARDEN?

Domestic gardens cover a huge area around our towns, cities and urban fringes. This is a potentially fantastic resource for an otherwise denuded habitat. Keeping your garden free of harmful chemicals gives you a head start in attracting wildlife and, with a little planning, you can create a habitat that will welcome a diverse range of creatures. The visitors in turn will repay you by acting as predators, helping to control the level of problem-causing pests in your garden. Knowing that your patch, no matter what its size, is providing a haven for wildlife will give you a closer connection with the natural world. Just to be able to enjoy watching birds feeding can lift the spirits and improve your sense of wellbeing.

Encouraging natural cycles in your garden will promote biodiversity. The more soil life there is, the more insects will come to feed on it. Birds will come to feed on the insects, as will amphibians and mammals. In this way, food webs will gradually recover in the absence of pesticides.

Making your own garden compost, instead of using peat, for instance, prevents damage to a fragile habitat that cannot be re-created. Collecting rainwater and using this in the garden will reduce the consumption of mains water. Huge amounts of energy are wasted on cleaning and transporting this precious resource and it is often extracted from rivers at levels that threaten the local wildlife. The careful gardener can encourage the creation of wildlife habitats in their own backyard and prevent habitat destruction somewhere else.

CREATING THE RIGHT HABITAT

Much of the wildlife that thrives in a garden does so under the care of a gardener who is not unduly tidy. The best wildlife gardens

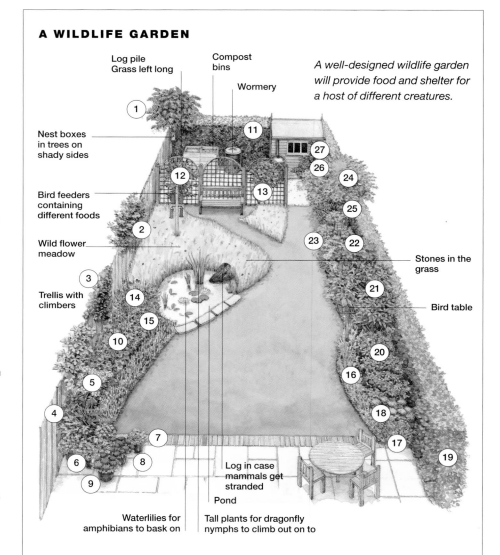

A WILDLIFE GARDEN

Log pile
Grass left long

Compost bins

Wormery

A well-designed wildlife garden will provide food and shelter for a host of different creatures.

Nest boxes in trees on shady sides

Bird feeders containing different foods

Wild flower meadow

Trellis with climbers

Stones in the grass

Bird table

Log in case mammals get stranded

Pond

Waterlilies for amphibians to bask on

Tall plants for dragonfly nymphs to climb out on to

1 *Sorbus aucuparia*
2 *Lonicera periclymenum* 'Belgica'
3 *Hedera helix* and *Humulus lupulus* 'Aureus'
4 *Echinops ritro*
5 *Lavandula* hedge
6 *Phlox paniculata*
7 *Nicotiana alata*
8 *Phacelia campanularia*
9 *Heliotropium* in pots

10 *Verbena bonariensis* and *Origanum vulgare*
11 Hedge of *Ilex aquifolium*
12 *Pyracantha*
13 *Clematis tangutica*
14 Mixed planting of *Perovskia* 'Blue Spire' and *Echinacea purpurea*
15 *Centranthus ruber*
16 *Nepeta* 'Six Hills Giant'
17 *Eschscholzia californica*

18 *Sedum spectabile*
19 *Fagus sylvatica* hedge
20 *Buddleja* 'Lochinch'
21 *Syringa* × *prestoniae*
22 *Aster* × *frikartii*
23 *Ribes sanguineum*
24 *Crataegus laevigata* 'Paul's Scarlet'
25 *Mahonia japonica*
26 *Cotoneaster horizontalis*
27 *Jasminum officinale*

leave room for decay. This approach – and it is one that is good for organic gardens in general – involves piling up old logs and autumn leaves in a quiet shady corner to create a home for insects and hibernating hedgehogs. Do not confuse this with making leaf mould pits; these stay in place and gradually rot down. Log piles can also be overplanted with ivy to enhance both their appearance and attractiveness to insects such as stag beetles.

Consider planting native trees, shrubs and flowers so that native creatures will have a familiar food source or nesting site. Plant as many suitable flowers as possible to attract bees, butterflies and other insects that will enhance your wildlife garden. Many beneficial species are attracted to a garden that is effectively a feeding station for them. For the larger visitors, such as small mammals and birds, you can plant flowering and berrying trees and shrubs.

Ponds provide a rich habitat for a variety of wildlife. Many familiar creatures, such as frogs, toads, newts and dragonflies, depend upon ponds to breed. Many urban gardens have become havens for these creatures. Even a small pool will provide somewhere that birds and other visitors can come to drink. If you have no space for a pond, try introducing a suitable container that can be utilized as a drinking or bathing area for birds, mammals and even insects.

Just leaving the lawn uncut for a few weeks in mid-summer will give many of the plants you do not normally see the opportunity to flower. An area of longer grass also benefits butterflies, moths and many other insect species by providing food and shelter. Many of these insects will

Above: Wildlife thrives in natural wetlands, many of which are threatened by domestic water use.

fall prey to larger garden occupants such as songbirds and hedgehogs, so diversifying and enhancing the food web in the garden.

The barriers and structures in your garden also provide very useful habitats. Hedges are a sanctuary for all sorts of wildlife, where they can breed, feed and take shelter. These hedges are easy to maintain, as they should only be cut once in the winter to avoid interfering with spring and summer nesting birds. Cutting is done on alternate sides in alternate winters. If one side is cut this winter, then the opposite side is cut the next. This ensures that only one side is clipped before the growing season. The unclipped side flowers and provides nectar and fruit for wildlife. Dry-stone walls

Above: Recycling organic material through composting reduces the need to use substances such as peat.

Above: Looking at natural habitats such as woodlands can provide inspiration for your own garden.

are another garden feature that can provide homes for hibernating amphibians, lizards, insects and bees and are best left undisturbed throughout the winter.

If you are lucky enough to have a few trees in your garden, you could try to re-create a woodland habitat. Larger gardens may actually contain a small area of woodland but most are more likely to have a shady patch under a few trees. Choose plants that mimic a woodland floor: bluebells, anemones and sorrel are just a few of the handsome plants that will thrive in these conditions. Planting a few understorey shrubs (those that grow below the trees) such as holly and hazel will complete the effect and may well tempt the shyer woodland birds into your garden.

WILDLIFE CORRIDORS

A wildlife garden is often likened to an oasis in an urban desert. Gardens are the only chance of cover that many creatures have to migrate between larger blocks of suitable habitat such as parks or a greenbelt. If these important habitats become totally isolated then they begin to lose much of their diversity. Town gardens play a vital role in protecting the health of the wider urban habitat, while rural gardens play a similar role in areas denuded by intensive farming. Try putting up a few bird or bat nest boxes and providing nesting areas for insects and mammals. The greater the year-round diversity, the more useful your garden will be.

WOODLAND GARDENS

Woodland can be one of the most interesting and diverse natural habitats. Those with smaller gardens may think that such a feature would be too large for them to create. However, even a few trees in the corner of the garden can provide ample opportunity for the creation of a small wooded area and provide a rich and diverse habitat for a range of visiting wildlife. Try to select native trees or species that have nectar-rich flowers or berries.

Above: *Woodlands are home to many of our favourite garden flowers such as these primroses (*Primula vulgaris*).*

WHAT IS WOODLAND?

Woodland is a very variable habitat and its exact character will mostly depend upon the prevailing climate. It is often a more open environment than that of a forest, having clearings, glades, pools and streams that break up the monotony of tree cover.

Large trees such as oak (*Quercus*), beech (*Fagus*) or plane (*Platanus*) are known as the woodland canopy. Beneath the canopy are smaller trees such as holly (*Ilex*) and hazel (*Corylus*), known as understorey species. They are often shade-tolerant trees, but grow best under gaps in the canopy. Beneath this, a shrubby layer develops in more open woodland, possibly consisting of bushes such as hawthorn (*Crataegus*) and elder (*Sambucus*).

The floor of the woodland is called the herb layer. The plants that live here tend to be seasonal, taking advantage of early spring sunshine to grow and flower, although some, such as mosses and ferns, grow through the summer. It is also where all seedlings grow and is mulched each year with the falling leaves of the trees.

CREATING A WOODED AREA

Gardeners who have a few trees (even if they do not provide a continuous canopy) can easily make a small woodland area. Visit some woods in your area to gain some inspiration and emulate natural growth if possible. Think how the existing tree cover can be linked, maybe by planting more canopy species and some understorey trees.

Woodland environments are often havens for plants and animals, with many containing an enormous diversity of species. This is most pronounced where there is a "mosaic" of open ground and trees. This is because it increases the "marginal areas" – the point between woodland and more open habitat. The places where two habitats meet are always the most diverse. Layered woodland (one with canopy, understorey, scrub and ground herbs) is beneficial for wildlife as it provides ample feeding and shelter for a range of creatures. Any additional planting should always be aimed at achieving or maintaining this layered structure and providing the highest number of habitats.

You can think of woodland as a collection of diverse habitats. Even those that have only a few types of tree are capable of supporting a great number of species that live on or within these trees. Oak trees in Britain, for instance, are known to provide homes for over 400 insect and other invertebrate species. This does not mean, however, that simply planting an oak tree in your organic garden will guarantee all 400 will appear at once. If you aim to create a woodland that is similar to others in your area, then species will be able to migrate from these to the one in your garden.

You may need to provide additional help for wildlife if it is to establish successfully in the woodland area. Nesting boxes, log piles, rocks and a long grass area linked to your pond can all help to encourage wildlife to use your planting as a habitat. Make sure that you include plants that provide food and be prepared to give additional sustenance, especially in the winter for non-hibernating foragers such as blue tits and other woodland birds. As the woodland develops, so will the diversity it contains. Let nature do its work and give a helping hand from time to time.

PLANTING WOODLAND FLOWERS

In most deciduous woodland, the ground is a riot of colour from late winter until early summer as showy woodland species grow, flower and set seed before the leaves in the canopy cast too much shade. As a consequence, most "woodland gardens" are at their best from late winter to early summer. The edges and clearings provide the chance for later colour, of course, but

Left: *Shady and partly shaded wooded areas can provide the perfect habitat for a host of creatures.*

Above: *Foxgloves (*Digitalis*) thrive in shady woodland corners and are very easy to grow from seed.*

Above: *Bluebells (*Hyacinthoides*) naturally grow and flower in the spring before the trees shade them.*

these boundaries are as long as possible. Fashioning them into "scalloped" or bay shapes will usually achieve this and each scallop or bay may contain different plants or shrub species. The clearings inside your woodland (if it is large enough) are also important. When you create these clearings, ensure that they are sufficiently long to allow plenty of sunshine into each one. Woodland glades should not be less than 7m (23ft) across and are best if they are irregular in shape.

Remember that the direction of the sun in your garden will affect the type of plants that you can grow at the woodland edge, and butterflies, for example, will prefer a sunny aspect. If the bays or clearings in your woodland area are mainly intended for long grass, then this may only need cutting every two to five years unless, of course, you wish to have a secluded seating area that may need more frequent mowing to maintain access.

some of the showiest species are to be found among the spring flowers. Choose species that grow in your own area, where possible, because these will be of most benefit to wildlife.

Primroses (*Primula vulgaris*), bluebells (*Hyacinthoides*), snowdrops (*Galanthus*) and wake robin (*Trillium grandiflorum*) are all guaranteed to give a good display, especially at a time when there are fewer colours in the rest of the ornamental garden. Later flowers such as foxgloves (*Digitalis*) should be planted at or near the edge, where they will still get sunlight once the leaves have appeared on the trees. Climbers such as honeysuckle (*Lonicera*) or clematis are also best situated at the woodland edge where you can appreciate the plants as they bloom. It is advisable to always obtain your seed or plants from a reputable source that does the propagation themselves. Never buy bulbs or plants that have been collected from the wild. Your aim is to create a habitat, but not by destroying another.

ASSOCIATED PLANTING

Perhaps the easiest way to mimic a woodland habitat in a smaller garden is to link a few trees with shrubs and understorey trees in order to provide the shelter and food plants that wildlife needs. These shrubs – particularly if they are deciduous – can provide a larger space in which to plant "woodland herb layer" species. Doing this

will also widen the edge of the habitat and provide extra coverings around the base of trees. There is, of course, no problem in having a few decorative species in or around your woodland. Try a few rhododendrons, mahonias, lilacs and hydrangeas to provide additional colour and interest if you have enough space. They will all provide shelter and look attractive when they are in flower.

EDGE ENHANCEMENT

Woodland edges are often the most valuable area in many types of woodland for a variety of wildlife and plants. The trick with any wildlife-friendly area is to make sure that

Above: *Hellebores and* Anemone blanda *make an ideal under-planting for trees, providing colour in early spring.*

Left: *Hornbeam (*Carpinus*), grown as a decorative hedge, can be underplanted with a selection of woodland flowers for added interest in the spring.*

WILD FLOWER LAWNS

Compared with a closely mown pristine lawn, an area of rough grass with flowers growing in it can provide a rich haven for a diverse range of wildlife. In nature, many attractive and species-rich habitats develop over time but in the garden, things may need a helping hand. You do not have to let the whole of the turfed area go untouched. Simply leave an area of grass uncut for some of the year and plant it up with your own choice of wild flowers to create a rich habitat.

Above: *Lawns and areas of long grass can easily be transformed into a stunning display of summer flowers.*

PLANTING AND MAINTAINING A WILD FLOWER MEADOW

Small areas of flowery grassland seem to work best when co-ordinated with hedges, shrubs or trees. They are not necessarily spectacular from a distance and need close inspection to appreciate the detailed tapestry of colour and form. Think carefully about where you would like to site such a feature. Always choose a simple mix of species that are well adapted to the conditions in your garden. Take a walk around your home area to see which local or well-adapted species thrive in similar soil types and aspects to your own.

ANNUAL FLOWERS OR PERENNIALS?

Many annuals have attractive flowers and seem ideal for flower-rich lawns but most require yearly soil disturbance and open ground. Poppies and cornflowers are good examples of showy annual plants that benefit from such conditions. Annuals are usually better treated as a separate display. Try planting some wheat or other grain along with the annuals and leave this for foraging birds and mammals. Don't try and harvest the wheat, just cut it down in late autumn and rotavate the plot ready for the spring.

Wild flower meadow species are perennials, which are adapted to life in permanent grassland. The easiest way to make a wild flower lawn is to plant small wild flower plants, directly into an existing lawn. Many wild flowers are easily raised from seed that is available from specialist suppliers. Sowing and growing this is generally the same as for any other herbaceous plant but you should use potting mix that is low in nutrients for the best results. A late autumn or early spring sowing will provide plants that are large enough to plant out in early to mid-summer.

HOW TO SOW WILD FLOWERS

1 *The most satisfactory way to create a wild flower meadow is to sow a special mixture of wild flower seeds. Remember to completely clear the ground of all perennial weeds before you start.*

2 *To bury the seeds, simply rake in one direction and then in the other. It does not matter if some seeds remain on the surface. Keep the area well watered until the seeds germinate. Protect from birds if necessary.*

ADDING INTEREST TO NATIVE GRASSLAND

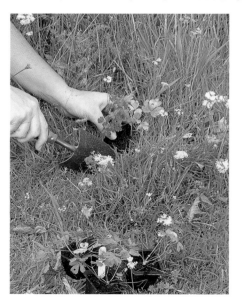

1 *For a very small area, wild flower plants may be more convenient. You can raise your own from seed or buy them. Plant into bare ground or in an existing lawn.*

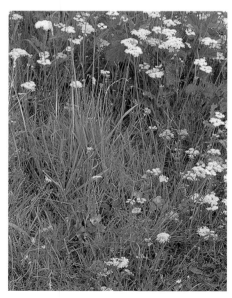

2 *Keep the plants well watered until they are established. Several years of successional planting may be needed to fully establish your wild flower lawn.*

Plant these out about 10–20cm (4–8in) apart in groups of 9–15 to ensure that the group can compete with the grass. Mark where you plant them so that you can see which ones have succeeded later.

If your plants do not establish the first time around, then it is worth trying again. Two failures should tell you that they are not suited for your conditions. You can always try a few non-native plants that have proven wildlife value. Prairie plants such as *Echinacea* are very useful in long grass. Try to avoid rare species, as they are likely to be particular in their habitat requirements, and always consider the attractiveness of plants to insects, birds or other wildlife when deciding what to grow.

NATURALIZING BULBS IN GRASS

Bulbs are potentially one of the easiest plants for flowery lawns. Many early-flowering species are suitable, including crocus, iris and snowdrops. Others, such as *Narcissus*, *Puschkinia*, fritillaries and *Leucojum*, provide good displays later in the spring. Planting bulbs is quite simple. Planting holes can be dug singly with a trowel or spade to the required depth – usually two to three times the height of the bulb. Bulbs should be placed with the base plate firmly in the bottom of the hole. An alternative method for large groupings of small bulbs like crocus and snowdrops is to cut an "H" shape in the grass surface and

Above: *Daffodils (*Narcissus*) are an ideal bulb to naturalize in lawns, giving spectacular early-spring interest in the wildlife or ornamental garden.*

HOW TO NATURALIZE BULBS IN A LAWN

1 *Lift an area of turf to create an H-shaped cut. Slice beneath the grass until you can fold back the turf for planting. Loosen the ground, as it will be very compacted. If you want to apply a slow-acting fertilizer, such as bonemeal, work it into the soil at the same time. Scatter the bulbs and plant them where they fall for a natural effect.*

3 *Special bulb planters can be used for large bulbs. The planters remove a cylindrical core of soil.*

2 *Use a trowel or a bulb planter for large bulbs, making sure that the bulb will be covered with twice its own depth of soil when the grass is returned. Firm down the soil and then return the grass. Firm once again if necessary to make sure that the grass is flat, and water well. Water the grass again in dry weather.*

4 *Place the bulb at the bottom of the hole on a bed of gravel to improve drainage, if necessary, and replace the plug of earth.*

peel the grass back in two "flaps". Place the bulbs underneath with the top uppermost and gently replace the flaps, firming them carefully. Any group of bulbs should be denser at the centre, gradually becoming wider spaced toward the outside, as this will give a natural appearance. Bulbs such as *Narcissus* may survive for many years but some smaller types – crocus being a prime example – may be eaten by rodents.

CARE AND MAINTENANCE

The time of year that you mow your meadow will influence the species you can grow and also when it will look good. If bulbs are not being grown in the grass then a spring cut can help keep a summer wild flower area tidy, especially after a mild winter. A high cut is best, especially if wild flowers have started to produce leafy growth. Cutting in mid-spring will produce a flowering peak in mid-summer. A slightly later cut in late spring will delay the peak of flowering by a few weeks.

Once flowering has finished, the long grass should be cut down. Spring-flowering meadows are best not cut until after flowering. If bulbs are included then the area should not be cut for six weeks after they have flowered. A second cut in mid-autumn will tidy the area ready for the winter. Summer meadows are usually cut from late summer to mid-autumn. All cuts must stress the grasses but minimize damage to wild flowers. Cuts should be between 30–70mm (1¼–2¾in) in order to achieve this.

Cuttings should be removed to help reduce fertility (as this will help your wild flowers) and to prevent long cuttings smothering the plants below. The cuttings should be left on the ground for three to five days, though, to allow insects to move back into the cut grass below. A portion of lawn may be left completely uncut to protect over-wintering insects, but the portion left must be rotated each year to make sure that the wild flowers survive.

WILDLIFE PONDS

Water is a key element in a wildlife garden. Garden ponds attract an enormous range of living creatures, such as dragonflies, newts and birds, to name just a few of the insects and animals that will visit the garden. Some will come to drink or bathe, others will set up permanent residence there, adding to the beauty and diversity of your garden. A pond not only provides an attractive feature in your garden, but also has far-reaching benefits to wildlife.

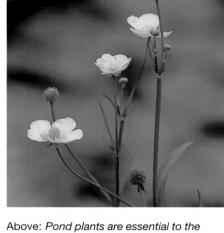

Above: *Pond plants are essential to the health and balance of the habitat as well as being highly attractive.*

CREATING A HEALTHY ENVIRONMENT FOR A POND

There are a number of points that you must be aware of if you want to provide a safe and healthy environment for wildlife. A pond is always best sited in a sunny position. This is because many pond plants will not prosper in shade, while the water may also be rather cold until the early summer. Shade within the pool is best achieved by surface vegetation, although a pond may have up to a third of the surface in shade if the remainder is well lit. You should also avoid a site near to overhanging trees whose shade can cause the water to be colder for longer in the spring. Falling leaves can cause a build-up of nutrients and increase the potential for toxic tannins in the water. The roots of some species may also interfere with the lining of the pond and can, in extreme cases, cause serious damage.

WATER FOR THE POND

Never fill your pond with tapwater, which often contains many additives, most notably chlorine. Much tapwater can have a high pH and may contain phosphates or nitrates. These can raise the pond's nutrient levels and promote algal growth. Water runoff from nearby lawns or borders can have much the same effect. If the water level becomes very low during the summer it is possible to use solarized mains water to top up your pond. This involves filling large containers with tap water, partially covering the tops and leaving them to stand in the sun for a couple of days. It removes chemicals like chlorine and, although not as good as rainwater, it will stop your pond from drying out. The majority of pool life requires a still environment, so avoid introducing pumps, fountains or filters.

POND SIZE

Even small-scale ponds can support an amazing diversity of life. The shallows are the most important areas for wildlife but a depth of at least 60cm (24in) must be reached in some parts to give creatures a place to which they can escape in extreme heat, cold or drought. The greater the surface area of a pool, the deeper it has to be (at its deepest point) to maintain an even temperature throughout the year. The average pool will need to be about 1m (3ft) deep.

STOCKING A POND

Ponds that are designed to attract wildlife should be colonized naturally within a couple of years. This is the best method for stocking your new pond in the first instance as it is providing a breeding place or hibernating area for those creatures already established in your area. Introducing frog (or other amphibian) spawn can sometimes spread diseases such as red leg that can devastate populations of frogs and other amphibians. Never attempt to introduce adult amphibians to your pond. They have an amazingly strong homing instinct and can die in the process of finding their way back.

A CROSS-SECTION OF A WILDLIFE POND

Displayed below are some of the more common inhabitants of the garden pool *which go towards forming a healthy and balanced ecosystem.*

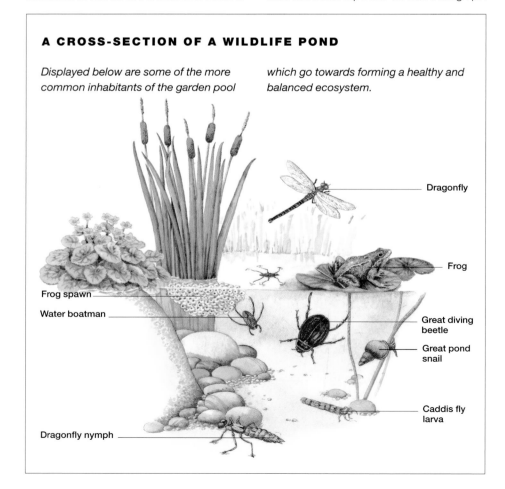

Dragonfly

Frog

Frog spawn

Water boatman

Great diving beetle

Great pond snail

Caddis fly larva

Dragonfly nymph

A WILDLIFE POND

Wildlife ponds depend upon correct planning. Ponds must be both deep enough and possess the right balance of plant types.

These plants will provide habitats, shelter, and maintain a balanced environment for the wildlife in the pond.

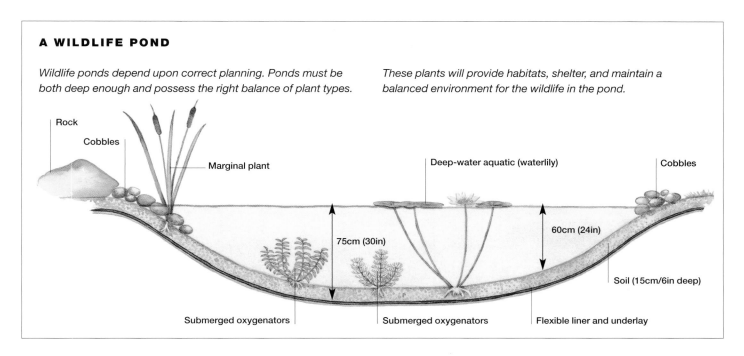

Rock

Cobbles

Marginal plant

Deep-water aquatic (waterlily)

Cobbles

75cm (30in)

60cm (24in)

Soil (15cm/6in deep)

Submerged oxygenators

Submerged oxygenators

Flexible liner and underlay

Avoid introducing fish to small wildlife ponds, as they can exclude other wildlife. Sticklebacks can wipe out the tadpoles of frogs and newts. Fish also eat valuable water-living crustaceans that help to control the growth of water algae and their droppings promote algal bloom.

PLANTING

Bank-side vegetation provides cover for animals entering or leaving the pond. Choose a selection of marginal plants, submerged plants and plants with floating leaves. Leaving long grass around a pond will also provide important cover for wildlife. Gently sloping sides make it easier for creatures to climb in and out of the pond.

Pond dwellers, such as dragonflies and caddis flies, need vegetation to climb out of the water so that the adult may emerge. Small reeds such as the lesser bulrush are ideal but any plants that grow about 40cm (16in) or more above the normal water surface will do.

A log pile nearby will provide a place for hibernating frogs and toads, as well as being a habitat for many other creatures. Add an escape log to help small mammals get out of the pond if they fall in.

Ideally the water surface should have a third or more covered with plant leaves such as water lilies, water soldier, frog-bit or even

Right: Even a small garden will benefit from a tranquil wildlife pond where animals can come to drink.

duckweed. These help keep the water cool, provide shelter and breeding cover for wildlife and help to prevent the development of algae in the water.

Plants that are to form part of your pond habitat should always be grown in a nutrient-poor potting mix. Slow-release fertilizers effectively act as an algal "time bomb", steadily releasing a supply of nutrients that encourage green water and blanket weed development.

Oxygen is essential for the growth and development of pond-dwelling creatures and can easily be boosted by the inclusion of plants that release it directly into the water. These are plants that are entirely aquatic and do not emerge above the water

surface. Plants such as milfoil and Canadian pondweed are often used for this purpose.

Native plants should be a first choice for a pond. Many are showy and often rare or endangered in the wild. If you decide to use natives, never take them from the wild. Always buy them from a reputable nursery or take small offsets from a friend's pond.

Some plants are just too vigorous to be included and will rapidly outgrow their situation. Reedmace (*Typha latifolia*), reeds such as phragmites, floaters such as duckweed (*Lemna*) and the *Azolla* fern are all potentially problematic and should only be included where space permits. They are the equivalent of aquatic weeds and may cause maintenance problems.

PROVIDING SHELTER

As well as needing water and food, wildlife occupants and passing visitors to the garden need a secure place in which to shelter, where they can feed, nest, breed or escape from predators. Almost every part of the garden can potentially shelter wildlife and the key is not only to provide the right kind of cover but also to make sure that it is not disturbed once it is occupied. These sites can take the form of natural plantings or man-made shelters.

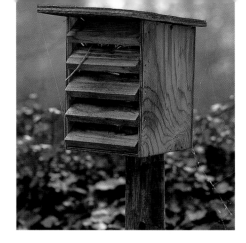

Above: *Providing winter cover such as this lacewing hotel for beneficial insects ensures a healthy population for next season.*

TYPES OF SHELTER

In nature, evergreen trees and shrubs provide year-round cover from weather and predators, while deciduous ones give summer cover for nesting and protection. Dead trees provide habitats for owls, woodpeckers and bats, while fallen logs are host to a wide array of ground dwellers such as wood-boring beetles and other insects.

Centipedes and ground and rove beetles that are active all year round need undisturbed soil, stones and logs. Frogs, toads and newts hibernate through the coldest months, often overwintering in damp hidden sites. Place stones and logs near to a pond and ensure that it has shallow edges and sloping sides. Newts prefer overhanging vegetation to shield them on entering and leaving.

Think about where specific creatures live in nature and aim to mimic these habitats. Sometimes this will involve using the natural landscape or erecting a purpose-built shelter.

Left: *Logs and branches, left over from pruning or tree felling, can be left as a habitat or winter shelter for wildlife.*

LOG PILES

These are an essential part of any wildlife garden because they offer shelter and food for a wide range of different organisms and insects that will in turn provide food for other visiting animals.

Log piles make an excellent place for frogs, toads, lizards, hedgehogs and other wildlife species to shelter, find food, and raise their young. Build a permanent log pile in a shaded area, and let it decay naturally. The logs form food for fungi and insects, while providing shelter for reptiles and small mammals. Dead wood on the ground and especially up in the trees is a very important source of nourishment for insect-feeding birds, such as woodpeckers and tree creepers.

Left: *A shady part of the garden, under the cover of trees, is the ideal place for a log pile. Log piles are both useful for hibernating animals and as a food source for beetles.*

TIDINESS

You should not be in too much of a hurry to clear and tidy up your garden in the autumn, as this will provide shelter during the winter months for a wide variety of garden wildlife. Always be selective, preferably removing only piles of diseased debris. The later you can leave your winter clearance, say until early spring, then the greater the numbers of animals there will be successfully overwintering.

WHICH SPECIES SHOULD YOU SHELTER?

There is a wide range of species that can benefit from cover in your garden. However, you should always try to assess the likelihood that these creatures will actually visit your garden in the first place. There is little point in putting up luxury accommodation for creatures that will never even see it, much less shelter within. The following are some of the creatures that may benefit from a shelter in your garden.

Above: *It is advisable to position shelters for beneficial insects near to a suitable habitat or to a source of food so that they can find them easily.*

Above: *Pollinating insects such as bees need both shelter and protection. Bees are very important inhabitants of a wildlife garden; honeybees pollinate plants in the garden.*

Bats These are probably the most elusive of our garden visitors and because of their nocturnal lives we know very little about them and often, rather unfairly, fear them. Bats roost during the day in tree hollows, in dense shrubs or climbers, and in buildings, although during winter they hibernate, often in deeper, solid places with an even, cool temperature. These fascinating mammals are declining in number due mainly to the loss of roosts and feeding areas, and the increasing use of pesticides. One of the easiest ways to help bats is by putting up bat boxes. These should be located in a sheltered position that gets morning sun and afternoon shade.

Birds The lively activity around your bird table or feeders shows that it can be easy to attract more birds into your garden. Birds need more than just a source of food, though, and suitable nesting sites can be essential for some common garden species. Trees, shrubs and climber-covered walls and fences will provide shelter and nest sites.

Though the term nesting box implies birds may nest in them, only a few species use natural or man-made cavities. Most look for shelter in vegetation, with shrubs being perhaps more valuable than trees for this purpose. You should note that regular close pruning of shrubs might cause growth that is too dense for birds to navigate easily. Try to use native species where possible. Hedges that also produce berries are a good source of food for birds in the colder months.

Butterflies These also require shelter from the elements and a place to roost. The foliage of shrubs is useful as an overnight roost, as are patches of tall grass. You can also provide a place for butterflies to roost, perch, or even hibernate by building a log pile and stacking the logs crosswise to create as many open spaces as possible. The ideal log pile size is about 1.5m (5ft) tall and 2m (6½ft) long. You can also buy a butterfly hibernation house, although there is little evidence that these are ever actually used by butterflies.

Hedgehogs If you lean a sheet of wood at an angle against a wall and stuff it with dry leaves, this will provide a suitable nest for hedgehogs. They will also nest under raised sheds and beneath hedgerows, as long as there are plenty of dry leaves for bedding. You can also provide a winter box in an old compost heap or leaf pile for hibernation.

Above: *You can encourage butterflies into your garden by planting wildlife-friendly plants such as these purple verbenas.*

Reptiles and amphibians Rocks, logs, and leaf piles offer cover for small mammals, reptiles, amphibians and insects. In the autumn, try constructing small rock piles that can provide lizards, reptiles and amphibians with a warm winter retreat. If you have a pond, leave brushwood and leaves or rock piles near the bank to provide shelter for amphibians as many of these hibernate in damp areas on the land.

Pollinators Bumble-bees can overwinter in a small terracotta pot filled with moss or finely shredded newspaper. Bury the filled pot upside down and protect the hole from rain with stones, but leave a tiny gap for the bee to get in and out. Masonry bees can be encouraged to take up residence by tying a bundle of bamboo canes together – lengths of about 25cm (10in) are ideal – and then placing them inside a length of old plastic pipe that is about 5–7.5cm (2–3in) longer than the canes. They will make nests inside the hollow bamboo canes and lay eggs within these that will hatch out the following spring. Always place the pipe in a sunny sheltered position where rain will not reach it. You can also buy purpose-built masonry bee shelters.

Predators Lacewings will shelter in a similar construction to that used for masonry bees. Ready-made lacewing hotels are available and are impregnated with a pheromone that attracts the adults in the autumn. Ladybird (ladybug) shelters are also marketed commercially for the same purpose. You can also buy the pheromone with which to impregnate your own home-made shelters.

PLANTS TO ATTRACT WILDLIFE

Plants are the single most important factor when it comes to attracting wildlife into your garden. They provide a food source and shelter for visiting bees, butterflies, moths and a whole host of beneficial insects. Even if your garden is tiny, you can still introduce a selection of useful plants by planting tubs of brightly coloured and nectar-rich summer flowers and pots of sweet-smelling herbs such as lavender and rosemary.

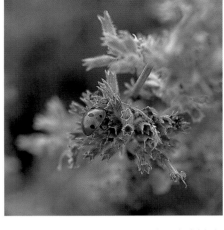

Above: *Beneficial predators such as ladybirds (ladybugs) will be attracted to the garden if you include the right species of plant.*

PLANTS FOR FOOD AND SHELTER

Planting colourful, nectar-rich plants attracts butterflies and other beneficial insects. Choose plants that will provide the visitors with nectar from early spring to late autumn. This of course has the added benefit that your flower beds will be brimming with colour for most of the year. Combine selected species of herbs, wild flowers and cottage garden plants in a herbaceous border to create a butterfly or bee border.

To encourage breeding insects, allow a few nettles and grasses to grow in a secluded corner of the garden or let ivy trail up your fence. These will provide sites for female butterflies to lay eggs and a food source for caterpillars.

Wild or single-flowering varieties of plants are often best for wildlife. You should not be too eager to dead-head plants in autumn.

Many birds feed on spent flower heads such as those of forget-me-nots and pansies. Leave perennial flower stems in autumn, as birds will be attracted to them, searching for seeds and hiding insects. Nesting birds need insects to raise young, so try early-flowering plants such as aubretia that attract aphids and provide a source of food.

Left: *Plants with composite flower-heads, such as thistles and daisies, readily attract insects to the garden.*

A hedge that is left relatively undisturbed by the gardener can prove a rich habitat for a diverse range of wildlife. Dense hedges give birds protection from predators and provide windbreaks. The thick undergrowth encourages many species of small bird to take shelter and unclipped hedges of all types have more chance of bearing flowers and fruit.

If your garden is large enough to have at least one large tree then this will provide perches and nesting sites for many birds. Native trees are valuable to insects, birds and other animals as they provide better shelter and food than introduced species. The best trees are those that produce

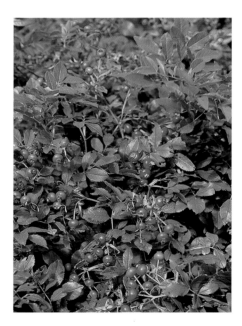

Above: *Choose plants such as roses that have berries or edible fruits for birds and mammals to feed on.*

Above: *Sunflowers (*Helianthus annuus*) provide food for insect pollinators as well as late seeds for overwintering birds.*

Above: Knautia macedonica *can be used in flower borders or in wild flower lawns in order to attract insects such as bees.*

seeds or fruit, as these are often a valuable source of food for many birds in autumn or winter.

Shrubs provide shelter for birds, enabling them to nest safely. Choose shrubs such as *Pyracantha*, *Cotoneaster* and *Viburnum* that produce a good crop of berries for the birds to feed on. Climbers are attractive to birds, especially if they are late flowering or bear fruit and seeds for winter food.

Annual species, planted on vacant patches where quick reliable displays of colour are required, will produce an outstanding array of colour, and their nectar and seeds provide valuable food for many types of insect.

Meadow-plant species will provide colour while the foliage of naturalized bulbs withers down. A fine early display can be created under deciduous trees before the soil becomes too dry and shaded, and grassy banks provide a marvellous opportunity for creating a mini meadow. An informal lawn is the intermediate step between a formal lawn and a meadow and is often created adjacent to a formal lawn and sown at the same time. It contains species tolerant of close cutting and if mowing is relaxed in summer, an enchanting display of flowers can be enjoyed for many weeks. When mowing is recommended no harm will come to the plants, and the practice can be repeated annually.

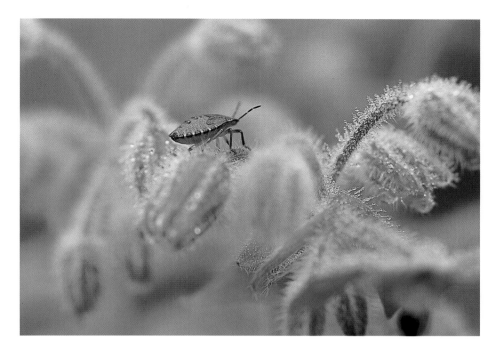

Shaded areas of the garden often present a problem for gardeners, but there are many varieties of woodland plants – often including some of the most beautiful wild flowers such as anemones and foxgloves (*Digitalis*) – that will thrive in these conditions. A woodland area planted with native trees and shrubs is the ideal backdrop for bulbs and woodland wild flowers. This habitat provides a continual source of interest throughout the year and attracts insects, birds and mammals.

Above: *Encouraging beneficial insects into your garden by including insect-friendly plants can help to create a natural balance.*

Plants growing along and in hedgerows are particularly useful to attract wildlife, especially if the hedge is made up of native species. Plants for sun, shade or semi-shade should be selected depending on the aspect of the hedgerow. New hedgerows should be allowed to establish free of competition for two to three years before associated plants are introduced. Hedges provide corridors for wildlife and sources of interest throughout the year, with attractive foliage in spring, flowers in summer and berries, hips or leaf colour in autumn and winter.

Plants that grow in or around ponds act as a magnet to surrounding wildlife. Damp soil borders and marshy areas are the ideal habitat for many species of wild flower.

Dry-stone walls can also be exploited by planting up nooks and crannies with wild flowers adapted to the conditions, adding interesting foliage and colour.

Combinations of wild flowers can also make excellent subjects for patio tubs, pots and hanging baskets, as many of them are tolerant of drought and have a spreading habit, making them ideal for low-maintenance containers.

Left: *As its common name of butterfly bush suggests, buddleia is a particularly excellent source of nectar for butterflies.*

TOP 20 GARDEN PLANTS TO ATTRACT WILDLIFE

There are literally thousands of plants that all have the potential to attract various forms of wildlife to the garden. Some plants, however, are more effective at this than others. Twenty of the best plants for attracting wildlife that are easy to grow are listed below.

PLANT		WILDLIFE ATTRACTED	BENEFITS TO THE GARDEN
Achillea millefolium (Yarrow) A vigorous herbaceous perennial that grows to a height of 60cm (2ft). Flower colour ranges from white through to reds and oranges.		An abundance of hoverflies can be found nectaring on the flowers in summer. Also attracts bees and bumble-bees.	Hoverfly larvae are an excellent addition to the garden, providing efficient control of aphids. The larvae can eat vast amounts of aphids during this part of the life-cycle.
Angelica archangelica (Angelica) A tall, upright, herbaceous perennial, more often grown as a biennial, which grows to 1.8m (6ft). The architectural flower-heads bloom in early to mid-summer.		Bees, butterflies, hoverflies, insects and birds all congregate around the huge flower heads of this garden bloom.	This plant can be likened to a supermarket where many species gather to stock up on food. Count the number of species on one bloom, it is amazing.
Aster novi-belgii (Michaelmas daisy) The flowers of this herbaceous perennial provide a rich source of late nectar. A full range of sizes and colours are available.		In late summer and autumn butterflies and bees visit the flowers. Birds eat the seed after ripening.	This plant provides a valuable late source of nectar. Butterflies will use this food to strengthen them up for winter hibernation or to produce eggs to overwinter.
Aurinia saxatilis (Golden alyssum) Also known as *Alyssum saxatile*, this herbaceous perennial forms a carpet of yellow flowers in spring.		Butterflies, bees and early flying hoverflies are attracted to the bright yellow flowers of this popular rock garden plant.	A very useful source of nectar for all early insects, especially early season or overwintering butterflies.
Buddleja davidii (Butterfly bush) This deciduous shrub is often quoted as the saviour of the British butterfly population due to the high quantities of nectar it produces.		As the name suggests, this is an excellent plant for attracting butterflies. Also useful for a variety of nectar feeders, including bees and moths.	Like asters, this is an excellent feeding stop for migratory and resident butterflies. The caterpillars are a good source of protein for birds.
Centranthus ruber (Red valerian) A herbaceous perennial that grows to 60cm (2ft). It performs well in poor dry soils and does especially well in seaside locations.		One of the best flowers for butterflies, providing nectar for small tortoiseshells, peacocks, red admirals and white and yellow butterflies.	Butterflies are a good indicator of the health of the environment. Their caterpillars are a good source of protein for nesting songbirds.
***Cerinthe major* 'Purpurascens'** A small herbaceous perennial that flowers in spring. Produces fantastic blue flowers with lilac bracts. It self-seeds freely.		Bees love the blue flowers and congregate in vast numbers while the plant is in flower.	This early flowering perennial gives a boost of nectar to resident bee populations, which are good pollinators.
Eryngium giganteum (Miss Willmott's ghost) A short-lived herbaceous perennial that reaches a height of 90cm (3ft) and has beautiful steel-blue flowers.		This plant hums with bees and bumble-bees during its long summer-flowering period.	An outstandingly beautiful plant that attracts bees which will pollinate your plants. Good for naturalizing in wild areas.
Eschscholzia californica (Californian poppy) An annual that produces striking orange, cream, red or yellow flowers which will bloom all summer. This is a small plant, reaching 45cm (18in) in height.		Hoverflies, bees and bumble-bees are attracted to this plant. Once it is sown, it will self-seed freely round the garden.	The bright orange flowers attract hoverflies, the larvae of which are extremely voracious predators of aphids.
Eupatorium cannabinum A tall plant that produces large heads of fluffy pink flowers in late summer. This herbaceous perennial is a must for the wildlife garden.		Attracts butterflies and bees. As well as looking fantastic, this plant is one of the best for providing nectar to adult butterflies.	From mid-summer onwards, this decorative plant offers a rich and steady source of nectar and is a firm favourite with visiting butterflies.

PLANT		WILDLIFE ATTRACTED	BENEFITS TO THE GARDEN
Helianthus annuus **(Sunflower)** If you want to make a statement, grow a few of these in your garden. They have enormous yellow, red or orange heads with some tall varieties easily reaching 2m (6½ft).		Birds such as greenfinches and bullfinches will eat the seeds. Also visited by honeybees and bumble-bees when in flower.	The seeds provide a late-summer boost to the diet of birds and some small mammal species. Good for encouraging birds into your garden.
***Humulus lupulus* 'Aureus'** **(Golden hop)** A vigorous climber with twining stems. It is unusual in that it dies down every year. The female plants produce hops that are used in flavouring beer.		Caterpillars of the beautiful comma butterfly and button snout moth feed on the golden foliage.	Food plants for caterpillars and larvae are an invaluable part of a wildlife garden, otherwise we would not be graced with the adult butterflies.
Lavandula angustifolia **(Lavender)** A compact bushy shrub that sports many varieties to choose from. It produces fragrant pink to purple flowers in early summer.		The fragrant blooms attract many different species of bees, bumble-bees and also white and blue butterflies.	Insect-eating birds are attracted to feast on the insects drawn to nectar on these fragrant bushes.
Lonicera periclymenum **(Honeysuckle)** A climber with twining stems reaching up to 6m (18ft). It bears sweetly scented, pink and cream flowers in early summer, with red berries appearing later.		Nectar provides food for bumble-bees, bee hawk moths as well as elephant, lime and privet hawk moths. Fruit-eating birds will feast on the berries.	A superb plant for night-flying moths that should be placed next to the house so you can enjoy both the fragrance and watch these night-flying beauties. The moths are also a good source of protein for birds and bats.
Nymphaea alba **(Waterlily)** An aquatic plant that has large round floating leaves with beautiful white flowers in the summer months.		Adult frogs and dragonflies use the floating leaves of this aquatic plant for basking on. The leaves also provide cover for tadpoles of newts and frogs.	Adult frogs eat slugs and snails. The tadpoles help to control algae in the pond, as it is part of their diet.
Phlox paniculata The lovely, sweetly scented flower heads provide a colourful display in late summer. This 90cm (3ft) herbaceous perennial prefers a moist soil in light shade.		This plant will attract adult butterflies and moths, which will appreciate the nectar from the flower heads in late summer to early autumn.	The moths nectaring on this plant will provide a tasty meal for wandering bats. Butterflies flying during the day will provide a meal for hungry birds.
Rosmarinus officinalis **(Rosemary)** A dense bushy shrub with aromatic foliage growing up to 1.5m (5ft) tall. It bears purple to blue flowers in mid-spring to early summer.		Almost unrivalled in its ability to attract honeybees, butterflies and hoverflies to its nectar-rich flowers.	Honeybees pollinate many garden plants and trees. They are welcomed by farmers into fruit orchards.
Sedum spectabile **(Ice plant)** This small herbaceous plant is one of the best butterfly plants. It has thick succulent leaves and stems that are well suited to growing in hot well-drained positions.		An old favourite for the herbaceous border, Sedum is extremely useful to butterflies, bees and hoverflies as a late summer source of nectar.	Provides a good source of nectar late in the season that is a positive benefit for overwintering butterfly species to build up their energy.
Sorbus aucuparia **(Mountain ash)** A wonderful tree for the small garden. It has attractive white flowers in the spring and bears red fruit in the autumn. It can reach heights of 12m (36ft).		The flowers are excellent for feeding bees and other insects in the spring whereas the berries are consumed by many species of birds.	The tree can attract up to 30 different species of insect, not including the birds and small mammals it feeds, providing a meal for many.
Verbena bonariensis **(Tall verbena)** This versatile plant can be grown as an annual or short-lived perennial, reaching up to 1.8m (6ft). The purple-flowering spikes bloom in late summer until the first frosts.		This is a fantastic plant for nectaring butterflies such as the small tortoiseshell, peacock, red admiral and comma. It is perhaps more effective than the more well-known buddleia.	Good for planting in large groups throughout the garden to attract large numbers of butterflies and bees to pollinate plants and to provide food for garden birds.

THE KITCHEN GARDEN

The kitchen garden is a paradise for gardener and cook alike. Few pleasures in life can compare with the satisfaction of harvesting and eating fresh produce from your own garden. There are many design possibilities when planning a kitchen garden. Some gardeners prefer to lay out their vegetable plot in neat rows; others choose an edible landscape that is ornamental as well as functional. There is also a seemingly endless choice of varieties in seed and nursery catalogues which can be confusing, but merely reflects the popularity of home-growing.

Left: *Kitchen gardens can provide a summer spectacle as well as a wealth of fresh, home-grown food for your table.*

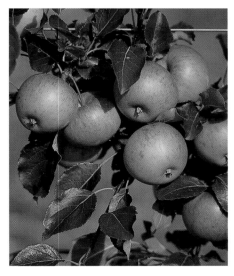

Above: *Fruit such as pears and apples is one of the most welcome delights of autumn in the kitchen garden.*

Above: *Companion planting helps to keep plants healthy and also looks attractive throughout the summer.*

Above: *Kitchen-garden plants can be just as decorative as those grown for their ornamental qualities.*

PLANNING A KITCHEN GARDEN

Growing your own vegetables, herbs and fruit ensures that the food you eat is fresh, tasty and chemical-free. The healthiest food is found closest to its source, so freshly picked produce from your garden is both tastier and better for you than that which has travelled long distances by air, sea or road. Your garden will also be more appealing when it is planted with a wide selection of plants that will attract an equally diverse range of wildlife.

Above: *A well-planned kitchen garden, with companion planting, can be a feast for the eyes as well as the table.*

WHAT DO YOU WANT FROM YOUR KITCHEN GARDEN?

An ideal starting point is to make a list of all the vegetables and fruit that you eat on a regular basis, adding in a few that you are curious about and would like to try. The next stage is to look at the size of your garden and consider if there is enough room to grow everything that is on your list. Think about the quantity needed to feed your family. There is no point in planting ten apple trees for a family of four. It is a good idea to start with a few easy crops to build your confidence and progress from there.

Many edible plants, especially vegetables and herbs, are easy to grow and can be ready for harvesting in a short space of time. Children love to sow and grow less difficult crops, such as spring onions (scallions), radishes, carrots and lettuce. Growing fruit is usually a longer-term investment, as many types, such as apples, pears and blackcurrants, for example, will take several years to crop. Once they start to produce fruit, however, your investment will pay off, as they will continue to crop for many years to come and are less time-consuming than vegetables.

Furthermore, you do not need acres of space to enjoy growing your own fresh fruit and vegetables. In fact, even a small garden will support an edible crop or two. You could grow potatoes in barrels, herbs in pots and fruit trees in ornamental containers. If you live in an apartment, you can use window boxes and containers to grow fresh herbs and vegetables. Try planting hanging baskets with trailing tomatoes, herbs or fruits such as strawberries to overcome space difficulties. Edible gardening involves using any space that is conveniently available. It also promises a colourful garden and unusual ways to feed your family.

DESIGNING THE GARDEN

There are a number of points that you will need to consider in order to get the most out of your kitchen garden and to ensure that the food you produce is safe and fresh. Siting your crops next to a busy road, for instance, can mean eating produce that is polluted by cars. When siting the crops, think carefully about your own garden environment. Each garden is different and

has specific requirements for growing various crops. Check the pH of your soil before getting underway as vegetables such as cauliflowers and cabbages will not grow well if the soil is too acidic (under pH of 6.5). As well as testing the pH level, test the soil for nutrients. The results will indicate if there is any need to improve the soil before planting.

The aspect of your garden is also critical in the siting of your plants. Fruit, for example, needs plenty of sun exposure in order to ripen properly and develop flavour. Fruit trees are also often best sited over a lawn to facilitate fruit collection.

Any design needs to consider the difference between annual and perennial crops. Annual vegetable crops, such as potatoes, carrots, cabbages and beetroot, need to be rotated within the vegetable garden to deter soil-borne pests and diseases from attacking them. Strawberries are a good example here, as they are effectively an annual, needing to be divided every year. A strawberry bed that you rotate with flowers and annual herbs (such as basil or dill) is useful for avoiding soil-borne pest problems.

Perennial crops, such as asparagus and rhubarb, may well merit their own distinct areas and are not rotated like annual crops. Raspberries and blackberries, which are both perennial, are best sited permanently on a wire trellis. Avoid putting them in a huge expanding clump that can take over your garden.

Consider, too, how difficult a particular plant (or the produce it offers) is to grow. Peaches, for example, can be challenging. They are disease-prone and require lots of care and attention. Unless you are a committed gardener with time on your hands, it may be best to purchase a few organically grown fruits from a local shop.

Left: *Peas and beans can easily be trained up supports, giving height and structure to the kitchen garden.*

PLANTING THE KITCHEN GARDEN

If you have recently moved into a new home, then you will have the luxury of starting your kitchen garden from scratch. If your garden is already established, there is no need to uproot everything to grow your own produce. Gardens need not be exclusively made up of just edible or ornamental plants. You may wish to start by planting a few annual vegetables and herbs among your ornamental plants. Indeed, you can easily incorporate edible plants into the garden, even mixing fruit, vegetables and herbs in ornamental beds. This planting arrangement avoids crops grown in visually uninspiring mono-cropped rows.

If you are planting vegetables in new beds, then they can be interplanted with ornamentals and herbs. Fragrant plants such as English marigolds (*Calendula*), French marigolds (*Tagetes patula*) and oregano (*Origanum*) are excellent choices for attracting beneficial insects, and interplanting with plants such as these will help to keep pests to a minimum. Large blocks of the same vegetable are likely to attract high concentrations of pests, whereas interplanting tends to confuse and dissuade them.

If you need to remove an ornamental tree or shrub that has died or outgrown its site, consider replacing it with a fruit-bearing tree or shrub. There are many possibilities, including apples, currants, raspberries, crab apples, plums and cherries, which can all provide valuable colour and texture in the garden as well as a source of food. Apart from feeding the household, excess fruit from these trees will also provide food for a range of birds and insects.

It is worthwhile researching the eventual height of plants in the planning stages. Some will simply look out of place if they are grown in the wrong location, such as planting tall plants in front of smaller ones. Many large ones will also need some form of staking or support.

Lettuce, chives, pansies and parsley create excellent borders along the edges of raised beds. Tall plants such as dill, sunflowers, daylilies, fennel, valerian, peas and beans are best grown at the back of beds or at the centres of containers. Provide trellises and other supports where needed. Choose edible flowers such as nasturtiums and chives wherever possible because they are a natural addition to gardens and make salad bowls look and taste wonderful.

You may wish to consider an edible lawn, in which some (or even all) of the lawn is given over to a groundcover such as strawberries. Strawberries are a very attractive crop because they produce fruit for most of the summer and tolerate marginal soils and light shade. However, large patches are likely to attract pests, so they should be interplanted with strong-smelling herbs like thyme and oregano which also form good groundcover. It may be an idea to keep a permanent cover of herbs and rotate the strawberry crop on a two- or three-year cycle.

PLANTS USED AS FENCES, SCREENS AND BARRIERS

Plants can be used in a number of imaginative ways. Instead of erecting plain wooden fencing or mesh barriers why not consider planting a living one?

Above: *Onions, with their tall stems, can be grown for their decorative appearance in ornamental beds and borders.*

Gooseberries, raspberries or currants are readily trained along a fence and apples can be trained as an espalier cordon or fan along a wall. Climbing plants, such as hardy kiwi fruits, trailing nasturtiums, broad beans, or sugar snap peas, can all be grown over a fence or trellis work to provide an ornate screen. Hedges can also form useful and attractive edible barriers. Shrub roses, such as *Rosa rugosa*, create an attractive, but impenetrable barrier, producing large red rose hips that contain 60 times the vitamin C of an orange. The hips can be used to make tea, jam, syrup or jelly. Currants and other fruit can also be included on the sunny side.

When designing your kitchen garden, bear in mind that the garden is for everyone in the household. Hold family discussions to involve everyone in the planning and design stage. It is worthwhile taking everyone's needs and tastes into consideration when undertaking this extremely important stage of development.

Right: *Cloches and low tunnels can increase the range of early crops that can be grown in the kitchen garden.*

CROP VARIETIES

There is a seemingly endless array of seeds available to the home gardener. Each supplier makes claims that their variety is better than all those that went before and any others currently available. Others claim to have older, more choice varieties saved from extinction and representing a time when everything was purer and more wholesome. Personal preference usually decides the best varieties for you, but an understanding of what you can expect from the seed in a packet can be very useful.

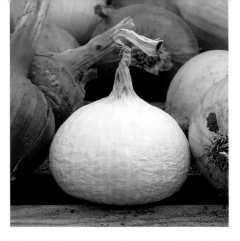

Above: *Onions come in a range of attractive colours and can be grown for their ornamental value in beds and borders.*

WHAT ARE HYBRIDS?

Often when we purchase seed, we respond more readily to the picture on the front of the packet. We may not notice whether it is marked with the terms "F1" or "hybrid". A hybrid is the result of a cross between one variety with pollen from another specific variety. The breeder chooses parent varieties that will produce first generation offspring (F1 hybrids) with known characteristics. The crossing is done in a very controlled manner so that no pollen from another variety is able to pollinate the flowers. As a result, all of the plants that are grown from the hybrid seed will be genetically identical.

Hybrids may be bred to be more widely adapted to environmental stresses such as heat, cold, disease or drought than non-hybrids. They also have more uniform characteristics, making crops more predictable in their qualities. They also have

"hybrid vigour" and may grow faster or be more disease-resistant than either of the parents. They may also give better yields than open-pollinated varieties. They will not breed true, however, meaning that seed collected will not produce plants that are the same as the parent (F1 hybrids). For this reason, seed cannot be saved from F1 hybrid plants by the home gardener. Seed for hybrid varieties must be purchased year after year from the seed companies or nurseries, unless you want to gamble and grow an array of offspring.

WHAT ARE OPEN-POLLINATED VARIETIES?

Open-pollinated varieties are traditional varieties that have (in some cases) been grown and selected for desirable traits such as taste, yield or disease-resistance for many years. They often grow well in organic kitchen gardens as many were originally selected under organic conditions. These plants can mutate and adapt to the local ecosystem, as the seed is often collected and re-used by the organic gardener.

If a seed packet is labelled "heirloom", "open-pollinated" or has no special markings, then it is most likely a standard or traditional variety. The majority of lettuce, bean and pea varieties for domestic use are open-pollinated, while most cabbages, broccoli, tomatoes, cucumbers, melons and Brussels sprouts are hybrids.

Right: *Allowing a few of your crops to flower will also provide you with seed for growing next year's crop.*

Left: *Unusual crop varieties can often be grown from seed that you have collected yourself each year. This is a striking variety of kohl rabi.*

Hybrid seeds can dominate the garden seed market, but open-pollinated varieties are more or less stabilized in their characteristics, remaining fairly consistent and producing seed that will grow into plants that are more or less like the parent plants. They are a little less uniform than hybrids, but the home gardener can safely collect seed and grow plants from them that will be essentially the same as the original plants. Open-pollinated varieties either self-pollinate or are pollinated by wind or insects and they usually produce viable seed.

There have been various claims that open-pollinated varieties do not taste as good as hybrids. It is also claimed that they are smaller and not as uniform and, in many cases, this may be true. However, where matters of taste in varieties are concerned, the only real answer is to try them and see for yourself.

Right: *Old varieties of tomato tend to have varying sizes of tastier fruits that crop over a long period of time.*

WHAT ARE HEIRLOOM VARIETIES?

In the 1970s the European Community brought in regulations to encourage the breeding of new vegetable cultivars and the standardization of older ones. This resulted in a list of approved cultivars being drawn up and it became illegal to sell any cultivar that was not included on this list. It is very expensive to have a single cultivar tested in order to then register it on the list. This meant that many old cultivars were put in grave danger of being lost forever, as the funds to test each variety were not available. It was due to this legislation that HDRA, the Organic Organisation, in England, a society which was established to promote organic issues, founded the Heritage Seed Library (HSL). This seed library ensures that old or "heirloom varieties" are kept safe for posterity by distributing its seed. Although HDRA grow some of the seeds themselves, they also employ contract growers and seed guardians to make up the bulk of the seeds that are supplied.

Each year a catalogue is sent to HSL members from which they can select up to six varieties free of charge. This distribution set-up overcomes the clause of selling only approved cultivars. This service is also available to members in the United States.

The best heirloom cultivars can be traced back fifty years or longer. Many of these early varieties have been lost already, making those that remain all the more precious. A number of these cultivars have been collected and saved by families and ethnic groups dating back many years. This practice protected the genetic make-up that made each variety successful within a given environment. These base characteristics have become invaluable and the genetic strains of these vegetables are the backbone of modern disease- and drought-resistant hybrids. It is this that makes the collection and preservation of these cultivars so important.

Left: *Many heirloom varieties have been selected for the way they perform in local garden conditions, rather than for crop size or uniformity.*

CROP ROTATION

This is the practice of grouping and growing related plants together and rotating them around different areas of land in a regimented fashion from year to year. Rotating your crops in this way has many advantages, including helping to prevent pest and disease problems from arising in the first place. This method of gardening is fundamental to successful organic growing. It has been practised for thousands of years and developed into a system that is easy to follow.

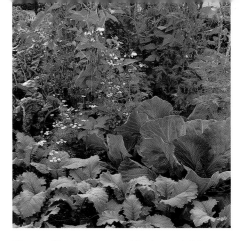

Above: *The secret to achieving a thriving and healthy kitchen garden is to rotate the crops on a regular basis.*

WHY ARE CROPS ROTATED?

Continuous cropping in the same area puts both plants and soil at risk. It not only allows large numbers of soil-borne pests and diseases to build up, but, because crops require the same nutrients from the soil year after year, the practice can deplete nutrient levels. A poor infertile soil produces weak unhealthy plants, which, in turn, will be more prone to pest and disease attacks. All these problems amount to reduced yields and even complete crop failure.

When crops are rotated, the groups are divided up into closely related plants that are prone to similar pests and diseases. For example, carrots, parsnips, beetroot and potatoes are members of one group and prone to carrot fly, whereas cabbage, kale, broccoli and Brussels sprouts, which are members of another group, can be prone to clubroot and cabbage root fly. If the groups are grown in different areas on a rotational basis, it can help to prevent the establishment of soil-borne pests and diseases.

Combined with regular additions of compost and manure, crop rotation will make the soil richer, replace certain nutrients and help prevent pH imbalances that can result from repeated crops of the same type of vegetable. Companion planting will also aid a rotational plan, particularly if the species improve pest control.

MAKING A ROTATIONAL PLAN

The basic rules of crop rotation are simple. If you are planning a four-year crop rotation, the plants you have selected are split up into five groups. Group one contains the legumes (peas and beans); group two contains the brassicas (cabbages, Brussels sprouts, broccoli, kale etc); group three contains the onion family and others (onions, lettuce, garlic, sweetcorn etc); group four includes root crops (potatoes, parsnips,

---

BENEFITS OF CROP ROTATION

There are many benefits to be gained from rotating your crops regularly.

- Prevents the build-up of soil pests and diseases
- Helps to prevent nutrient depletion from heavy-feeding crops
- Rotated crops produce higher yields
- Results in a healthier soil

---

carrots, beetroot etc); and finally group five houses permanent crops such as asparagus and rhubarb.

The vegetable plot is then divided into five sections. The permanent crops are given a specific area and are not moved or included in the rotational cycle. The remaining four groups are allocated an area in which to grow. Every year each group is moved on to the next plot, making it four years before the crops are grown on the same area of land again; hence the name crop rotation.

If space is limited, crops can be grown on a three-year rotation. Quite simply, the crops are split into three groups, plus the permanent ones. The plant groups are divided up as before except group three is incorporated into group one.

There is no need to grow each crop in every year of a cycle. Remember that it is the vegetable groups that dictate the cropping cycle according to their soil needs and any associated problems. Rotating the crops helps provide the correct soil requirements for certain crops. For example, cabbages and the rest of the group grow well in soil that has been manured the previous autumn, whereas carrots and other root crops (not including potatoes) do not. Where carrots are to be grown, then the plot will need to be dug deeply in readiness for them.

It is important that you plan where the crops are to be every year, so that you know their position for the following year. A comprehensive cropping plan can help you to maximize the yield on a year-round basis by working out successional sowings and intercropping and catch cropping. The plan needs to include not only the crops that will be grown but also the companion plants and the soil amendments that are needed to support the best possible growth of your plants.

COMMON DIFFICULTIES

When planning the cycle, you may encounter certain problems. Careful planning will show that potatoes often take up more space in a vegetable bed than any other crop and finding enough room to grow them in their allocated area may prove difficult. Other problems you may come across include overwintering brassicas or plants left in the ground for seed collection. This is when you find that practising crop rotation in a small garden is difficult and that you may not be able to practise a strict rotation.

If space is proving a problem, consider some of the following strategies. Keep brassicas together as a group and never plant them in the same ground two years running. Keep potatoes together every year; if you have planned a lot of potatoes, move all the other members from group four into group three. Also bear in mind that some root crops, such as potatoes, are manure-friendly, while others, like parsnips, are not. Finally, alternating shallow-rooted plants like cabbages or lettuce with deep-rooted plants like tomatoes or squash will allow the plants' roots to do much of the soil loosening that would otherwise have to be done by hand. This will help to preserve the health of the soil, while causing minimal disturbance to its ecosystem.

FOUR-YEAR CROP ROTATION

Divide the vegetables you have decided to grow into the five groups (plots 1–5) shown in the table. Draw a plan to indicate which group of crops goes where, using a different colour for each group. (Remember plot 5 is for the permanent crops.) Next year, move the crops in each group on to the next plot.

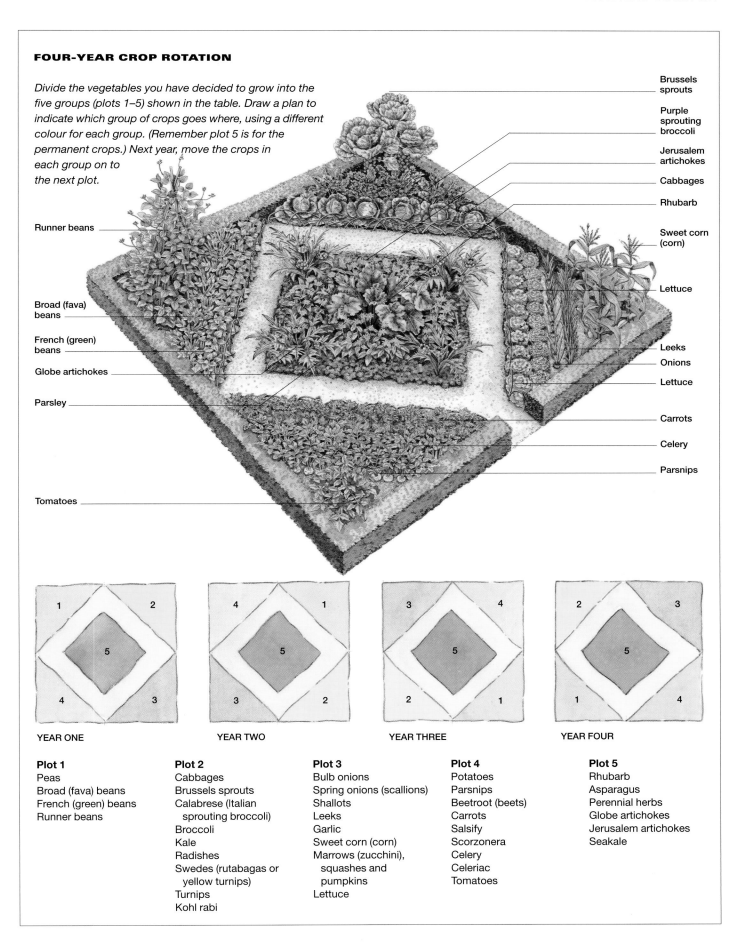

YEAR ONE

YEAR TWO

YEAR THREE

YEAR FOUR

Plot 1
Peas
Broad (fava) beans
French (green) beans
Runner beans

Plot 2
Cabbages
Brussels sprouts
Calabrese (Italian
  sprouting broccoli)
Broccoli
Kale
Radishes
Swedes (rutabagas or
  yellow turnips)
Turnips
Kohl rabi

Plot 3
Bulb onions
Spring onions (scallions)
Shallots
Leeks
Garlic
Sweet corn (corn)
Marrows (zucchini),
  squashes and
  pumpkins
Lettuce

Plot 4
Potatoes
Parsnips
Beetroot (beets)
Carrots
Salsify
Scorzonera
Celery
Celeriac
Tomatoes

Plot 5
Rhubarb
Asparagus
Perennial herbs
Globe artichokes
Jerusalem artichokes
Seakale

GROWING METHODS

There are many different ways to grow your crops. You can try the traditionally practised method of sowing crops in rows or be more adventurous and grow them in blocks. The crops you have chosen to grow can be planted into a number of different types of vegetable bed: flat beds, raised or edged beds and no-dig beds. Each method and type of bed has its own advantages and disadvantages, which are described here, so choose the one that best suits your needs.

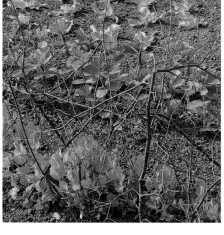

Above: *Twiggy sticks provide an ideal support for young climbers such as peas. They also look very decorative.*

PLANTING IN ROWS

This is the most traditionally practised and popular form of vegetable growing. It is an effective method because the spacing of the plants allows the crop to grow without excessive competition. In addition, it is relatively easy to add supports and protection such as cloches to the crops. However, this type of planting does have the disadvantage of needing relatively high maintenance. Due to the large amounts of bare earth left between the rows, the conditions are ideal for weed growth. Rows are spaced according to the optimum growth of the plants and so rows of pumpkins need to be much wider than those for carrots. Setting out rows in this way allows free movement of air along the rows. This results in fewer disease problems which can occur with more closely grown methods such as block plantings.

The rows are quite easily maintained by regular hoeing but can be wasteful of space, particularly in smaller gardens. They will produce sizeable vegetables, but this is offset by the actual yield per unit area being smaller than more intensive systems.

BLOCK PLANTING

In this method plants are grown in squares or rectangles rather than in straight rows. Blocks of plants are grown next to each other, for example in dimensions such as five plants by five plants. The numbers of plants grown can be larger or smaller than this. Block plantings use space efficiently, producing many more plants in an area than if grown in rows.

Well-tended soil can support planting that forms a close network of foliage over the soil. The soil will retain moisture extremely well underneath the canopy. It also stops weed seeds from germinating, resulting in a less weedy environment than

other growing methods. However, a close canopy of leaves can have disavantages, resulting in poor air flow and high humidity which are ideal for attracting diseases such as botrytis. During dry spells watering is essential for the health of the crops. Double check all watering that has been done because water easily runs off the dense cover of the leaves and never reaches much of the root system.

Blocks can be planted and managed at ground level or in slightly raised beds. They suit modestly sized vegetables, such as root and salad crops, that are usually grown in rows. You may have to be inventive with crop protection for early-sown crops, as cloches and low polythene tunnels do not cover the area well. The blocks are edged with permanent paths for easy access to the centre from any side so you need never walk on freshly cultivated soil. As a result, the soil does not get compacted and the closely grouped plants make maintenance and cultivation easier.

Seeding a block involves sowing the furrows thinly along close rows. For example, instead of the usual 30–40cm

(12–16in) distance between carrot rows, this can be reduced to 20–25cm (8–10in). Further space savings can result from growing as much as you can vertically, rather than sprawled over the ground. Wire fencing, netting or poles and tepees take up less space than blocks of climbing vegetables. This will also keep the climbing plants dry and free of disease.

FLAT BEDS

As the name suggests, flat beds are constructed at the natural ground level of your garden. They are the traditional way of cultivating ground for growing vegetables and are most suitable for gardens that have good soil. Flat beds will naturally raise the level of the soil, especially where organic matter is added on a regular basis as part of the cultivation regime, but the bed remains effectively at ground level. This form of gardening is relatively labour-intensive because all of the bed is cultivated, with large areas then being used as paths between the vegetables. With raised beds, there are no paths and only the growing areas are dug.

Left: *The close planting of crops in rows or blocks helps to retain soil moisture as well as reduce the growth of weeds.*

Above: *Plants such as beans can be trained over an arch in order to provide an ornamental and productive feature.*

RAISED AND EDGED BEDS

These can be freestanding garden beds or beds with wooden or brick walls constructed several inches above the normal ground level. Raised bed gardens not only look good but they also can help solve many problems associated with soils that are difficult to manage. Problems with soil are often aggravated in urban and suburban settings, where topsoil and vegetation may have been removed or the surface level changed during building work.

Raised bed gardens improve the environment for plants by lifting their roots above poor soil. The growing medium can be amended by the incorporation of manure and/or garden compost. Soil in these beds warms up earlier in the spring, allowing the seed sown to germinate quicker than if it is grown in flat beds. Beds should be located where they will receive full sun and with protection from prevailing winds. Do not site the beds in frost pockets or where air circulation is poor.

Drainage is important. Build the beds so that the crops will not become waterlogged, as good drainage is especially important when growing vegetables. If the bed contains clay soil, incorporate sand, grit or organic matter to improve drainage. Construct the bed so that it slopes about 2cm (¾in) per metre (yard) of horizontal distance away from any structures, or away from the centre of the bed.

NO-DIG BEDS

As the term suggests, no digging is involved in this method, which is a good way to retain good soil structure within a vegetable garden. Weeding is kept to a minimum and because the soil is not disturbed it will be alive with worms and other organisms. The bed is made on top of the ground and can be built over existing beds, lawns and even hard or rocky ground. Situate the bed in a sunny area that receives morning sun and has good drainage. It can be any size or shape, depending on your space. Start with a small bed – about 2 x 1.5m (6½ x 5ft) – but with a view to expanding in time.

When preparing the site it is not necessary to pull up the lawn or existing garden if the soil conditions are good, but if the ground is very poor, compacted or the drainage is bad, initial digging may be necessary.

Above: *Containers are an ideal way to grow a variety of crops where space is limited. These pots contain courgettes (zucchini).*

The outside wall of a no-dig bed is formed using logs, old planks, tiles, bricks or stones. Line the bed with a layer of plain wet newspaper, at least 6mm (¼in) thick. This layer should cover the enclosed area completely and overlap slightly, so as to kill off any weeds and stop new ones growing. Spread out a thin layer of hay or straw, ensuring that there are no gaps. Place a layer of good organic fertilizer, such as chicken manure, 20mm (¾in) thick, on top. Cover with a 20cm (8in) thick layer of loose bedding straw. Follow this with a 2cm (¾in) layer of good organic fertilizer and complete the bed with a top layer of garden compost, about 10cm (4in) thick. Make sure the bed is watered in well. Once it is settled you can plant out seedlings, but not seeds. Sowing seeds can begin when the bed has matured and the soil has become fine and crumbly.

No-dig beds that have been recently created are best for growing crops such as potatoes, lettuce, brassicas and cucurbits, whereas root crops grow better when the bed is mature. No-dig beds are best suited to planting vegetables in small blocks of different varieties rather than in long rows.

Left: *Vegetable beds need not be rectangular to be functional. This kitchen garden uses simple geometric shapes to provide interesting effects.*

COMPANION PLANTING

This is when two or more crops are grown together for the benefit of one or all. This technique creates a colourful landscape, made up of different species, which mirrors nature itself. Plants are grown together for several reasons, including to attract beneficial insects or to give off odours that deter or confuse pests. This is so different from large fields planted with only one crop, a monoculture that allows large numbers of pests and diseases to build up rapidly.

Above: *Nasturtiums have edible leaves and flowers as well as being a colourful companion plant.*

HOW COMPANION PLANTING WORKS

Plants have natural affinities with others of their kind. The smell of volatile oils from many plants discourages certain pests, making them excellent companion plants. A good example of this is the well-known relationship between the tomato plant and the French marigold (*Tagetes patula*). The scent of the French marigold is said to deter whitefly from entering the greenhouse and therefore avoids a whitefly attack on the tomato plant.

Plants such as yarrow (*Achillea*) and hyssop (*Hyssopus*) are just a couple of plants from a list of many that attract beneficial insects like hoverflies. The hoverflies will lay their eggs around these plants and, after hatching, the larval stage of the insect will start to eat adult aphids. So greedy are these larvae that they can eat up to 800 aphids before pupating. Many organic gardeners grow trays of single-flowered French marigolds to dot around their gardens, both in the vegetable and

Right: *Companion plants can provide welcome splashes of colour in the kitchen garden.*

BENEFITS OF COMPANION PLANTING

A mosaic of plants offers many benefits to the organic garden, some of which are outlined below.

- Creates a colourful landscape.
- Plants can attract benefical insects.
- Plant odour can deter harmful insects.
- A variety of plants together confuses pests from locating host plants.
- Plants attract birds that prey on pests.
- Flowers attract pollinators.

ornamental areas, in order to encourage these eating machines. This is both very effective and quite stunning to look at.

Certain distinct qualities of a plant have a proven benefit to others, such as fixing nitrogen in the soil. Clover in grass will fix nitrogen, offering the excess nitrogen produced to the surrounding grass which improves the yield. By the same token,

others are less suited as partners. It is never wise, for example, to plant two vegetables side by side that attract the same pests, as this effectively doubles the chances of attack. It is advisable to practise crop rotation or use companion planting in between them.

BENEFICIAL COMBINATIONS

There is little scientific evidence of these associations working, but if you talk to any organic practitioner, they will certainly provide plenty of anecdotal evidence. Tomatoes, for instance, like to be grown near basil and parsley plants. This is, of course, useful for cooks as well as gardeners. Separating rows of cabbages, broccoli or other brassicas with rows of onions has always been a popular combination, possibly due to the onion's strong scent confusing cabbage pests. Tomato plants also grow well next to cabbages and seem to deter caterpillars. Other beneficial combinations include leeks near carrots as they repel carrot flies, while Swiss chard thrives near carrots and beetroot. Never plant carrot and dill close by each other. This makes the carrots woodier and stronger-flavoured, and the dill milder and with weaker stems.

DECORATIVE COMPANION PLANTS

Certain flowers and flowering herbs offer potential benefits for a variety of vegetables. French marigolds (*Tagetes patula*) are cited as a wonder flower by many organic gardeners and the bright flowers make a colourful companion crop. They deter many pests, and seem to spur growth in roses. They are also said to reduce the number of soil nematodes, while attracting hoverflies and their larvae which eat aphids. French marigolds are frequently planted with pot marigolds (*Calendula officinalis*).

CROPS AND THEIR COMPANION PLANTS

While it is not an exact science, any practitioner of companion planting will tell you that individual crops have their "preferred companions".

Experience is the best guide, but the list below outlines some plant combinations that work well in most situations.

Apples Chives, foxgloves, wallflowers, nasturtiums, garlic, onions

Apricots Basil, tansy, wormwood

Asparagus Tomatoes, parsley, basil

Beans Carrots, cucumbers, cabbages, lettuce, peas, parsley, cauliflower, spinach, summer savory

Beans (broad/fava) Potatoes, sweetcorn (corn).

Beans (dwarf) Beetroot, potatoes

Beetroot Onions, kohl rabi, lettuce, cabbage, dwarf beans

Brussels sprouts Nasturtiums

Cabbages Beans, beetroot, celery, mint, thyme, sage, onions, rosemary, dill, potatoes, chamomile, oregano, hyssop, wormwood, nasturtiums, tansy, coriander (cilantro)

Carrots Peas, radishes, lettuce, chives, sage, onions, leeks

Cauliflowers Celery, beans, tansy, nasturtium

Celery Tomatoes, dill, beans, leeks, cabbage, cauliflowers

Chives Parsley, apples, carrots, tomatoes

Courgette (zucchini) Nasturtiums

Cucumbers Potatoes (early crop only), beans, celery, lettuce, sweetcorn, Savoy cabbages, sunflowers, nasturtiums

Kohl rabi Beetroot, onions

Garlic Roses, apples, peaches

Grapevines Geraniums, mulberries, hyssop, basil, tansy

Leeks Carrots, celery

Lettuce Carrots, onions, strawberries, beetroot, cabbages, radishes, tagetes

Onions Carrots, beetroot, lettuce, chamomile, kohl rabi, courgettes

Parsnips Peas, potatoes, peppers, beans, radishes, garlic

Peaches Tansy, garlic, basil, wormwood

Peas Potatoes, radishes, carrots, turnips

Potatoes Peas, beans, cabbage, sweetcorn, broad beans, green beans, nasturtium, marigolds, foxgloves, horseradish, aubergine (eggplant)

Pumpkin Sweetcorn

Radishes Lettuces, peas, chervil, nasturtium

Raspberries Tansy

Spinach Strawberries

Squash Sunflowers

Strawberries Borage, lettuce, spinach, sage, pyrethrum

Sunflowers Squash, cucumber

Sweetcorn (corn) Broad beans, potatoes, melons, tomatoes, cucumber, squash, tansy

Tomatoes Asparagus, celery, parsley, basil, carrots, chives, marigolds, foxgloves, garlic, sweetcorn

Turnips Peas, nasturtiums

White alyssum (*Lobularia maritima*), by reseeding frequently, helps to break up the soil and adds to its organic content, while chrysanthemums reduce nematodes, making for healthier soil. Mint almost always works with various types of squashes and brassicas to aid plant growth, although it can become invasive. Tansy (*Tanacetum*

Left: *Foxgloves (*Digitalis*) make excellent companion plants for growing under apple trees.*

vulgare) is said to repel ants, aphids and plant beetles although this, too, can become invasive if not regularly checked.

Chamomile (*Chamaemelum nobile*) is known as the "plant doctor" by some organic gardeners because of its alleged ability to encourage other plants to increase their production of essential oil, making plants such as rosemary and lavender taste and smell stronger. Chamomile is easy to grow and looks beautiful anywhere, although it should be kept well trimmed to avoid a straggly look. It is also thought that chamomile can help to activate the composting process if it is added to the compost heap.

Lavender (*Lavandula*) is a general insect repellent and makes an excellent small hedge. It is a great addition to the garden, attracting bees and numerous white and blue butterflies.

Plants that produce berries such as cotoneaster and the rowan tree (*Sorbus*) will attract birds into the garden. Birds, in turn, eat many pests, such as protein-rich

aphids, caterpillars and various flies. Thrushes are the unsung heroes of the garden because they decrease the snail population quite considerably.

Be prepared to experiment before committing to a companion species. Nasturtiums have been cited as an effective aphid control, although many wonder if they do this by attracting all the aphids to themselves. What works in one area may not always work elsewhere and experimentation is the key to success in this interesting yet uncertain area of organic gardening.

CROPS AND THEIR ANTAGONISTS

Some plants are highly antagonistic to one another. You should always avoid planting the following combinations.

Asparagus Onion and potato

Beans Chives, fennel or garlic

Carrots Dill

Carrots, cauliflower or potatoes Tomatoes

Peas Onion, garlic and shallots

Potato Pumpkin and summer squash

MAKING THE MOST OF YOUR SPACE

There are three basic growing techniques that you can use to make the most of your space. These are known as intercropping, catch cropping and successional sowing. By adopting the latter two practices, you will extend the cropping season instead of harvesting a crop all at once. You will also make use of the available space, therefore increasing yields. All that is needed is careful planning to work out which crops to sow and when.

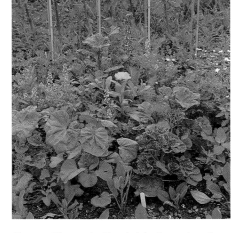

Above: *Close planting in blocks makes the most of available space and allows more crops to be raised in a season.*

INTERCROPPING

This kitchen-garden technique increases productivity and also helps to keep the numbers of weeds down. It refers to the practice of planting a fast-growing crop, such as carrots, radishes and lettuce, between main crops that are slower growing. These include vegetables such as cabbages, peas and potatoes.

Intercropping involves harvesting the quicker-growing crop first before the slower-growing one achieves total foliage cover of the soil or shades out the area. A good example of intercropping is to grow a crop of spring onions or lettuce between tomatoes. Similarly, spinach or radishes can easily be planted out early between sweetcorn or, alternatively, radishes can be planted between cabbages.

Intercropping can also be used to increase productivity. It ensures that no space is left unused and makes the most efficient use of light, nutrients and moisture. It will also reduce the amount of weeds in the vegetable patch by maintaining a continuous plant canopy over the soil.

One slight variation on the theme is to combine the benefits of a green manure with a crop. This can be useful in the case of winter crops because the green manure doubles up as a cover crop, protecting the soil from erosion and leaching as well as stabilizing soil temperatures. If a leguminous green manure is planted in late summer or early autumn in a bed along with leafy crops such as Brussels sprouts, it can provide nitrogen throughout the remaining growing season. It will also provide a boost for early crops that will be planted out after the green manure crop has been dug into the soil. While intercropping requires careful planning, it can increase the productivity of even a relatively small vegetable plot.

CATCH CROPPING

This technique is when fast-maturing vegetables, such as radishes and lettuce, are grown in an area of ground that has just been cropped and has a vacancy until the next crop is either sown or planted. The sowing of the catch crops can be done in between the main ones or after harvesting at the end of the season if there is time. It is important to know how long a crop takes to mature when planning catch cropping so that you do not sow anything that takes too long to mature in between the main crops.

Left: *Successional sowing in rows allows the same space in the vegetable plot to be kept productive throughout the growing season.*

ADVANTAGES OF INTERCROPPING AND CATCH CROPPING

Making the most of your space is not only productive, but it also has environmental advantages.

• Suppresses weed growth in the kitchen garden
• Increases the productivity of the vegetable patch
• Planting green manures enriches the soil with nitrogen
• Helps to protect against the erosion of the soil
• Helps prevent leaching

SUCCESSIONAL SOWING

This is the practice of sowing the seeds of fast-maturing vegetables at regular intervals several times during the growing season. This practice will ensure that you have a continuous supply of crops such as lettuces, carrots and spinach throughout the season. Successional sowing is also useful where crops are sown directly outdoors early in the season where they may be prone to frost damage. Early crops

Above: *The close spacing of rows and successional sowing of new rows allows the maximum use of space on your plot.*

such as lettuce and radish can be sown under the cover of, for example, a cloche where they will begin to develop earlier than would otherwise be possible. Subsequent sowings outdoors will mature later, thus extending the growing season for harvesting.

Gardeners with small plots can use this method by sowing only a half a row at any one time. This process is then repeated a week or so later, with further sowings as often as you like. This way you will have fresh vegetables for several weeks and will avoid a sudden glut.

Above: *Sweetcorn (corn) is a late-maturing crop that can be intercropped with fast-growing, early salad crops. This enables you to make the most of your growing space.*

SOWING IN THE OPEN

There can be nothing more satisfying than sowing seeds and watching in anticipation for them to germinate. Watching the seedlings grow in your kitchen garden, making it come alive with leaves, flowers and insects is a fantastic experience. One of the drawbacks of sowing out in the open is that you are at the mercy of the weather, but you can manipulate your garden environment by using cloches, small plastic bottles and polythene tunnels to increase your chances of success.

Above: *A dibber (dibble) is a very helpful tool to use when you are transplanting seedlings outside.*

SITE REQUIREMENTS

If you are a novice kitchen gardener, be assured that sowing seed is easier than you may think. In order to germinate successfully seeds need water, air, a suitable temperature and a place into which they can root in order to support the top growth that will follow. For this reason, good soil preparation is everything to organic success. Most garden soils are able to supply all the necessary elements and only slight modifications are usually necessary. However, it is important that the ground is prepared in a way that will enable the seed to germinate evenly and grow in a uniform environment. The prior preparation of a seedbed can provide the seed with the environment that it needs and has the added bonus of making the task of seed sowing easier.

Preparing a seedbed is simple. Following cultivation, the ground is levelled using a rake, held at a shallow angle, to break down any large clods. The art of levelling is to keep the rake angle shallow and move the high spots over into the low spots with even strokes. Hold the rake firmly at the rear and let the shaft run smoothly through the front hand. All stones and large objects, including organic matter such as twigs or previous crop debris, should be removed by combing them out with the teeth of the rake, while holding the tool in a near vertical position. The soil is then firmed with light treading. A light shuffle across the bed is best. Once firmed, lightly rake the soil again at a shallow angle to produce a light "fluffy" surface that runs freely through the teeth of the rake. This is the perfect environment for sowing and growing seeds.

SEED REQUIREMENTS

The conditions that seeds require to germinate are easy and straightforward to create. A well-aerated moist soil environment is almost all that the seed needs. Most seeds will germinate quite successfully once the temperature gets above 7°C (45°F). Seeds carry their own food supply that provides them with everything they need for those first crucial days following germination. Once the plant begins to establish and grow, it needs soil-borne nutrients. This means that the soil in which it is growing needs to be of the right fertility for the plant. Poorer soils can benefit from the addition of a base dressing with fish, blood and bone prior to sowing to give the boost that the developing plant needs, although loamier soils need only be properly dug and prepared to support germination.

SOWING SEEDS OUTDOORS

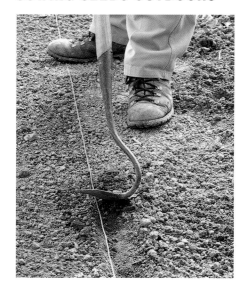

1 *Set a tight string line where you intend your crop row to be and make a shallow drill with the edge of a swan-necked hoe.*

2 *Water dry soil using a watering can fitted with a fine rose about an hour before sowing and allow to drain.*

3 *Sow the seed thinly along the length of the row. Larger seed may be station sown at regular intervals.*

Some seeds can benefit from being soaked for a short period in tepid water just before planting to help them take on the water they need for germination. This is especially true of beets, but other large seeds also benefit from this treatment.

SOWING IN ROWS

Seed is usually sown in rows. Using a tightly drawn garden line as a guide, draw the corner of a swan-necked hoe along the line to create a shallow drill of about 1–2cm (⅜–¾in) depth, depending upon the seed's individual requirements. Dry ground can be watered after the drill is made. Sow the seed thinly and mix fine seed with silver sand to make it easier to distribute evenly. Mark the end of each row with a label before moving on to the next.

STATION SOWING

Seeds of larger growing plants, particularly those with seed that is large enough to handle, benefit from station sowing. This involves sowing two or three seeds at intervals that will be the eventual crop spacing. If all three germinate, then the two weaker ones are removed or transplanted to gaps where none has germinated.

WIDE ROWS

Certain seeds, particularly peas and beans, benefit from being planted in wide rows. Two rows are effectively station sown at

once, one on each side of a drill that is 15cm (6in) across. The drill is made with the flat of the hoe and after sowing the soil is carefully raked back. Make sure that you do not disturb the seeds from their stations.

BROADCASTING (BLOCKS)

Broadcasting is an ancient method of seed sowing that was used to sow large areas of crops. It involves a "broadcasting" action that separates the seed to an even spacing. The easiest way to do this in small vegetable plots is to split the seed into two halves, mixing small seed with fine sand. Scatter the seed carefully, letting it run from your hand in even arcs as you move your arm from side to side. Sow each half of the

Left: *Station sowing is ideal for larger seeds or seedlings that resent disturbance. Use a marked stick to set the spacing of the seed.*

seed at a 90-degree angle to the other, thereby assuring an even distribution. Gently rake the seed in once sown and lightly water if needed.

PROTECTING SEEDLINGS

Seedbeds, with their fine "fluffed" earth, act as magnets to birds and animals. Some may take the seed from the ground, but, in truth, most will find it more attractive as a dust bath or litter tray. Once the seedlings emerge, however, some birds find them irresistible. They must be kept out with some form of barrier. One of the easiest methods is to form a low tunnel of chicken wire, supporting this on hoops. For larger areas, a series of stakes in the ground can be covered with netting to keep birds at bay. Sticks with thread or string stretched between them are also effective, but less easily removed for you to tend the crop.

LABELLING

When you sow a row or area of seeds, label it straightaway. Re-usable plastic labels are the best option. Each label should have the name and variety of the plant sown. You may also wish to record the sowing date and if the seed was pre-treated.

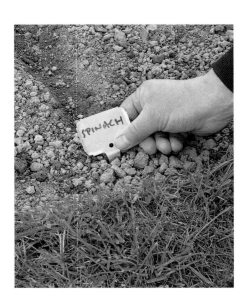

4 *Place a label at the end of each row, showing the crop name, variety and the sowing date, before you start a new one.*

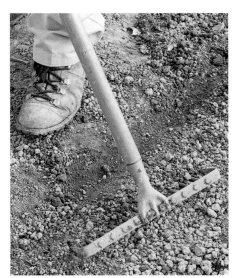

5 *Gently cover the seed using a rake. Take care not to disturb or move the seed in the row when you cover it.*

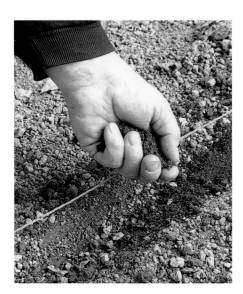

6 *Alternatively, seed can be covered using a soil and potting mix. This is useful on heavy soils and avoids capping (surface hardening).*

SOWING UNDER GLASS

Sowing seed under glass extends the growing season and enables you to raise tender crops that only survive outside in warmer months. It is also ideal for rapidly establishing plants to use as catch crops and as early companion plants. In short, it offers variety and choice for your cropping regimes. Plants raised under glass can be grown on until they reach a size where they are better able to resist pest attack. They can also be planted out at their final spacing, thereby avoiding thinning or gaps in rows.

Above: *A propagator is a useful piece of equipment for raising your seed in ideal growing conditions.*

HEAT REQUIREMENTS

Most seeds have a preferred temperature range within which they will grow. A heated greenhouse, a conservatory or even a warm living room will often provide this, although seeds needing a constant high temperature may need a propagator. Such seeds are mercifully rare among vegetables, although cucumbers, tomatoes and peppers are good examples of crops that will benefit if they are first started off in a propagator.

CHOICE OF CONTAINER

There are a variety of containers that may be used to sow seed under glass. The most common form is the plastic seed tray which has now largely replaced the wooden seed tray. Although more attractive, wooden trays are difficult to keep clean and may harbour plant diseases. Plastic trays can be made of durable polyurethane or sometimes a more flimsy, thin, moulded plastic which is intended for single use. They are available in a variety of sizes, although small 9cm (3½in) pots may be more suitable when you are raising only a few plants.

Modular seed trays are another option. These are made up of individual cells, and a single seed is sown into each one. Seeds that are sown in these trays have the advantage of not suffering any root disturbance when they are planted out in their eventual position. The same is true of some biodegradable pots, which are formed out of paper and coir. These are better (environmentally speaking) than those made from peat, but any recycled material used for these trays is acceptable in the organic kitchen garden.

Inventive recycling can also provide an array of useful sowing containers. Re-using plastic cups, vegetable packing trays and

any other throw-away items that might otherwise end up on a landfill site are all possibilities worth exploring. Old plastic bottles make good individual propagation cowls for small pots and plastic bags can also be used to cover the tops of pots and trays in order to maintain humidity.

PROPAGATORS

These are, in effect, mini-hothouses that help to keep the seed in a warm, moist, stable environment both above and below the soil line. Expensive propagators involve the use of electric soil-warming cables and some have thermostats to control the soil temperature. Many are designed for use in the greenhouse, but

Above: *Modular trays are ideal for planting large seeds and avoid disturbance to roots when planting out or potting on.*

Left: *Many propagators have ventilators on the top in order to aid the flow of fresh air to the seedlings.*

some models are narrow enough for use on a windowsill inside the house. Alternatively, instead of buying the whole propagator, you can purchase a heating mat on which the seed trays can stand in order to receive heat at the bottom. This system has the advantage of being mobile and easily moved about from area to area. Another cheaper method is to buy soil-heating cables to bed into sand. The seed trays sit on the bed of heated sand to receive an even supply of bottom heat.

AFTERCARE OF SEEDLINGS

Once seeds begin to germinate, they can be moved gradually into a less humid environment. The trays are freed of plastic covers, or the propagator vents or lids are opened and, after a few days, the lid is removed completely. As soon as the seedlings reach a size at which they can be handled, they are carefully pricked out into individual pots or larger boxes and trays. Always handle the seedlings by the leaves,

Above: *Individual pots can be used for large seeds. Plant two seeds per pot and remove the weaker seedling.*

SOWING IN TRAYS

1 *Fill a seed tray with propagation potting mix that has been thoroughly mixed. Fill the tray to overflowing and do not firm in the potting mix.*

2 *Using a straightedged piece of board, level the surface of the potting mix by carefully moving the board across the top of the tray.*

3 *Water the tray and leave to drain for about 20 minutes before sowing the seed on the moist surface of the potting mix.*

4 *Larger seed can be placed on the surface of the potting mix at regular intervals. Regular spacing will prevent overcrowding.*

5 *Once the seed has been sown, use a sieve to cover the surface with a fine layer of potting mix.*

6 *Do not cover the seeds of plants that require light for germination. Always check the growing requirements of plants before sowing the seed.*

gently lifting each one from beneath, using a dibber (dibble). Never hold them by the stems because this can cause a great deal of damage to the developing plant. They should be spaced at least 5cm (2in) apart to allow for subsequent development. Water

Above: *Growing vegetables in pots under glass can extend the growing season and also provide a colourful greenhouse display.*

the transplanted seedlings with a fine upturned rose attached to a watering can that has been filled with water overnight, thus bringing it up to room temperature and not giving the transplants a shock of cold water. Keep the seedlings on a warm and sheltered windowsill or in a greenhouse or conservatory. A constant temperature will promote healthy growth.

HARDENING OFF

Plants that have been grown in a greenhouse cannot be put straight outside because their growth is too soft to withstand the cold. They must be gradually hardened off and acclimatized to outdoor conditions. The young plants are hardened off by moving them from the greenhouse and into a cold frame, planted out under cloches, low polythene tunnels or horticultural fleece. Open up the cloches and cold frames or remove the fleece

during the day and replace at night for a week or two before planting out or removing the cloches completely. Remove low polythene tunnels after a couple of weeks depending on the weather conditions. If these are severe, leave in place for longer.

Above: *Watering from below by pouring the water into the base of the seed tray will prevent damage to newly emerging seed.*

THINNING AND TRANSPLANTING

Thinning seedlings not only allows the plants left in the soil to develop and mature into their natural shape and habit, but it is an essential process for good plant health. Thinned seedlings can be transplanted into bare areas or more often special seedbeds are set up or crops are grown under glass and the whole batch of seedlings are transplanted into their final destination within the vegetable garden.

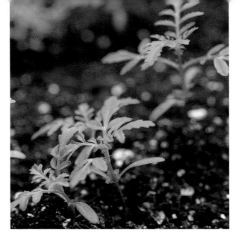

Above: *Growing plants from seed is one of the most satisfying ways of producing new stock for the kitchen garden.*

WHY THIN SEEDLINGS?

All plants need space to develop and grow. Plants that are growing too closely compete not only for space, but also for light, water and important nutrients. In addition to this competitive stress, they also become prone to a variety of fungal diseases, as the air is not able to move around them. Thinning the seedlings helps to counteract these problems and will result in larger, stronger and healthier plants.

HOW TO THIN SEEDLINGS

Thinning is essentially two processes in one. Firstly, you are removing all the plants that are excess to requirements and at the same time you are selecting the biggest, healthiest and strongest plants that will be retained to form the crop.

Before starting to thin, dry ground must be watered, preferably the night before you intend to thin. A measuring stick, marked with the appropriate crop distance, can be used to show the approximate position of

Above: *Rows of seedlings are often too crowded and need to be thinned when the plants are young.*

Left: *Seedlings grown elsewhere in the garden can be lifted and replanted in their eventual positions. This method is good for crops that need wide spacing.*

stressed if their roots are disturbed. The alternative, in this case, is to snip off the seedlings at ground level with a pair of sharp scissors, thereby avoiding root disturbance.

the individual plants. Remove all the plants in between each of the markers, selecting the healthiest plant at or near the mark on the stick. If there are no plants at the marked point, then you can transplant one of the seedlings that is excess to requirements into this position. When you are removing the excess plants, place a finger on the soil at either side of the seedling that is being kept. This protects it from root disturbance. Once you have finished, water the remaining seedlings with a fine rose on a watering can to re-firm the soil around the plants. The seedlings that have been removed can be put on the compost heap.

Avoid thinning with this method on hot dry days or in windy conditions, as the remaining seedlings may become water-

THINNING DISTANCES

The following measurements are the distances that need to be left between thinned seedlings.

Beetroot	7.5–10cm (3–4in)
Broad beans	
(fava beans)	23cm (9in)
Carrots	7.5cm (3in)
Dwarf French beans	
(bush green beans)	20cm (8in)
Florence fennel	25cm (10in)
Kohl rabi	20cm (8in)
Lettuce	23cm (9in)
Parsley	15cm (6in)
Peas	5cm (2in)
Parsnips	15–20cm (6–9in)
Radishes	2.5–5cm (1–2in)
Runner beans	25–30cm (10–12in)
Salsify	15cm (6in)
Scorzonera	15cm (6in)
Spinach	15cm (6in)
Spring onions	
(scallions)	5cm (2in)
Swedes (rutabaga	
or yellow turnip)	30cm (12in)
Swiss chard	30cm (12in)
Turnips	15–20cm (6–8in)

TRANSPLANTING SEEDLINGS

1 *Water your row of seedlings at least an hour before transplanting and preferably the night before if no rain has fallen.*

2 *Using a fork to loosen the soil, gently lift the seedlings. Take care to handle them by their leaves and never touch the stems.*

3 *Using a tight line, straight edge or notched planting board, replant the seedlings at the appropriate spacing for that crop.*

4 *Gently water the seedlings immediately after sowing. Never let roots dry out at any stage during transplanting.*

COMMON PLANTING DISTANCES
Always allow the correct spacing between crop plants so that they will grow into healthy specimens.

Asparagus	30–38cm (12–15in)
Aubergines (eggplant)	60cm (24in)
Broccoli	60cm (24in)
Brussels sprouts	50–75cm (20–30in)
Cabbages	30–50cm (12–20in)
Calabrese (Italian sprouting broccoli)	15–23cm (6–9in)
Cauliflowers	50–75cm (20–30in)
Celeriac	30–38cm (12–15in)
Celery	23–30cm (9–12in)
Courgettes (zucchini)	60cm (24in)
Cucumbers	60cm (24in)
Garlic	15cm (6in)
Globe artichokes	75cm (30in)
Jerusalem artichokes	30cm (12in)
Kale	60cm (24in)
Leeks	15cm (6in)
Marrows (zucchini)	60cm (24in)
Onion sets	10cm (4in)
Peppers	45–60cm (18–24in)
Potatoes	30–38cm (12–15in)
Pumpkins	90–180cm (3–6ft)
Rhubarb	75–90cm (30–36in)
Runner beans	25–30cm (10–12in)
Seakale	30cm (12in)
Shallots	15–18cm (6–7in)
Sweetcorn (corn)	30cm (12in)
Tomatoes	60cm (24in)

TRANSPLANTING SEEDLINGS
The most common way of transplanting seedlings involves planting container-grown plants into open ground. Early vegetable crops can easily be raised in this way. The other method is to raise seedlings in open ground near to where they are to be planted out. Transplanting outdoor seedlings means that a smaller area of the vegetable plot is needed for sowing and, in consequence, a smaller seedbed is required. Transplanting seedlings is a good way of growing plants such as lettuce that are to be used in catch-cropping beds or where plants are to be planted out in no-dig beds.

The ideal time for transplanting outdoor seedlings is during damp overcast weather because this helps to prevent the seedlings' roots drying out. As is the case when thinning the plants, the seedlings will need watering the evening before. It is best to dig up only a few plants at a time, discarding any that are weak, damaged or appear to be sick. Seedlings can be placed in a plastic bag to maintain humidity around them while they are out of the ground.

A garden line can be set out in the vegetable patch in a similar manner to the way in which it is placed for preparing a seed drill. The position of the plants can then be determined using a measuring stick. Use a dibber (dibble) or thin trowel to plant the seedlings, firming lightly around the base before moving on to the next transplant. Once the row is completed, it is important that you water them in.

For catch cropping or planting among other plants, the surrounding crop may well determine the spacings between the transplants, although the procedure remains exactly the same.

AFTERCARE

The aftercare that your crops require is essential to ensure healthy plants that produce high yields. There are a number of different techniques that are listed below to help you on your way. Just remember that the more effort you put in then the better they will taste. As well as judicious watering and feeding, you will also have to weed the vegetable plot and provide some form of plant protection and support. But the reward of such care and attention is delicious home-grown produce.

Above: *Regular cropping of vegetables such as this ruby chard will encourage the development of new growth.*

WATERING

Vegetables need watering if there is no significant rainfall. This is especially true when the crops are young and only have shallow roots. Having a soil that is rich in organic matter is an advantage because it conserves water in the soil, particularly if the soil is sandy. You can enrich the soil by digging in organic matter, growing green manures or by continuous mulching.

If you have a large garden, mulching around the crop with straw, farmyard manure, garden compost or another similar substance can help to limit water loss. When you water, it is best to give the plants a thorough soaking, allowing the water to penetrate deeply. Giving a light watering will just encourage shallow surface roots that are easily damaged by prolonged drought. Prolonged dry periods also encourage plants to bolt, thus ruining the crop.

Certain plants such as cabbages and lettuces are naturally shallow rooted, whereas others such as tomatoes and squash are naturally deep rooted. Shallow rooters especially benefit from mulching and may need watering often in hot summers.

FEEDING

This is generally only necessary for heavier feeding plants such as pumpkins and marrows, but can provide a tonic for any crop during the growing season. Specific nutrient deficiencies are rare in the garden if a regular crop rotation and soil enrichment programme is followed, but if specific shortages are noticed, they must be countered immediately. Good liquid feeds can be made in your back garden. Try making compost tea or "worm liquid", as these are an excellent choice for actively growing plants.

Above: *The effort you put into protecting and caring for your crops will be rewarded at harvest time.*

Apply these feeds once every week or two. Many plants are given their main feed annually. This type of feeding is normally applied to fruit trees and bushes in the spring and is best applied in the form of a slower-release fertilizer such as bonemeal.

WEEDING

Check your plants regularly and try to keep them as weed-free as possible. Remember that weeds compete with your plants for light, space, water and nutrients. It is better to weed a little and often than to weed irregularly. Even areas that have been mulched or have close cropping regimes need regular checks and weeds removed.

PLANT PROTECTION

Pests and diseases come in many different forms. Over time you will learn which specific problems your garden is prone to. Keep a yearly notebook of all the things that affect your crop each season, noting what control measures you used and how effective they were. In time you will have a record of how and when to manage pests and other problems in your own garden.

Above: *The careful harvesting of crops is essential if they are to store well. Here, carrots are being lifted with a garden fork.*

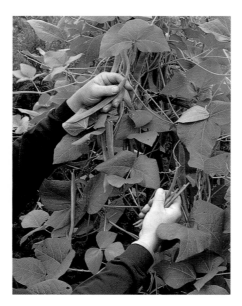

Above: *The regular harvesting of peas and beans will help to extend the length of the harvest period.*

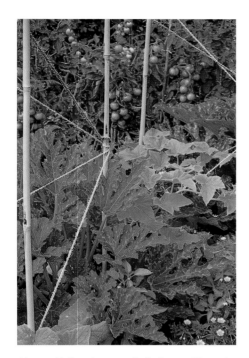

Above: *Taller plants and climbers will need some form of support. Canes or sticks with twine tied between them provide ideal temporary supports.*

PROVIDING SUPPORT

Plants may need supporting, especially climbers such as peas and beans. This support must begin at an early age, using twiggy pea sticks or hazel sticks, both of which can look ornate. Bamboo canes can be used for a host of climbing plants, but it is more ethically correct to use local materials rather than to use a product that has been transported thousands of miles. Squashes can be grown up fancy supports made from stakes and strong string or rope, making a curious garden feature. Other plants such as globe artichokes and Florence fennel can benefit from individual supports for their stems.

Above: *Marrows and pumpkins are easily stored in trays that should then be kept in a cool dark place.*

HARVESTING AND STORING

When harvesting, it is tempting to pick the good specimens and leave the rest, but remember to pick and compost poor or rotten ones as well as the best of the crop. Diseased or damaged crops can begin to rot and may infect the remaining harvest.

Freshly picked vegetables are higher in nutritional value than stored ones. So, during the growing season, pick what you need and store the surplus. Choosing when to pick a certain vegetable is a matter of taste. Some prefer to pick produce such as beans when they are young, small and succulent, whereas others prefer the beans to be more mature.

Crops can be stored in a number of ways. Root crops can be left in the ground in all but the coldest winters, lifting them as they are needed. Some crops, such as parsnips, actually develop a better taste after they have been subjected to frost. Alternatively, root crops can be stored in a cool dark place. They should be cleaned and stored in sand and a sterile organic substance such as coir, untreated sawdust, fine leaf mould, fine bark or sterilized soil.

Store other vegetables on shelves or boxes, ensuring that they do not touch. Onions and garlic are best kept in open sacks or in strings. Cabbages can be kept in nets until needed for up to two to three months. Other brassicas such as Brussels sprouts and swedes are best kept outside in the ground, harvesting them as needed.

Freezing is another storage option. Some vegetables, such as asparagus, beans and cauliflowers, are best blanched in boiling water for a couple of minutes before freezing. Alternatively, you can cook the vegetables and then freeze them, as is the case for marrows and Jerusalem artichokes.

Above: *Store root crops such as carrots in a cool dark place and cover them in sterile sawdust, leaf mould or coir.*

CROPS FOR STORING OVER WINTER

Harvest time often brings the problem of a crop glut. Storage can enable you to enjoy this bounty for longer.

Asparagus Best consumed fresh. Cook or blanch before freezing
Aubergines (eggplant) Cook before freezing
Beetroot (beets) Shelf storage or pickling
Broad (fava) beans Freezing or drying
Brussels sprouts Freezing. Leave on plant until needed
Cabbages Freezing or shelf storage. Leave in ground in mild conditions
Carrots Leave in ground in mild conditions. Shelf storage
Cauliflowers Blanch before freezing. Shelf storage if hung upside down in dark and misted
Celery Cook before freezing. Limited shelf storage
Courgettes (zucchini) Cook before freezing. Limited shelf storage
Dwarf French beans (bush green beans) Freezing
Garlic In sacks or strung
Kale Harvest through winter
Kohl rabi Leave in ground if mild or protected, medium shelf storage
Leeks Freezing, leave in ground in mild conditions, shelf storage
Marrows (zucchini) Cook before freezing, shelf storage
Onions In sacks or strung
Parsnips Leave in ground until needed or late winter
Peas Freezing or drying on plant
Peppers Blanch before freezing. Pickle or dry
Potatoes Store in paper sacks once cleaned and dried
Pumpkins Cook before freezing. Good shelf storage if fully ripe
Rhubarb Cook before freezing
Runner beans Freezing
Shallots In sacks or strung
Spinach Cook then freeze
Swedes (rutabaga or yellow turnip) Leave in ground until needed (may go woody by late winter)
Sweetcorn (corn) Freezing or pickling
Tomatoes Cook before freezing. Pickle
Turnips Leave in ground until needed

GROWING HERBS

Herbs are valued for their culinary, medicinal, decorative and aromatic properties. They come in a diverse range of sizes, shapes and habits, ranging from ground-creeping thyme through to the tall architectural stems of angelica. The choice of herbs is so great that there is always something to offer a gardener with only a window box, hanging basket or a small space. A herb garden offers a treat for the senses and these fragrant plants are also easy to grow in the organic garden.

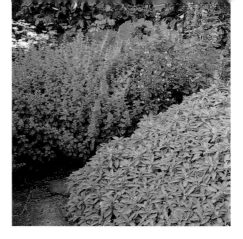

Above: *Herbs are easy to grow given the right growing conditions. They provide an attractive, often fragrant, display.*

WHERE TO GROW HERBS

Herbs can be grown in a range of settings, such as custom-designed herb gardens and ornamental borders. They can also be grown as companion plants in the vegetable garden and are eminently suited to growing in containers, hanging baskets and window boxes. They are especially useful if grown near the kitchen.

Herbs range from tall showy herbaceous plants such as fennel (*Foeniculum vulgare*) and tansy (*Tanacetum vulgare*) to ground-hugging cushion plants such as thyme (*Thymus vulgaris*). The majority of herbs originate from dry sunny environments and so need sunshine to help them develop their essential oils. It is best to site herbs in an open, sunny spot in the garden where they will thrive.

SOIL PREPARATION

Drier sites suit most herbs, and the sunnier and hotter the site the better they will taste. The taste and smell of herbs is usually due to the production of essential oils within the plants. If they are grown in hot conditions, then the concentrations of essential oils will be greater. Growing herbs in very moist rich soils can accelerate their growth, but will result in a milder flavour. They will also look better and flower less than their "hot-site" counterparts and be easier to harvest.

Herbs are, however, best grown in a soil that is loamy with some added organic matter. The ideal pH is 6.5 to 7.0, which means that herbs can easily be planted among vegetables in the kitchen garden.

Above: *You can restrict the spread of invasive plants such as mint (*Mentha*) by planting them in pots or buckets that are then buried in the ground.*

SOWING HERB SEED

Herbs may be sown directly in the soil outdoors, just like vegetables. The preparation of the seedbed and the sowing techniques are exactly the same, and they can easily be interplanted or block planted among other vegetables.

Alternatively, herb seeds may be planted under cover, raising them in the same way as early vegetables and bedding plants and then hardening them off before planting out in the garden. This method is especially useful for more tender, leafy herbs such as basil or coriander (cilantro).

Left: *Herbs are an important element in both ornamental and kitchen gardens, being decorative as well as useful.*

Above: *Pinching out newly planted herbs such as this bay (*Laurus*) will encourage bushy, leafy growth.*

Basil (*Ocimum basilicum*), for example, associates well with outdoor tomatoes, both in the garden and in the kitchen. These can be planted out together from an indoor sowing and the crop will be mutually complementary. Indoor sowing can also provide you with herbs that can be cropped earlier in the season, effectively extending the useful life of your organic herb garden.

PLANTING HERBS

1 *Excavate a planting hole that is about a quarter to half as big again as the plant's rootball. Make sure it is deep enough.*

2 *Ensure that the top of the compost is the same level as the surrounding soil. Refill the gap around the rootball and firm the soil.*

3 *Water the plant immediately after planting. Keep the plant well watered until it is fully established into the surrounding soil.*

PLANTING HERBS IN THE GARDEN

Herbs can be sited anywhere in the garden as long as it is sunny. They have a range of forms and colours and often make valuable additions to the ornamental garden. Foxgloves (*Digitalis*), sage (*Salvia officinalis*) and the curry plant (*Helichrysum italicum*) are a few examples of herbs that can be used in annual and herbaceous borders as well as in the kitchen garden. Some herbs, such as mint (*Mentha*) and lemon balm (*Melissa officinalis*), can become very invasive if they are not contained in a pot or sunken sink when growing among other plants in an ornamental border. Remove the flower-heads from the mint before they have had a chance to seed, as the seed will germinate all over your border.

PLANTING HERBS IN CONTAINERS

Herbs make excellent subjects for use in pots and containers and are wonderful for patio gardens that catch plenty of summer sun, although you need to make sure that the potting mix never dries out. Raised beds, which provide good drainage, are also good areas for growing herbs. Always plant them in a free-draining potting mix that will not become waterlogged. There are numerous cultivars of culinary herbs that can be used for ornamental purposes, and groups of pot-grown herbs can be extremely decorative as well as supplying you with a range of fresh flavourings. Thyme, rosemary, lavender and sage are all good choices to grow in pots, either outdoors or on your windowsill.

Above: *Herbs are easily grown in a container which will provide an excellent focal point in the kitchen garden.*

Herb pots require little maintenance, save for watering and the occasional feed during the growing season. Most are rarely long term and are best restarted yearly or every other year. Herbs that are permanently in pots, such as bay trees, will need repotting every year. Spreading subjects like thyme can be lifted and both top-pruned and root-pruned prior to repotting.

Mint and other spreading herbaceous subjects may need dividing and repotting from time to time. This is done by splitting the crown of the plant into smaller pieces and then repotting one of these back into the container with some fresh potting mix. Dividing in this way is best performed annually for very vigorous herbs. Harvesting on a regular basis is often enough to control the growth of many potted herb arrangements (where a number are planted in one container), but a light trim may also be necessary from time to time.

Potted herbs may also be grown in the greenhouse to ensure a supply both earlier and later in the season. Try growing basil (*Ocimum basilicum*), coriander (cilantro; *Coriandrum sativum*), chives (*Allium schoenoprasum*) and dill (*Anethum graveolens*) in pots because this will save money if you spend a lot on fresh herbs. Pots raised under glass can be brought into the kitchen for ease of use. A series of successional sowings under glass will ensure that you have fresh herbs for most or even all of the year, both indoors and out.

Above: *Planting spreading herbs such as thyme (*Thymus*) in pots will help to control them and can also be decorative.*

HARVESTING AND STORING HERBS

Many commonly used culinary herbs such as basil, coriander (cilantro), chives and parsley can be grown indoors on a windowsill or conservatory during the cooler winter months if you have space. If you are not able to spare growing room for these, most are easily stored for use later. Herbs are easily harvested and most of the storage techniques are simple and straightforward.

Above: *Aromatic herbs such as rosemary* (Rosmarinus officinalis) *can be used to flavour bottles of olive oil.*

HOW TO HARVEST HERBS

Various parts of herbs, including the leaves, flowers, fruits and seeds, are gathered at different times, depending upon the plant and the part that provides the desirable properties. Annual leafy herbs such as basil (*Ocimum basilicum*) and parsley (*Petroselinum crispum*) should be carefully picked, never taking more than about 10 per cent of the growth in a single picking.

The same is true of perennials such as sage (*Salvia officinalis*), thyme (*Thymus vulgaris*) and rosemary (*Rosmarinus officinalis*) because severe pruning or over-stripping of the leaves will weaken the plant. It is important that you not remove more than one-third of the growth at any one time. If you harvest carefully, you will get a more vigorous leaf growth that will result in healthier plants.

As a general rule, pick herbs just before the plant is about to flower, which is when they have the strongest flavour. Pick the leaves when they are fresh and at their sweetest, selecting blemish-free, upper leaves. Collect the leaves in early morning or late evening, provided they are dry, rather than in bright afternoon sun when the plant's sap is rising. This is when the aroma of herbs is at its strongest and is easily lost if picked during this time of day. Flowers such as borage (*Borago officinalis*) and lavender (*Lavandula*), however, are best picked just before they reach full bloom and once they begin to open in the heat of the day.

Rhizomes, like ginger and turmeric, are collected in autumn, just as the leaves begin to change colour and the maximum amount of nutrition has been stored. Use a fork to gently free the roots from the soil and always avoid "hand-pulling" them. Choose only the best ones and use a vegetable brush to gently loosen any dirt. If you do need to wash them, do so quickly in cold water and avoid soaking them, as this can result in lost flavour.

Harvesting seeds tends to vary from plant to plant. Some seeds, like those of borage, simply fall to the ground as soon as they are ripe. Thyme seeds are very small and hard to see. Parsley and coriander seeds shake off very easily, and frequently the plants will have sown next year's crop for you before you realize they have gone to seed. One method of harvesting any seed that is difficult to collect is to tie a small paper bag over the flower head when the seeds start to form, ensuring that you can collect the seed without losing any. It would be advisable to use this method for collecting from plants with small seed as they can drop off when ripe or sometimes spring from the plant.

Above: *The best time to harvest herbs is usually just before they flower. This is when they have their strongest flavour.*

Above: *Herbs can be dried for later use by hanging them in bunches in a dry place out of direct sunlight.*

DRYING HERBS AND FLOWERS

Store herbs in a cool, dry place with minimum exposure to air and sunlight. One of the most popular methods of preserving them for use during the winter months is drying. This method can actually improve the flavour of some herbs, particularly the leaves of bay trees (*Laurus nobilis*). Herbs may be dried in bundles secured with a rubber band or string and hung upside down from a rack in a dry location such as an airing cupboard or shed.

When drying the herbs, the temperature of the area should not exceed 30°C (86°F) because the plants' essential oils will evaporate at or above this temperature. Do not dry your herbs in the kitchen where they will be spoiled by the humidity caused by cooking.

Fresh herbs can also be placed in brown paper bags. Remember to label the bags because it will be hard to distinguish between the herbs once they have dried. Store in a dry, dark, cool place until the herbs inside are dry, shaking the bags occasionally so that the plants dry evenly. Remove any stems and store the dried herbs in airtight jars. Keep the jars away from light to protect the colour and flavour of the herbs. Roots are best chopped into small pieces and dried in an oven. In general, you can expect those that you have grown and dried yourself to last at least two years.

STORING HERBS

Herbs can also be preserved in other ways, so that you can use them in cooking throughout the year.

Herb salts In a cool oven, spread a layer of ground salt on a sheet of greaseproof (waxed) paper. Sprinkle the chopped fresh herbs on top of the salt and bake for 10–20 minutes. When the herbs are dry, let them cool and place in a jar. Chives, oregano, thyme, lemon balm, lemon thyme, parsley, rosemary and basil can all be treated this way.

Puréeing This method involves mixing approximately 60ml (4tbsp) of olive oil with 2l (8 cups) fresh basil leaves which have been washed and dried. These are blended in a processor until puréed before being transferred to a jar. Stir each time you use it and top with a thin layer of oil afterwards. The purée should keep for up to one year in a refrigerator.

Above: *After herbs have been hung up to dry, separate the seeds from the dry flower heads before storing in tightly sealed jars.*

Freezing herbs Herbs such as dill, fennel, basil and parsley freeze well. The herbs should be cleaned and put into separate, labelled freezer bags. Alternatively, chop the leaves and freeze them with a little water in ice-cube trays. Chop the herbs finely, filling each cube, half with herbs and half with water, before freezing. Transfer the frozen cubes to plastic bags and label. Frozen herbs are best used within six months.

HERBAL INFUSIONS

You can also make a hot infusion of leafy herbs by placing the herb and any fine-quality olive oil in a glass bowl. This is then placed over a pan of gently simmering water and heated gently for about three hours, ensuring that the water in the pan does not dry out. The strained oil, once it has cooled, should be stored in airtight bottles or jars.

A cool infusion of flowery herbs involves using fresh herbs such as chamomile which are ground with a pestle and mortar and packed into a large jar and covered with oil. The sealed jar is then left in a warm, sunny place for two to three weeks and shaken occasionally. It is then strained and placed into airtight jars or bottles where it can be stored for up to a year.

A simple way of creating aromatic olive oil is to simply add a large sprig of your chosen herbs – rosemary and mint are good choices – to a bottle of olive oil. Store the bottle in a cool dark place for about ten days before using.

You can also make you own herbal vinegars by adding fresh herbs such as tarragon or rosemary or cloves of garlic, slices of ginger, chillies or peppercorns and all-spice powder to white vinegar. Crush about a quarter litre volume (1 cup) of loosely packed fresh herbs for each litre of vinegar. If you are using dried herbs, use half the amount of herb stated above. It is important that you use only commercially prepared vinegars, as homemade vinegar may not have a low enough pH to prevent bacterial growth. Place the vinegar in a pot on the stove and heat, but do not boil. Place the herbs in a clean, sterilized jar and slightly crush them. Pour the vinegar over the herbs and cover the jar tightly. Let the herb-vinegar mixture steep in a dark place at room temperature, shaking the jar every couple of days. After a week, strain the vinegar and place in bottles and store for up to six weeks.

DRYING AND FREEZING HERBS

1 *Pick seed just as it is ripening. Place the seeds on a tray or in a paper or muslin bag. Leave in a cool, dark place for a few days until the seed is completely dry.*

2 *Herb seeds that have been dried can be stored in old glass jars with an airtight lid. Store the jars in a cool, dry, dark place and label them for future reference.*

3 *Herbs can be frozen in ice-cube trays. Fill the trays with water after you have added the herbs to make ready-to-use cubes. Herbs can also be packed into freezer bags.*

GROWING FRUIT TREES AND BUSHES

Freshly picked fruit from the organic garden tastes absolutely delicious. The warm taste of a juicy sweet raspberry or the crisp flavour of a tree-ripened apple would tempt many a gardener into growing their own fruit produce. The tastes can be quite different from shop-grown produce where storage, handling, packing and off-the-tree ripening all take their toll on the quality and taste of the fruit.

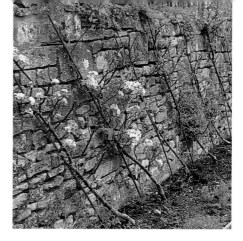

Above: *A sunny wall provides an ideal location for growing fruit trees, such as this pear, that need warmth.*

WHERE CAN FRUIT BE GROWN?

Fruit trees and bushes can be grown wherever there is space. Strawberries can be used in hanging baskets or tubs, dwarf apple trees can be planted in ornamental containers and a number of fruits, such as cherries, white and red currants and figs, can all be grown against walls. Fruits not only provide produce for the kitchen table but many of them have ornamental qualities and can blend well with other plants in the decorative garden.

CHOOSING A SITE

The best site for fruit, both indoors and out, is a sunny one. Sunlight is essential, not just for the ripening of the fruit itself but also for flower bud formation and flowering. In addition, fruit trees and bushes often appreciate a sheltered spot where even exotic fruit can be raised. Within the garden a sheltered sunny wall can provide the ideal place to grow peaches, apricots or figs. If cold winters are a problem, then provide winter protection in the form of a portable frame or, alternatively, grow the plants in a greenhouse. It is worth noting that providing your plants with the ideal conditions for healthy growth will reap its rewards in the

end. Not only will you harvest heavier yields, but, more importantly, your plants will be less prone to pest and disease attacks, which is an obvious advantage when growing organically.

SELECTING THE RIGHT PLANTS

Variety selection should not be based purely on hardiness but on personal preference. You may also wish to consider how easy the fruit tree or bush is to grow, fruit size, taste and the time of harvest. Selecting more than one variety can result in having fresh fruit over a longer period due to a succession of ripening.

Some fruit trees combine the best qualities of two plants. Grafting utilizes the qualities of the variety as top growth (scion) and other desirable qualities from a rootstock that may be absent from the variety. The scion is the fruiting variety that is budded or grafted on to the rootstock which is selected for certain characteristics such as dwarfing, nematode insect resistance, soil type, cold hardiness and disease resistance.

The most commonly grown rootstocks for amateur gardeners are the apple semi-dwarfs and dwarfs. Grapes are also grafted on to clonal rootstocks, although they are often supplied on their own roots. Figs, olives and various types of berry are also usually supplied as plants on their own roots.

Dwarf apple trees are very useful in small gardens and are eminently suited to container growing. They produce fruit of the same size, colour and quality as larger standard trees and require the same pruning, nutritional and care regimes as a standard-size tree.

Left: *Most fruit bushes will benefit from a generous application of well-rotted manure or compost early in the year.*

Dwarf trees fruit much sooner after planting and bear less fruit per tree. When harvesting the fruit, you can reach all parts of the tree from the ground without using a ladder and the trees are easier to train and prune on an annual basis. Grafting the desired variety on to special clonal rootstocks "dwarfs" apples. The most popular dwarfing rootstocks for apple were developed in England and are designated as either EM or M (for East Malling) or MM (for Malling Merton). Dwarfed trees must be pruned annually or size control may be lost. In addition, loss of fruit by frost or pests will also increase growth so necessitating summer pruning.

PLANTING FRUIT TREES AND BUSHES

As with any other type of tree, good ground preparation and careful handling are essential steps to successfully establishing your fruit trees and bushes. The cheapest option when buying fruit trees is to purchase bare-rooted plants. The disadvantage is that they are only available during the dormant season. The most important factor in handling bare-rooted plants is not to let the roots dry out. When you buy trees always check the condition of the roots and packing material. Heel in plants by covering the roots with moist soil in a cool environment outdoors if they are not to be planted immediately.

Dig a hole slightly wider and deeper than the spread and length of the root system, making sure the sides of the hole are not "glazed" over as this will result in a root girdling. After trimming diseased, dead, broken or extra long roots, place the tree in the hole and spread out the roots. For larger trees, place the stake in the hole and drive it in (remembering to first remove the tree and cover the roots). Place the tree back into

PLANTING A FRUIT TREE

1 *Dig a hole in the ground that is at least half as large again as the rootball of the fruit tree. Loosen the sides and the base of the planting hole with a garden fork.*

2 *Remove the pot and check the rootball for girdling roots. Tease these out by hand or with a garden fork.*

3 *Use a straightedge to make sure that the plant is at the right depth in the hole. Fill around the roots with soil, firm it down and water well.*

4 *Hammer in a stake at an angle of about 60° in order to avoid the rootball and place a tie on the tree. Saw off the end of the stake. Nail the tie to the stake to secure it.*

5 *The tree should remain staked for approximately one year. As the diameter of the tree stem increases, loosen the tree tie as required.*

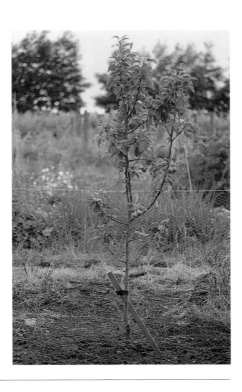

the hole and return the soil, firming in layers of about 30cm (12in) as you go. This avoids large air spaces being left around the roots and ensures that it is set firmly. Trees should be planted at the same depth as they were grown in the nursery. Make sure the bud union (for trees on rootstocks) is about 5–7cm (2–2¾in) above the soil line. Do not place fertilizer in the planting hole as this can be added later. Mulch the newly planted tree with well-rotted manure or compost to suppress weeds. Container-grown nursery stock can be transplanted any time of the year. Site preparation is the same as for bare-rooted stock. Make sure that you check the roots as they can become distorted or root bound if they are

grown in containers for a long period of time. Teasing these roots out can help avoid root girdling, but the best way to do this is to use field-grown (bare-rooted) stock.

PRUNING NEWLY PLANTED STOCK

Fruit trees must be pruned when they are planted for a number of reasons. If planting bare-rooted stock, the top of the tree must be pruned to counter-balance the loss of the root system which would have been severed in the nursery during lifting. Pruning also forces the growth of laterals from which the future framework of the fruit tree will be selected. Branches that are desirably located can be retained as part of the framework whereas undesirable branches are removed.

FRUIT TREE POLLINATION

Pollination is the transfer of pollen from the male part of the flower to the female part of the flower (the stigma) to allow fruit to set and seeds to develop. Seeds cause the fruit to develop properly. If both the pollen and stigma are from the same flower or from another flower from the same variety, the process is called self-pollination. Fruit trees that set fruit as the result of self-pollination are called self-fruitful, whereas those relying on pollen from a different variety are called self-unfruitful. The latter needs two varieties near to each other for fruit set to occur. This is called cross-pollination.

Apples Apples generally need two varieties for good fruit set. This can be another apple variety or a crab apple that blooms with the edible crop.
Apricots Self-fruitful
Berries (all types) Self-fruitful
Cherries Sweet cherry is self-unfruitful and needs two varieties for good crop set. Sour cherry varieties are self-fruitful.
European plums Self-fruitful
Figs Self-fruitful
Japanese plums Self-unfruitful as a rule with the exception of Santa Rosa which will set fruit fairly well without cross-pollination.
Nectarines Self-fruitful
Peaches Self-fruitful with the exception of 'J.H. Hale' which has to be pollinated by another variety.
Pears These always need two varieties to ensure good fruit set.

SUPPORTING FRUIT TREES AND SHRUBS

Many of the fruits that we grow, such as free-standing apple or plum trees, require support only in the early stages, whereas other fruits, like the raspberry, need this throughout their lives. Supports benefit the plants in a number of different ways. They help in establishing strong roots and can prop up trained specimens such as cordons and espaliers. This helps to maintain healthy vigorous growth and increase fruit yields.

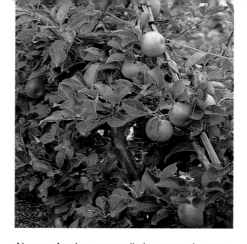

Above: *Apples can easily be grown in rows as cordons that are supported by a framework of stakes and wires.*

WALL AND FENCE FRUIT

The training of fruit on a wall or a fence is carried out to gain the maximum production of high-quality fruit in a limited space. As well as being ideal for a small garden, this can also look extremely decorative. Numerous training systems, based on the art of espalier which originated in France and Italy about 400 years ago, have been devised. The most useful training systems used in gardens today are the fan, espalier and cordon. Apples, pears and plums are all suited to this method of training, which is usually supported by a wall, fence or wire trellis. The plants are normally held to the wall or fence using wires which are held in place by vine eyes, positioned 60–90cm (2–3ft) apart. The wire is led through the holes in the vine eyes and secured at both ends. The wires should be no more than 30–45cm (12–18in) apart.

FREESTANDING WIREWORK

Raspberries, blackberries and other hybrid berries are all grown on a permanent framework. They are usually grown on a freestanding structure that supports the loose growth of the plants. To build such a structure, insert a post at least 60cm (24in) into the ground at the end of each row. Brace each end post with another post set at a 45-degree angle. Insert intermediate posts between the two end ones at a distance of every 2m (6½ft). They are set in at the same depth as the end posts, but no bracing posts are needed. Fix the wires on to the posts so that they run the length of the support. Place the first wire 60cm (24in) from the ground, pull tight and attach to the posts using staples or eye-bolts. The other wires are attached at 30cm (12in) intervals until they reach the top of the support. The final height depends on the height of the fruit.

INDIVIDUAL SUPPORT

When they are first planted, all free-standing trees require support to help them to establish a strong healthy root system. You can use a stake to support a fruit tree, ensuring that the stake is placed on the windward side of the tree. The stake is inserted before the tree is planted and is driven well into the ground. The general rule is to have a stake that is one-third the height of the tree showing above the ground. The tree is then tied to the stake using a tree tie. Do not use string or rope because this can damage the bark. A low stake such as this will allow the top part of the tree to move about freely and so help the tree to thicken and strengthen its trunk. For most fruit trees the stake should only be left in the ground for approximately one year and not for several years as is commonly practised.

STAKING A FRUIT BUSH

1 *Using a large mallet, drive a strong wooden post into the ground at the end of a row of the fruit bushes to a depth of about 60cm (2ft).*

2 *Fix another strainer post at a 45-degree angle in order to support the upright. Place this on the side the wire is to run and nail it firmly.*

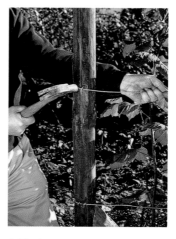

3 *Fix the wires to one of the posts and then stretch these tightly along the row, stapling them at each post along the row as you go.*

4 *The fruit bushes can be fastened to or trained along these wires. Take care not to tie stems too tightly as this will damage them.*

PROTECTING FRUIT

There can be few more frustrating events in the kitchen-garden calendar than losing your fruit crop (or a fair portion of it) to birds. However, we have to remember that birds are a strong ally in the fight against pests in an organic garden and should be encouraged into fruit-growing areas when the bushes are not fruiting. Protection for the fruit crops will therefore need to take the form of moveable cloches or fruit cages where the netting can be removed after fruiting has taken place.

Above: *Cloches can be used to protect young strawberries from bad weather and also to keep pests at bay.*

FRUIT CAGES

This is perhaps the easiest way to protect tall fruit crops such as blackcurrants, raspberries and gooseberries because these plants can all be grown under the one structure. This makes it easy to maintain and harvest the fruit.

A permanent fruit-cage structure with removable netting is the ideal scenario because the netting can be put in place just before the crop ripens and then is taken down again after fruiting has occurred. This allows the birds to roam freely around the area at all other times, but without jeopardizing the crop at fruiting time. Alternatively, a series of small cages can be constructed over crops that ripen at different times, netting each of them individually as the fruit begins to ripen. This is a wildlife-friendly way of protecting the fruit, but it is also time-consuming.

Above: *A tunnel of wire netting is ideal for protecting ripening strawberries from pests such as birds.*

LOW-LEVEL PROTECTION

Smaller- or lower-growing crops, such as strawberries, can also benefit from a barrier to protect them from birds. This is easily achieved, as the structure does not need to be large, permanent or even particularly sturdy. One simple method is to form a low tunnel of chicken wire, supported on hoops that are bent into an inverted U-shape. For larger areas, a series of stakes hammered into the ground can be covered with netting to keep the birds at bay. Plants growing on wire trellises can be protected with netting draped over the stakes and top wires and weighted at the base with stones.

Left: *Fruit trees growing against a wall can easily be protected with a cost-effective frame that is covered with netting.*

Right: *Fleece stretched over a frame can help protect the blossom of wall specimens from late frosts.*

Larger bush fruit can be covered with netting and weighted down with stones. A little of the crop may be accessible to birds, but most will be protected.

PROTECTION WITHOUT BARRIERS

Most bird deterrents depend upon shocking the birds or mimicking something that they are naturally afraid of. Scarecrows are an age-old favourite. Other deterrents mimic the shape of hawks or make noises that will startle the birds. A relatively recent "innovation" has been to hang compact discs from wires stretched through the crop. Most of these deterrents tend to work very well at first until the birds get used to them. However, the only drawback is that when the birds get used to them, they resume their onslaught with a vengeance. The only way to overcome this is to keep changing the deterrents every few days.

PRUNING FRUIT TREES AND SHRUBS

The general purpose of pruning fruit trees is to regulate growth, increase crop yields and to improve fruit size and quality. The fruit trees also need to have all the dead, diseased and damaged wood removed as well as overcrowded areas thinned out. Pruning is also performed in order to establish a tree with a strong framework that is capable of supporting heavy crops without causing damage to the plant.

Above: *The careful pruning of trained specimens, such as this pear, will result in good blossom and improve fruit yields.*

WHEN TO PRUNE FRUIT TREES

If a fruit tree is pruned in spring, all the effort that the tree has put into bud production is wasted. The best time to prune is in winter when the plants are dormant and the sap has not yet started to rise. This applies to all fruit except for plums and cherries which are susceptible to silverleaf disease at this time and are best pruned in summer.

Summer pruning is also recommended if you wish to control vigorous growth in formally trained fruits such as fans, cordons and espaliers.

When pruning is underway, older fruit-bearing trees should be pruned first. Young, non-bearing apple trees and stone fruits can be pruned later to minimize the risk of winter injury.

BASIC PRUNING CUTS

Although there are different methods of pruning and training, the pruning cuts are the same. Always make the pruning cut just above a bud, ensuring that the cut is angled away from the bud. This will allow rainwater

---

BENEFITS OF PRUNING

Pruning fruit trees and bushes has many advantages, some of which are outlined below.

- Increased fruit yields.
- Can aid ripening of the fruit.
- Maintains healthy growth.
- Regulates growth.
- Improves fruit size and quality.
- Controls the spread of diseases.

---

to drip down the other side of the stem and away from the bud, thus protecting the top of the cut from rotting.

Larger branches will need to be cut with a saw. If the branch is very heavy, you will need to remove the branch in three separate stages. Cut underneath the branch first, 20–25cm (8–10in) away from where the final cut will be. Make the second cut on the top of the branch just behind the first undercut. Follow this through until the

weight of the branch makes the wood split and it falls off cleanly at the undercut. You will then need to make a third cut at the branch collar, cutting straight from the top to the bottom of the branch as there is no weight left to tear the bark.

Above: *Training can give rise to a variety of ornamental shapes. These pear trees have been trained into a cylindrical shape.*

PRUNING LARGE BRANCHES

1 *Make a cut about 20–25cm (8–10in) out from where the final cut will be on the underside of the branch. Cut about a third of the way into the branch.*

2 *Make a cut about 10cm (4in) nearer the position of the final cut, cutting until the branch snaps. The initial undercut prevents the wood splitting or bark from stripping.*

3 *Position the saw for the last cut to avoid damaging the swollen area at the base of the branch. The cut will heal in a couple of seasons. No wound painting is necessary.*

SUCCESSFUL FRUIT TREE AND SHRUB PRUNING

Pruning fruit trees is a very complex subject and, like so many areas of organic gardening, is the subject of opinion and hot debate. Despite this it is possible to apply certain guiding principles that can enable you to prune your fruit trees and bushes successfully.

1 Remove root suckers arising at the base of the tree
These compete with the upper growth for water and essential nutrients and their dense habit can harbour pests.

2 Always cut out dead, dying, damaged or diseased limbs first
Helps to maintain the plant's health and enables you to see precisely what needs doing next.

3 Remove low, drooping limbs
These will not bear fruit and will often be heavily shaded by growth above. They are an unproductive drain on the tree.

4 Remove upright growth or outward growth in the case of wall-trained bushes
Upright growth will produce a flush of growth at the end and will not fruit well. Branches growing away from the wall will shade the fruit behind causing poor ripening.

5 Remove crossing or dense parallel growth
Crossing growth will rub and can cause bark damage that will allow disease entry. Dense growth will also shade the developing fruits. This will slow and limit the ripening of the fruit.

6 Freestanding trees should have upper limbs cut back further than lower limbs
This will result in the development of a conical shape that will allow light penetration all the way down the side. Fruit will ripen more evenly.

7 Remove water sprouts as they develop
Water sprouts can quickly develop and cover the developing fruits, causing poor ripening and harvesting difficulties. They can be easily removed by hand. This is best done early in the season when the growth is soft and is therefore easily removed. Carry out regular inspections throughout the season to control the water sprouts.

8 Once the larger cuts have been made, thin out the smaller branches
Removing thick branches first allows you to see what remains to be done and also makes it easier to get to the remaining pruning work. Removing older wood encourages young growth to fill the gap. Remember to stand back and view what you have pruned as you go along.

9 Always make clean cuts above a leaf bud or close to the stem
Pruning cuts that are not performed cleanly or that leave a long stub will damage the plant tissue and encourage the entry of pests and diseases.

10 Avoid feeding with nitrogen for a season before and following heavy pruning
Both pruning and high nitrogen fertilizers promote the development of rapid growth flushes that can result in the poor development of the crop.

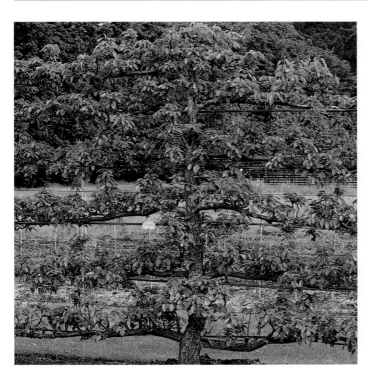

Above: *This well-established pear tree has been trained into an espalier on wire supports. Many fruit trees can be grown and supported in this way.*

Above: *This pear tree has been grown as a fan. Fans are an ideal way to train many species of fruit tree and are well suited for growing against a wall.*

HARVESTING AND STORING FRUIT

When harvesting your fruits, you will find that there is only so much you can eat fresh or give away. There is always surplus fruit left over and you are faced with the question of what to do with it. Leaving some on the plant to help feed the wildlife in your organic garden is a good idea, but storing the rest of the excess fruit using a variety of methods will ensure that you can eat your home-grown produce over a longer period of time.

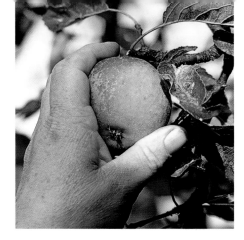

Above: *An apple is ready to be picked if it can be removed from the tree with only a single twist of the fruit.*

HARVESTING

The key to successfully storing fruit begins well before harvesting commences. Your first objective should be to grow fruit that is as healthy as possible because it will be the best for storage. Harvesting immature crops or attempting to save those that are in poor condition – due perhaps to a lack of water or nutrients or to pest and disease damage – can lead to many storage losses.

There are several ways that fruit can be stored and the condition of the picked crop will usually be the deciding factor as to which of these you should use. Top fruit such as apples and pears can often be stored fresh through most of the winter, whereas stone fruits and berries, such as peaches, strawberries and raspberries, must be quickly consumed, turned into a preserve or frozen.

Careful handling, both during and following harvesting, is essential because, from the moment they are harvested (and in many cases well before), crops have no

means of repairing any physical damage that they may suffer. Even firm, strong-looking fruit such as apples can easily be bruised, although the damage may well not show up immediately.

As well as good handling, a careful selection of the fruits during harvesting is essential for successful storage. You should inspect the picked fruits and select only those of the best quality for fresh storage. Reject any that have a broken skin or show any sign of pest or disease damage. Do not throw them on the compost heap yet, however, because damaged fruit may well be useful for making preserves such as jellies and jams or for freezing.

It is also a good idea to leave a small percentage of mature fruit on the plants when you are harvesting to help feed the wildlife in your organic garden.

STORING

In general, the storage area for fruit must be frost-free, safe from pests, rainproof and ideally kept at a constant temperature.

STORING FRUIT

To store surplus fruit and avoid the risk of rotting, make sure that you use the appropriate method.

Apples, pears and quinces
Store in a cool place for up to 12 months, depending on the variety.
All other fruit Eat immediately or freeze. Alternatively, preserve fruit by bottling or making into jam. Fruit can be kept for up to 12 months, depending on the method of preservation that has been used.

The long-term storage of any fruit calls for cool conditions with adequate ventilation. If you have space, consider having a separate refrigerator specifically for fruit storage, or choose an area with a low temperature that does not go below freezing. A garden shed or garage can be ideal, in many cases, but even these

Far left: *Pick soft fruits, such as strawberries, raspberries and gooseberries, carefully to avoid bruising the fruit.*

Left: *Pears can last for up to 12 months, depending upon the variety. Lay them in a recycled box, ensuring that the fruits do not touch and air can circulate around the fruit.*

Above: *Fruit trays, recycled from supermarkets, make ideal storage boxes for surplus fruit. The trays should be kept in a cool dry place such as a garage or shed.*

Above: *Soft fruit is best placed in small individual containers as it is picked to prevent it being squashed and spoiling. Store in a refrigerator or other cool place.*

spaces may need extra insulation if winter weather conditions become severe. Some houses have a basement, cellar or unheated room that may be ideally suited for the task. Attics are not recommended for fruit storage because of their wide temperature fluctuations and variable humidity.

It is worthwhile trying out a variety of different storage methods. This can be done by splitting the crop up and then trying out different locations in your home. You will soon find which are the best places to store fruit, and what areas are best for storing a particular kind of fruit.

Ensure that you check the stored fruit regularly, at least weekly, removing any that show signs of decay. Remember the old adage that "one bad apple spoils the whole barrel"? This can be true for your crop too unless you prevent rots from spreading. The unblemished parts can often still be used for eating or cooking. If lots of fruits begin to rot simultaneously, it could be that the storage conditions are not suitable, the crop has reached its maximum "shelf-life" or the fruit was not of sufficiently good quality to start with.

FREEZING AND PRESERVING

Freezing is an excellent way of storing all the surplus fruit that has been produced in your garden. Unfortunately, fruit tends to lose its firmness once it has been frozen,

although the taste will remain more or less the same. Raspberries, for example, are best used for making pies or flans after they have been frozen and will be of very poor quality if they are eaten raw. Most fruits can be frozen after they have been stewed or puréed; this is true of fruits such as apples and plums.

Fruits like strawberries and blackcurrants that are not suited to long-term storage can be made into jams, pickles and chutneys. You can find recipes for these in good cookbooks.

Above: *One of the simplest ways of preserving fruit is to freeze it, although once frozen most fruits are only good for cooking.*

Above: *Adding a favourite fruit such as these cranberries to good wine vinegar can produce interesting flavours.*

Right: *Bottling fruit in alcohol is an ideal way to preserve soft fruits such as peaches, nectarines and apricots.*

CALENDAR OF CARE

WINTER

THE ORNAMENTAL GARDEN

EARLY WINTER
- Continue cultivating the soil, if not already done, when the ground is not wet.
- Continue planting and transplanting on mild days.
- Press plants that have been lifted by frost back into the ground.
- Plant herbaceous perennials for next year.
- Last chance to plant roses.
- Move greenhouse plants to the house as they come into flower.
- Start pruning deciduous shrubs and trees during spells of fine, frost-free weather.

MID-WINTER
- Finish digging and trenching and fork over borders.
- Order seeds for coming season.
- Protect autumn sown annuals from frost.
- Prepare ground that is to be planted out with bedding plants with manure.
- Tidy up climbing plants and remove any dead wood.
- Firm down herbaceous plants that have been lifted by the frost and protect the new shoots of young tender plants.
- Plant evergreen and deciduous shrubs.
- Trim deciduous hedges and shrubs to start bringing them into shape.
- Take hardwood cuttings and layers of deciduous shrubs.
- Sow annuals in gentle heat.
- Take cuttings of tender shrubs and start under gentle heat.

LATE WINTER
- Tidy up unused ground and apply a top-dressing of manure or leaf mould.
- Protect bulbs from mice, snails and birds.
- Prune roses planted this month.
- Start to train and trim climbers.
- Divide herbaceous plants.
- Sow annuals in gentle heat.
- Transplant autumn sown annuals.
- Plant edgings such as box (*Buxus*) hedging, pinks (*Dianthus*) or thrift (*Armeria*).

SPRING

EARLY SPRING
- Feed lawns where the grass is thin and seed areas where the grass has been completely worn away.
- Prepare borders ready for biennials and perennials next month.
- Remove leaves and other debris from borders and fork over.
- Tidy up spring bedding plants.
- Sow hardy annuals when the weather is dry and mild.
- Start pruning roses.
- Trim box edging and damaged evergreens.
- Prick out annuals started last month.
- Start to harden off early seedlings ready for bedding out.
- Look for pests and diseases and deal with them as they occur.

MID-SPRING
- Hoe off weeds.
- Watch for signs of frost and protect young shoots.
- Watch out for pests and diseases.
- Give the lawn its first cut and tidy its edges.
- Stake and tie any plants that need it.
- Sow hardy annuals.
- Propagate hardy perennials, including water plants.
- Finish winter pruning and prune late winter/early spring flowering shrubs before they commence growth.
- Continue hardening off summer bedding and pinch out the tops.
- Trim and tidy up all climbers before they start into growth.
- Sow half-hardy annuals and take cuttings.
- Give box hedges their first clipping.

LATE SPRING
- Hoe off weeds.
- Finish off digging and rotavating to prepare the beds for planting.
- Water newly planted plants in dry weather.
- Keep an eye open for pests and diseases.
- Tidy bulb beds after the foliage has died down.
- Tie in sweet peas (*Lathyrus odoratus*) and check the support of other climbers.
- Finish sowing hardy annuals and plant out those raised under glass. Thin outdoor sowings and transplant where necessary.
- Plant half-hardy bedding plants when the danger of frost is over.
- Divide spring-flowering plants, like primroses (*Primula vulgaris*), for next season.
- Shrubs should have old wood removed and thinned out.
- Continue taking cuttings.

THE WILDLIFE GARDEN

EARLY WINTER
- Try to maintain a fresh supply of clean unfrozen water for wildlife.
- To keep some open water on ponds, put in a floating ball or anchored block of polystyrene, preferably painted black, to absorb the warmth of the sun.
- Leave tidying the garden until late winter to shelter overwintering insects.
- Leave log and leaf piles completely undisturbed until spring.
- Feed resident birds with high energy supplements such as fat balls.
- Order seed now for early sowings of perennials and annuals.

MID-WINTER
- Put plenty of food in the garden for resident birds.
- Hang nesting boxes ready for breeding birds.
- Build dry-stone walls with gaps to provide shelter for reptiles and amphibians.
- Look out for wildlife tracks in snow and position cat deterrents at entry points.
- Provide food for non-hibernating mammals if present.
- Keep a record of wildlife to help you target future feeding and habitat creation.

LATE WINTER
- Continue feeding resident birds.
- Put up a range of different nesting boxes and make each box as inconspicuous as possible. Reposition any nesting boxes that were unused last year.
- Stretch wires or heavy-duty cord at least 10cm (4in) proud of walls and fences and train climbing plants to form a screen with a gap behind it for nesting birds.
- Trim one side of hedges to encourage dense new growth as nesting cover, but leave some flowering stems on spring-blossoming species such as hawthorn (*Crataegus*) for nectar.
- Protect bulbs from mice, snails and birds.

EARLY SPRING
- Put plenty of food in the garden for resident birds.
- Create a wildlife pond ready to plant up next month.
- Supplement the diet of resident early nesting birds with mealworms and waxworms.
- Emerging hedgehogs will benefit from a feed of cat food near their nesting sites.
- Hang nesting boxes for solitary bees.

MID-SPRING
- Plant new garden ponds and replace dead plants in established ponds.
- Sow seeds of hardy annuals in a sunny spot to attract insects during the summer until late autumn. Mix them up with salad crops to act as helpful companion plants.
- Install a "cage" of large-gauge chicken wire around nesting sites to allow nesting birds in but keep out magpies, grey squirrels and other nest-robbing species.
- Keep one or two nest boxes sealed so as to prevent the entry of resident birds until migrant bird species arrive.
- Continue feeding garden birds.
- Continue feeding hedgehogs until natural prey increases in numbers.
- Propagate hardy perennials, not forgetting water plants.

LATE SPRING
- Plant pot-grown seedlings of spring-flowering wild flowers in an area of lawn where you can leave the grass uncut until mid-summer.
- Sow the seeds of wild flowers thinly on the surface of gritty potting mix.
- Divide spring-flowering plants, such as primroses (*Primula vulgaris*) and cowslips (*P. veris*), for next season.
- Continue feeding garden birds.
- Put up bat boxes to encourage bats to roost in the summer.

SUMMER

EARLY SUMMER
- Mulch round plants and shrubs that need to be kept moist.
- Keep an eye out for pests, and keep weeds under control.
- Cut down and tidy perennials as they finish flowering.
- Feed roses and sweet peas (*Lathyrus odoratus*) with manure or compost tea.
- Sow biennials and perennials.
- Plant out plants raised under glass, dividing and planting out those that have finished flowering in other areas.
- Thin out seedlings and stake carnations (*Dianthus*), dahlias and sweet peas.
- Sow hardy annuals for autumn planting.
- Spray the foliage of new trees with water in hot or dry weather.
- Tidy up rhododendrons and other plants by removing seedheads, unless leaving them for decoration and food for the birds.

MID-SUMMER
- Continue to hoe weeds and water newly planted specimens.
- Stake and tie plants.
- Layer or take cuttings from carnations.
- Pinch out the tops of chrysanthemums to prevent straggly plants.
- Water and feed sweet peas with a compost or manure tea.
- Sow perennial and biennial seeds for next year.
- Continue taking cuttings.
- Sow seeds for overwintering in the greenhouse.
- Pot plants that need repotting.
- Cut away dead and unwanted foliage on vigorous shrubs.
- Trim deciduous hedges.
- Propagate shrubs by cuttings or layering.

LATE SUMMER
- Continue watering, mulching and hoeing.
- Remove all dead flowers, stalks and leaves.
- Train and tie clematis, honeysuckle (*Lonicera*) and wisteria.
- Trim plants such as lavender and penstemons after flowering.
- Water and feed sweet peas with a compost or manure tea.
- Take cuttings of old-fashioned roses.
- Thin perennial seedlings.
- Divide and replant spring-flowering perennials.
- Take cuttings of fuchsias, pelargoniums, heliotrope, hydrangeas and all half-hardy plants.
- Remove dead flowers and stalks from summer-flowering shrubs, unless they are berry producing.

EARLY SUMMER
- Plant tobacco plants (*Nicotiana*) to guarantee interesting night-flying moths and the bats that feed on them.
- Check fruit nets each day to ensure no birds are trapped inside.
- Choose bedding plants with simple flowers and keep a note of which the bees and butterflies prefer.
- Leave seedheads on spring-flowering shrubs such as rhododendrons as food for birds.
- Continue feeding garden birds, with seed and waxworms or mealworms, especially if there is a dry spell.

MID-SUMMER
- Watch for night-flying moths on tobacco plants, late flowers on the honeysuckle, and tall yellow evening primroses.
- Continue to check fruit nets each day for birds.
- Take special care when turning compost heaps as grass snakes may be nesting and hedgehogs often sleep in them.
- Make log piles for wood feeding insects such as stag beetles.
- Lightly trim deciduous hedges if birds have finished nesting to encourage dense cover in the winter.
- Continue feeding garden birds, especially if there is a dry spell.

LATE SUMMER
- Plant early spring bulbs now for nectar next year, especially for overwintering insects.
- Lightly trim nectar-rich plants such as lavender (*Lavandula*) and nepeta after flowering to encourage new growth.
- Dead-head herbaceous plants to encourage fresh flowers that give an extra boost to pollinators in the early autumn.
- Leave seedheads and berries on summer-flowering shrubs for birds.
- Continue feeding garden birds.

AUTUMN

EARLY AUTUMN
- Hoe off any late weeds.
- Start tidying up for winter, but leave seedheads for birds.
- Put unwanted debris on the compost heap.
- Collect seeds and label for sowing next year.
- Start digging, manuring and rotavating heavy soils.
- Repair patches on lawns.
- Start collecting fallen leaves to make leaf mould.
- Tie and stake dahlias and tall shrubs.
- Cut back and support climbing plants.
- Sow spring-flowering seeds, starting with hardy annuals.
- Plant spring bulbs.
- Plant or transplant evergreen shrubs, conifers and herbaceous plants.

MID-AUTUMN
- Collect fallen leaves to make leaf mould.
- Prepare areas for planting.
- Repair and lay new lawns, repair paths and walkways.
- Make final plantings of bulbs.
- Collect seeds of late-flowering plants.
- Lift and store half-hardy bulbs, corms and tubers.
- Lift, divide and replant herbaceous plants.
- Sow early sweet peas (*Lathyrus odoratus*).
- Start planting out spring bedding.
- If moving deciduous shrubs, do so to encourage new root growth.
- Take cuttings until the cold weather sets in.

LATE AUTUMN
- Continue digging heavy and medium soils, leaving the light soils for spring.
- Spread surplus manure around flowerbeds if leaf mould is not available.
- Fork over herbaceous borders, leaving dead foliage until spring.
- Take cuttings of plants that may need replacing.
- Make final plantings of spring bedding.
- Take rose prunings from choice plants and push into the ground in a sheltered position where they may strike and give you more plants.
- Put bulbs for forcing under glass in pots.
- Plant flowering shrubs and trees for next season.

EARLY AUTUMN
- Let one or two old vegetables flower, such as leeks, carrots and almost any member of the cabbage family, to boost nectar supplies for autumn insects.
- Look now to see if there is a shortage of nectar and redesign flower borders accordingly. Remember to select single-flowered plants where possible.
- Build new log piles, rock piles and brush piles ready for overwintering insects, reptiles, amphibians and mammals.
- Place nest boxes outside for overwintering mammals such as hedgehogs.
- Continue planting spring bulbs for early nectar next year.
- Plant evergreens to provide dense winter cover for birds and mammals.
- Continue feeding garden birds.

MID-AUTUMN
- Start a new compost heap.
- Let hedge prunings, raspberry canes and other woody waste accumulate and leave them to become a hibernation heap for hedgehogs.
- Weed among and divide most pond plants before they die back. This removes excess nutrients from the pond and minimizes next summer's algal blooms.
- Pile weeds and thinnings from ponds at the side until the following day to give trapped pond dwellers time to escape.
- Place nest boxes outside for overwintering mammals such as hedgehogs.
- Continue planting spring bulbs for early nectar next year.
- Begin putting out high energy supplements such as fat balls for birds.

LATE AUTUMN
- Plant hedgerows using native shrubs and trees.
- Plant late-flowering nectar plants like English ivy (*Hedera helix*) against a boundary that catches autumn sun.
- Put in late bulbs at least 7.5cm (3in) deep and bury chicken wire just below the surface to avoid them being eaten by squirrels.
- Feed resident birds with high energy supplements such as fat balls.

WINTER

THE KITCHEN GARDEN

VEGETABLES

EARLY WINTER
- Hoe between crops on fine days.
- Examine stored onions and potatoes for any sign of disease and discard second-class seed. Any potatoes that are sprouting should be placed apart in dry trays.
- Protect more tender plants with leaves or cloches.
- Begin forcing rhubarb and seakale under a light-proof cover.
- Order seed catalogues and plan the new season's crops.

MID-WINTER
- Tidy up and put vegetable waste on the compost heap.
- Hoe between growing crops when dry.
- Sow broad (fava) beans and peas in warm sheltered positions.
- Sow early vegetables under glass or cloches.
- Start potatoes in a frost-free shed.
- Plant rhubarb in well-manured beds.

LATE WINTER
- Hoe weeds when the weather allows.
- Clear old beds ready for new season.
- Cut pea and bean sticks.
- Sow early vegetables under glass or cloches.
- Plant artichokes, garlic, shallots, lettuce (winter), potatoes (early), rhubarb and seakale.
- Plants overwintering under cloches should be hardened off and only protected when the weather is frosty.

FRUIT

EARLY WINTER
- Finish pruning fruit trees and bushes on frost-free days. Large standard trees will need pruning every second or third year.
- Firm newly planted trees where the frost has been at work.
- Do not plant any more trees until the spring; just prepare the ground.
- Currants and gooseberries should be pruned if not already done.
- Prune outdoor vines.
- Remove unwanted suckers from raspberry stools but do not prune until early spring.

MID-WINTER
- Start pruning hardier trees such as apples. Do not prune apricots, cherries, figs, nectarines and peaches.
- Prepare grafting material.
- Plant container-grown trees and cover soil with well-rotted manure.

LATE WINTER
- Prune damsons, pears, plums and quince.
- Spread manure around fruit trees and dig it in.
- Prepare new strawberry beds.
- Fertilize by hand the blossom of fruit trees grown under glass.

HERBS

EARLY WINTER
- Prepare ground for planting when conditions allow.
- Protect tender herbs under cloches.
- Continue to remove dead stems from herbaceous types.

MID-WINTER
- Prepare ground ready for planting.
- Force early growth under cloches.
- Make early sowings under glass.

LATE WINTER
- Remove dead stems from herbaceous types.
- Continue forcing under cloches.
- Continue sowing under glass.

SPRING

VEGETABLES

EARLY SPRING
- Hoe weeds when the weather allows.
- Prepare seedbeds.
- Protect early crops from birds.
- Begin sowing in sheltered places in the open.
- Sow early vegetables under glass or cloches.
- Plant out early crops raised under glass and early potatoes.
- Plant early broad (fava) beans out in the garden under glass.

MID-SPRING
- Hoe weeds regularly.
- Prepare beds for planting out.
- Feed cabbages with high-nitrogen fertilizer such as chicken manure.
- Potatoes need the soil drawn over their leaves to protect them from frost.
- Begin sowing remaining summer crops outdoors.
- Continue sowing more tender crops under glass.

LATE SPRING
- Hoe weeds regularly.
- Cut asparagus when shoots reach 15cm (6in).
- Maintain the succession of seed sowing to give salad throughout the summer season.
- Continue planting out summer crops.
- Sow late crops such as broccoli and plant out winter crops previously sown under cover.
- Last chance to plant late potatoes.
- Plant out cucumbers, pumpkins and melons in beds previously used for protected early crops.

EARLY SPRING
- Protect blossom with fleece on cold nights.
- Last chance to plant container-grown fruit bushes.
- Graft apples, cherries, pears and plums that were prepared in mid-winter.
- Finish pruning fruit trees and bushes.

MID-SPRING
- Continue protecting blossom.
- Wall trees will need moisture from now on.
- Watch for pests and diseases.
- Grapes will require thinning in order to swell their size.

LATE SPRING
- All fruit will benefit from a mulch.
- Apricots, peaches and Morello cherries should have fruiting spurs shortened back to three to four leaves.
- Limit raspberry suckers to around four to six to each stool.
- Put straw around strawberries to protect the fruits from the ground.

EARLY SPRING
- Continue sowing under glass.
- Plant out hardy herbs once hardened off.
- Prune shrubby types.
- Lift and divide herbaceous types until late spring.

MID-SPRING
- Continue sowing under glass.
- Continue planting out.
- Take basal cuttings.

LATE SPRING
- Sow herbs like parsley (*Petroselinum crispum*) and chervil (*Anthriscus cerefolium*) for winter use.
- Continue sowing under glass and planting out.

SUMMER

EARLY SUMMER
- Hoe weeds regularly throughout summer.
- Water all salad crops regularly.
- Feed heavy feeders like cauliflowers with liquid manure or compost tea.
- Keep picking peas to stimulate flowering.
- Harvest early potatoes and replace with winter turnips or late celery.
- Support runner beans.
- Sow the last of the outdoor salad crops and continue sowing seed of late or winter crops.
- Thin out seedlings.
- Plant late-season crops raised under cover.

MID-SUMMER
- Water all salad crops regularly.
- Remove debris, following harvest, to the compost heap until late summer.
- Potatoes and other crops may need earthing-up.
- Pinch out and stop tomatoes and marrows.
- Maintain the succession of seed sowing for late or winter crops.
- Thin out the beetroot crop so that the roots can form properly.
- Plant late-season crops raised under cover.

LATE SUMMER
- Water all crops regularly.
- Remove debris, following harvest, to the compost heap.
- Harvest seed from French (green) beans and onions.
- Garlic and onions can be harvested this month and then ripened.
- Potatoes for next year's seed should be dug up and dried in the sun.
- Maintain the succession of seed sowing for late or winter crops.

EARLY SUMMER
- Continue mulching trees and bushes to conserve moisture.
- Cut back untidy vigorous growth.
- Over-laden trees may need support. Aphids will appear, so take appropriate action.
- Throw nets over fruiting trees and shrubs to prevent the birds getting the fruit first.
- Peaches and apricots may need some thinning.
- Strawberries should have regular watering.

MID-SUMMER
- Thin trees and remove unnecessary growth.
- Hoe round the roots of fruit trees and water them.
- Fruit trees may be budded when the weather is moist.
- Espalier and dwarf fruit trees will need training and protection from birds.
- Strawberries and loganberries should be layered and clipped to the soil to secure their position.

LATE SUMMER
- Protect fruit on walls from wasps and birds as it ripens.
- Pruning can be started and trees budded.
- Apples, pears and plums may need the fruit thinning out if the crop is heavy.
- Cut down the old canes of loganberries and raspberries after harvesting.
- Cut off unwanted runners from strawberries and remove the old straw from round the crowns.

EARLY SUMMER
- Continue sowing under glass.
- Continue planting out until late summer.
- Harvest herbs for storing before they flower.
- Plant out tender herbs.
- Dead-head unless seed is required until late summer.
- Cut back herbaceous types to stimulate growth until late summer.

MID-SUMMER
- Cut mint (*Mentha*) and other sweet herbs for drying.
- Pull out parsley (*Petroselinum crispum*) unless it is being kept for seed.
- Propagate sage (*Salvia*) or savory (*Satureja*) from cuttings or division.

LATE SUMMER
- Harvest herbs as required.

AUTUMN

EARLY AUTUMN
- Hoe weeds regularly throughout autumn.
- Water all crops regularly.
- Harvest onions and bend down the necks of the remainder to prevent seeding.
- Continue to lift potatoes.
- Expose the fruit of outdoor tomatoes to the sun by removing the covering leaves.
- Maintain the succession of seed sowing for late or winter crops.
- Plant late season crops raised under cover.

MID-AUTUMN
- After beans and peas have been harvested, turn the soil over and leave it fallow over the winter.
- Lift root vegetables when their tops fade.
- Cut down asparagus foliage when mature.
- Onions and turnip beds should be thinned.
- Clear the last of the potatoes and store them.
- Earth up celery and leeks.
- Plant out late-season crops and protect tender types such as cauliflower.

LATE AUTUMN
- Get the soil ready for spring sowing.
- Protect crowns of tender crops with a mulch of leaves.
- Lift the last of the beetroot and carrots.
- Earth up celery and leeks if not already done.
- Spinach will continue to crop as it is thinned.
- Dry off the late potatoes for seed stock next year.
- Continue to plant out late-season crops and protect tender types such as cauliflower.

EARLY AUTUMN
- Wall fruit that has ripened will need protecting.
- Fruit trees may be budded and light pruning continued.
- Early varieties of apples and pears that do not keep well should be gathered.
- Prune currants and gooseberries to keep them in shape. Raspberry canes that have fruited should be removed to make room for the new growth.
- Strawberries should have unwanted runners removed to give space to the main plants.

MID-AUTUMN
- Look though the nursery catalogues and order fruit stock, then prepare the ground and remove stock to be replaced.
- Move any trees or bushes that are in the wrong place.
- Apples and pears can now be gathered.
- Apricots, cherries, currants and gooseberries should be pruned and the cuttings burnt.
- Loganberries and raspberries should be planted now.

LATE AUTUMN
- This is the time to plant fruit trees in well-prepared ground.
- Begin winter pruning of fruit trees.
- Plant currants and gooseberries.
- Figs will need thinning.
- Spread manure between rows of new strawberry plants.

EARLY AUTUMN
- Harvest seed as it ripens.
- Harvest leaves and stems as required.
- Cut back herbaceous types to stimulate new growth.

MID-AUTUMN
- Harvest seed as it ripens.
- Tidy away dead material.
- Protect tender herbs.
- Plant shrubby and herbaceous types until late autumn.
- Move tender container herbs under some protection.
- Divide herbaceous herbs until late autumn.

LATE AUTUMN
- Prepare ground for planting when conditions allow.

INDEX

ACKNOWLEDGEMENTS

Authors' Acknowledgements
We would like to thank the following people who worked as models for the photography: Joe Lovell, Debbie Hart for her willow weaving skills, Jane Dobson for her graft unions and Ian Gandy and Stewart Brown for the lawn maintenance shots. A big thank you to Writtle College and their staff for allowing the use of their grounds and glasshouses to take many of the photographs.

Publisher's Acknowledgements
The publisher would like to thank the following for kindly allowing photography to take place in their gardens:
t = top   b = bottom   l = left   r = right   c = centre

The Centre for Alternative Technology, Wales 8t; 32t; 33t; 61br; 104;114c; 121bc and br; 122t; 130t; 141bl; **Dean Court, Dorset** 16; 26b; 36; 37c; 65bl; **Edmondsham Manor, Dorset** 6; 9t; 10bl; 12t; 30t; 63t; 76c; 78; 92t; 96t; 106t; 109tl; 123b; 129tl; 137bl; **Fardel Manor, Devon** 30c; 55t; 62bl; 101tl; 107b; 113b; 115tl; 140c; 142bl; **Valerie Ferguson, Bath** 9b; 31t; 38bl; 42tr; 43t (all pictures in sequence); 56t and c; 72t; 75br; 77tl and cl; 114t; 125b; 129tr and b; 133b; 146t; **HDRA, the Organic Organisation, Coventry** 4t; 5bc; 8b; 11; 12br; 14c; 28tr; 56b; 60; 61bl; 73br; 74t, c and b; 77br; 105c; 107tl and tr; 109tr; 114b; 115tr; 122b; 123t; 125t; 130b; 141t;

Adrian Penrose 40t; 75t; **RHS Rosemoor, Devon** 7c; 10br; 17bl; 21br; 62t; 80; 96b; 108t; 126; 128t and b; 152br; 149br; 150t; 160; **RHS Wisley, Surrey** 62b; 120; **Peter Robinson** 12bl; 105r; **The Royal Society for the Protection of Birds, Bedfordshire** 72c; **Writtle College, Chelmsford** 5tl and b; 14b; 17br; 19tr; 26t; 29 (all pictures); 37br; 40br; 76t; 77bl; 81 (all pictures in sequence); 82; 84t and bl; 85bl and br; 86c; 87 (all pictures in sequence); 91t; 96c; 100t; 100–1 (all pictures in sequence); 101tr; 108b; 109b; 110t, bl and br; 111b; 132t.

The publisher would also like to thank the following picture libraries for kindly allowing their photographs to be reproduced for the purposes of this book:

The Garden Picture Library 67r (three from top; Sunniva Harte); 68t (Janet Sorrell); 69 (ten from top; Lamontagne); **Holt Studios International** 67l (four from top; Nigel Cattlin); 67l (thirteen from top; Nigel Cattlin); 67r (four from top; Nigel Cattlin); 67r (eight from top; Nigel Cattlin); 69 (seven from top; Nigel Cattlin); 69 (eleven from top; Nigel Cattlin); 71 (four from top; Nigel Cattlin); 118 (three from top; Primrose Peacock); 118 (four from top; Nigel Cattlin); 119 (six from top; M. Szadzuik/R. Zinck); **NHPA** 66br; 67tl; 67l (seven from top); 67l (eight from top); 67l (nine from top); 67l (ten from top); 67r (five from top); 69 (three from top); 67r (two from top); 67r (six from top).